Charles Sumner Seeley

The Spanish Galleon

Being an Account of a Search for sunken Treasure in the Caribbean Sea

Charles Sumner Seeley

The Spanish Galleon
Being an Account of a Search for sunken Treasure in the Caribbean Sea

ISBN/EAN: 9783743329829

Manufactured in Europe, USA, Canada, Australia, Japa

Cover: Foto ©ninafisch / pixelio.de

Manufactured and distributed by brebook publishing software (www.brebook.com)

Charles Sumner Seeley

The Spanish Galleon

THE
SPANISH GALLEON

BEING AN ACCOUNT

OF

A SEARCH FOR SUNKEN TREASURE IN THE CARIBBEAN SEA

BY

CHARLES SUMNER SEELEY

CHICAGO
A. C. McCLURG AND COMPANY
1891

COPYRIGHT,
BY A. C. MCCLURG AND CO.
A. D. 1891.

CONTENTS.

Chapter		Page
I.	The Island	7
II.	The Food Supply	17
III.	House-Building	28
IV.	Pig-Hunting	41
V.	Boat-Building	53
VI.	"Duke 2d, property of H. Senlis"	67
VII.	The Water-Glass	80
VIII.	Bread-Making	93
IX.	The Galleon Found	105
X.	The Castaways	116
XI.	Alice and her Father	129
XII.	The Problem	143
XIII.	The Abandoned Plantation	153
XIV.	A Remarkable Cure	166
XV.	Lost and Found	180
XVI.	A Bad Port	192
XVII.	The Waves in Harness	204

CHAPTER		PAGE
XVIII.	EMBAYED	218
XIX.	THE PEARL-FISHERS	231
XX.	THE CAPTAIN OF THE GANG	245
XXI.	SELF-BETRAYED	259
XXII.	THE CAPTAIN'S FATE	272
XXIII.	TREASURE TROVE	283

THE SPANISH GALLEON.

CHAPTER I.

THE ISLAND.

MY name is William Morgan, and I am a lineal descendant of that William Morgan who was a brother of the famous Welsh buccaneer, Henry Morgan. I mention this in no spirit of pride, — quite the contrary, — but because some may choose to trace in these adventures evidence of hereditary tendencies.

On the eighteenth day of August, 1886, as the sun was setting, I was floating in the Caribbean Sea. You may mark the place on the map as being approximately N. latitude 15°, and W. longitude 62° from Greenwich; or in other words, between one hundred and two hundred miles west of the French island of Martinique. A chest, well corded but partly filled with water, was all that kept my head above the surface. Without food or drink I had been floating thus since shortly after sunrise of the previous morning. At that time the sloop in which I was voyaging, capsized and sunk in a squall, drowning the negro captain and owner, and his son, who constituted the crew. In this little vessel I was bound for a small uninhabited island known as "Key Seven," which was in plain sight when the disaster occurred. For two days and a night, without sleep or refreshment, I had been struggling to push the floating chest toward this land.

Now as the sun was just about to sink exactly behind the trees on the island, I was so near that the sound of the waves on the beach reached my ear. The tide would soon turn, and I must gain a foothold on the sand before the ebb got fairly under way, or continue the struggle another night. My hands and arms were sore in places from chafing in the salt water against the chest, every muscle ached, cramps and pains shot incessantly through every limb, my eyes were on fire, the wolf of hunger gnawed at my stomach, my lips and mouth and throat were parched and dry. The fever of utter exhaustion and fatigue drove delirious dreams and fancies through my aching brain. Still on, on, on, compelling the unwilling and rebellious muscles to their automatic work, made sickening to the very soul by long continued repetition, I fought until at last my feet rested on the bottom. One final struggle and the wave left me with the chest upon the beach. But it was not until the last ounce of energy had been expended, that I staggered and fell on the dry sand among the parched bladder-weed that streaked the shore. There I lay for half an hour, completely exhausted.

When I rose to secure the chest by dragging it a little way — a very little way — beyond the reach of the waves, the sun had just sunk, night with tropical suddenness had fallen on the scene, and the stars burst out in all their brilliancy in the clear dark vault of heaven.

Here then I was at last at the end of my voyage, but in what a plight. Food and drink and sleep I must have, and that speedily, or death would shortly claim me. It was starlight, but too dark to see more than the dim outlines of things. I lay down again on the warm dry sand and tried to think what was best to do; but I could not think, for my dry tongue rattled in my mouth and my head ached as though it would burst with every feeble throb of the heart.

As I lay with my face turned toward the sea, listening in despair to the soft, monotonous lip-lipping of the waves, varied at regular intervals by the long, foaming crash of the swell as it broke and swept up the sands, there came presently in the eastern sky a faint silvery glow, and the full moon stole up from out the glistening water until it shone full and broad, making a burnished path down to the shore at my feet. No doubt, this saved my life. In an hour it was almost as light as day. I untied my shoes, which I had fastened to the chest while swimming, put them on to guard my feet, and started in search of drinking-water. Fortunately it was close at hand. A little brook flowed down to the sea not more than forty rods to the north of my landing-place. Had I been in condition to remember anything, I should have known this fact, because while floating in the sea I noted this stream by the low foliage that marked its course near the beach, and longed for a draught of the water which I knew must be there. Stumbling along the sands, I reached the stream, and lying down, buried my face in the clear, sweet water, and drank until I could drink no more. This was possibly an imprudent thing to do. Indeed it was followed by dreadful nausea. But this did not hinder me from taking another draught, almost as deep as the first.

He who has not experienced real thirst can never know how delicious is pure, sweet water, taken when every fibre and pore of the body is suffering for it. Each capillary and duct seemed to expand, and the heart soon began to beat stronger and fuller as though under the lash of a stimulant. Though I had fancied food was what I needed most, it was really the water that my system demanded, and I felt at once so much stronger and better that a desire to sleep came upon me, the fever left my veins, and I felt as though I could wait until morning before breaking my fast.

On the way back to the chest I picked up half a dozen shell-fish of some bivalve species, on the sands at the edge of the surf, and ate them. They tasted sweet as a nut to me, but were probably of little nutritious value, and possibly more or less indigestible. But they brought no harm, and seemed partly to fill what void the water had left.

At the landing-place I drew and rolled the chest still farther up the beach, took off my wet clothing, spread it out to dry, and buried my body in the warm sand, putting the chest between me and the gentle wind which was breathing steadily and softly in from the sea. Exhausted as I was, the sense of bodily rest and warmth was delicious; but as is apt to be the case when one is over-fatigued, sleep did not come to my eyelids. I was free from pain with the exception of the smarting of the raw wounds on my hands and arms, and lay listening to the rustling of the breeze, the sound of the sea, and the lonesome call of a night bird or a small animal of some sort that occasionally broke the stillness.

I thought over my desperate situation; of the disastrous ending of the voyage, from which I had hoped so much; how and when, if ever, I could get off the island and back to civilization to take a fresh start, — for as to giving up the great object of the expedition, that thought was not once entertained either then or at any other time. But now without a boat or the many necessary appliances for carrying out my plans, I could not hope to accomplish that object, though I was upon the very island that I had travelled over a thousand miles to reach. It would be necessary to go back at least to Martinique, if not to New York, to obtain what I needed.

Diving apparatus is not to be found everywhere. Besides the assistance of at least one person seemed absolutely necessary, and here I was alone. Yes, I must somehow go back and start over again, — that seemed clear. But how, and when? These questions were not easy to answer. Should I be able even to obtain food while a prisoner here, waiting such deliverance as chance might bring?

These and a thousand other thoughts passed through my mind while I lay looking at the stars as they paled before the silver shield of the moon. I thought of my plans so carefully laid, and now, at least for the time being, so utterly defeated. Thus I reviewed mentally the whole history of the enterprise I had undertaken. And perhaps this is a proper place to give the reader an account of what he will doubtless conceive to be the wildest scheme that ever was seriously contemplated. Listen, that you may judge.

On my twenty-first birthday, now only a few weeks past, I sailed from New York in one of the steamers plying to the Windward Islands, bound for Martinique and thence by country sloop to Key Seven, for the purpose of finding a Spanish galleon that sank in the open sea near that island, July 9, 1665, after a bloody battle with two vessels commanded by the buccaneer Welshman, Captain Henry Morgan. This galleon contained pieces of eight, gold and silver in bars and plate, and jewels, to the value of over three hundred thousand dollars. It had lain thus at the bottom of the sea, as I believed, for more than two hundred years. To find this sunken wreck and secure the treasure was the object of my expedition. How I succeeded in such a wild undertaking will appear hereafter.

Several years before, while I was at college, a desultory course of reading had awakened in me a deep interest in the early printed accounts of the lawless buccaneers and maroons who infested the waters and coasts of the Caribbean Sea, besieged and sacked the Spanish forts and cities, crossed the isthmus of Darien, and followed down the coast of South America, capturing the vessels and laying waste the towns of the Spaniards. Bartholomew Portuges, Brasiliano, John Davis, Francis Lolonois, and Henry Morgan, the brother of my ancestor, were noted leaders of these buccaneering crews and armies. Perhaps the last-named adventurer, who led the desperate expedition across the isthmus and captured the fortified city of Panama, was the most noted of all, as he was also not the least cruel, bloodthirsty, and avaricious. Fragmentary accounts by various authors, some of whom were actors in the scenes described, have been published in Dutch, French, Spanish, and English. So far as I could do so I had sought and studied these accounts. A translation into English, made more than a hundred years ago, of the most considerable Dutch and French accounts had enabled me to absorb them, and the numerous original reports of Spanish officials made to their government, and which are still preserved in the archives at Madrid, were rendered accessible to me by a fortunate circumstance.

Many years ago most of the documents bearing upon the history of America, from the time of Columbus down to the present century, had been collected and transcribed through the efforts of an American author whose charming histories have delighted all English readers. This mass of material had since its transcription been made use of by many others, and being in the charge of the college librarian, I obtained access to it. My enthusiasm may be imagined, when I say that in order to consult these transcriptions I actually learned to read Spanish. It was in one of these papers that I found the report of Don Josef Isabel del Velo y Campo, admiral of the Spanish fleet and at the time in command of the Spanish galleon La Magdalen. The admiral gave a full account of the loss of this galleon, of the desperate battle, of the tremendous bravery of the Spaniards under his command, and of his own escape with two others by swimming to the island of Trebucino near by. The vessel sank about a mile from the northern extremity of the island, bearing a little east of north from the point of rocks. The report was accompanied by an account of the cargo on board, as nearly correct as his memory and knowledge could serve him to give, and by a like statement of the money and treasure lost, concluding with a pious congratulation that if lost to Spain it at least had not fallen into the hands of Morgan and his murderous *hereticos*.

At the time of reading this report, it was to me a matter of idle wonder, to conjecture whether the noble galleon still held together at the bottom of the sea, and if the treasure was still there; to picture the many curious things that possibly lived and grew near the blackened and corroded silver and the untarnishable gold, the monsters of the sea that swam and crept over and about it, the seaweed, the sponge and the coral, the tides and the currents which swept by it, and the drowned sailors and cavaliers whose spirits possibly guarded it through the slow ages of decay and change.

Although I had looked up the island of Trebucino on the old charts, and had identified it as the bit of land now marked "Key Seven" on modern maps, yet at that time I had no thought of the possibility of recovering the treasure, much less of engaging in such a hairbrained enterprise myself. It was not until long afterward that the idea entered my mind of seeking the treasure, and then it was suggested by a serious misfortune that befell me.

Both my parents were dead, and I had no living relatives nearer than an uncle, my mother's brother, who was my guardian, and who from time to time sent me money as I needed it. When my father died he left his estate, consisting of valuable farming lands in the beautiful Mohawk valley, heavily encumbered with debt. The money sent me for expenses at college came from a small property that had belonged to my mother. I had always looked forward to the day when, free from school life, I could undertake the management and control of my father's farms, and return to live at the home farm, where I was born and where my early boyhood days were passed. The old Dutch-built brick house with its noble elms, the brook that ran through the meadow, so near that its murmur could be heard on still summer nights from my open bedroom window, the broad fields stretching up and down the valley as far as the eye could reach, the thousand acres under cultivation, and the thousand more of woodland and pasture, the sleek herds, the dairy, and all the joys of a farmer's life, made up the picture which was ever in my mind. To live this life had been my ambition, and I had tolerated school only because I was told it would better fit me for the work.

But all my hopes were suddenly dashed by a letter from my uncle advising me to be economical and saving with my money, as there was only seven hundred dollars left of the fund devoted to my education, and the whole of which he would in six months turn over to me in one sum. He told me I was now old enough to be informed of my exact prospects. It was better, he said, I should know that my father's estate would not sell for nearly enough to clear the mortgages on it, that it would require at least a hundred thousand dollars to meet and pay a debt due in three years. He offered to manage the property for me up to that time; but warned me that I could hope to realize but little from it, and that it would then have to go under the hammer. By this sad and unexpected news, my prospects in life were wholly changed. The thought of losing my old home and all the familiar surroundings was so dismal and distressing that I had no heart left to finish my college work. Could I not somehow get the necessary money to redeem the property? This thought came to me over and over. To get a hundred thousand dollars in the short space of three years! Alas! the accomplishment of such a feat must involve some extraordinary circumstances as well as great good-fortune. It was while thus cudgelling my brains in despair, that the idea of the Spanish galleon recurred to me. After weighing the whole matter coolly, and without any enthusiasm or prejudice, I concluded that there was a bare chance of raising this sunken treasure from the sea. I resolved to take that remote chance, and to spend my money and the three years, if necessary, in the endeavor.

It would be six months before I could get the seven hundred dollars that remained to me. This period I spent in planning and studying the enterprise, and in such physical preparation as I was able to make. Every day I visited the natatorium and gymnasium to practise swimming and to train and develop the muscles; so that when the six months had passed I was an expert swimmer and diver and my muscles were hard as steel. The money came duly to hand, and I left college at once for New York City.

There, after writing to my uncle that I was about to go on a voyage that might last three years, and bidding him an affectionate farewell, I bought such articles and appliances as I had determined would be necessary, and took passage for Martinique with exactly two hundred dollars in my pocket.

Then came, as we have seen, the wreck of the sloop, the drowning of my negro assistants, and my long struggle in the sea.

CHAPTER II.

THE FOOD SUPPLY.

THE sun was well up the eastern sky when I awoke in the morning, so numb and stiff that I could with difficulty unbury myself from the sand, the weight of which had almost stopped the circulation in some parts of the body. My clothing, which I had spread on the sand, had completely dried. After some chafing and rubbing I dressed myself and felt more comfortable than at any time since the loss of the sloop. The first thing to do was to get something to eat. I walked to the brook, bathed my face, and took a long drink of water, and began to be more and more impressed with the fact that the diet was thin. There were a number of cocoanut palms near by, growing within a few rods of the sea, and plenty of nuts on them, as could be plainly seen. But though I searched the ground with hungry glance I could find only one nut that had not been operated on by the land crabs, which are able in an ingenious manner to extract the contents through the three little eyes or holes in the shell. This one nut, the exterior husk of which had not been disturbed, I broke open by pounding it upon a rock, and found it to my bitter disappointment blackened, rancid, and quite unfit for food.

I had noticed a flock of gulls, or some species of shore birds, wheeling about and lighting and running on the beach near by. With a shotgun it would have been an easy matter to creep near and bag half a dozen at a shot. I watched them a little while and concluded that though it might prove a tough and unpalatable dish I must have one, or starve. It would be a good plan, I thought, to gather a dozen pebbles weighing three or four ounces apiece and try the effect of a shot into the thick of the flock from as near a point as I could reach. But as there would be no chance for more than one trial, I determined to fire the stones in a volley. To do this effectively I gathered some tough reeds and tied one to each stone until I had half a dozen stones so provided. By swinging these missiles at the end of the reeds they could be thrown a considerable distance with great velocity.

Trembling with expectation and excitement, I crept down toward the flock, keeping out of sight behind some rocks until I was as near as it was possible to go, when I let fly my volley of improvised slung-shots as well as I could direct them into the thickest of the birds. Running forward immediately, I found two lying on the sand struggling. One was hit squarely on the wing with a stone, and the other had a reed wound once around its neck. I secured both and wrung their necks. The idea at once occurred to me that the next time I had occasion to hunt gulls, I would contrive a bolas by tying a stone to each end of a cord; it seemed to me that this would prove even a more effectual instrument of destruction than the sling volley, as it would be almost certain to entangle one or more of the flock.

These birds were nearly as large as a guillemot, but of what species I do not know. As I had no fire to cook with, I immediately ate one of them raw. The other I cut into strips and shreds and laid them on a rock in the hot sun to dry. The experience of eating a raw unseasoned gull was such as to turn my thoughts forcibly to the necessity of some means for procuring both fire and salt. The salt would not be difficult to obtain, for if it could not be found somewhere along the shore or in the salt marsh near by, it would not be difficult to make some sort of a salt pan provided I could find clay or other impermeable soil with which to confine a shallow pool of sea water somewhere in the sunshine. The evaporation would speedily give the small quantity I should require.

In my vest pocket was a small metal match-box half full of matches, such as every smoker carries. But on examination it proved, as might be expected, that all the matches were wet and useless. Nevertheless when I got back to the landing-place, I laid them carefully out in the sun on a stone to dry, thinking that possibly one of them might be made to light.

I now turned my attention to the chest. This chest was one of four that contained my baggage; but which one of the four, or what this particular one contained, I could not conjecture. So I set about untying the rope wound around it, and soon had it free. There was fully forty feet of strong hempen halyard stuff in the line, and this in itself was a possession of value. The bunch of keys in my pocket enabled me without trouble to open the lock. When I raised the lid I found to my bitter disappointment that the chest contained those articles which would be of least value to me under the present circumstances. The contents consisted chiefly of books, stationery, sketching appliances, drawing tools and materials, and a photographic camera and outfit. Everything was, of course, soaked with water, and I hardly had the heart to take the things out to dry. The books and paper, as well as the photographic plates, were in a sad condition. The bellows of the camera came to pieces. I spread out the contents of the chest on the hot sand to dry, putting stones on such things as might blow away when they became dried. The lens of the camera I unscrewed, intending to use it as a burning-glass to start a fire, so that there might be no further need to eat raw gull. The burning-glass, which was of priceless value to me, and the rope were practically all the chest yielded that could be put to use, as I then supposed. The chest itself would of course be useful to me.

Eager to try the burning-glass, I collected some dry branches, leaves, and other fuel. In a ball or nest of dry grass, of the size of my two fists, I placed a little bunch of silky seed fibres collected from a weed. Upon this fibre I brought to bear the focus of the lens, concentrating the sun's rays to an intense white spot, which almost immediately began to smoke with the heat. Presently the material commenced to burn, and I whirled the ball rapidly around through the air, whereupon the whole burst into a flame, which being placed among the fuel was speedily a roaring fire. In this manner I obtained fire as long as I remained on the island. As a mere matter of curiosity I tried some of the matches which had been laid out so carefully to dry, but, as might have been expected, not a single one would light. It was very fortunate, therefore, that I had the lens, as otherwise I should have been reduced to the necessity of rubbing sticks together in the manner of the savages, and probably without being able to get fire as they are said to do. Of course I did not need the fire to keep me warm, for the air was excessively hot. But it seemed so like a new-found friend that I built it high, and when there was a mass of embers, carefully covered them with sand and ashes that they might last and be ready for future use.

It was now nearly noon and my stomach became more clamorous than ever. I therefore cooked and ate the flesh of the other gull, which had been laid on the rocks to be cured. Although the flies had begun to attack the meat, it was, as yet, in no wise tainted, nor very dry. By dipping the pieces into the sea water I gave it, as I fancied, a perceptible flavor of salt. At any rate, though tough and a little rank in flavor, it tasted good enough and my only regret was that there was not more of it. I could perceive the gulls in great numbers flying about out at sea, but none on the shore, and concluded that they came to the land only at certain stages of the tide, — probably at low tide, when their food would be exposed.

Determined to lay in a store of provisions, I next turned my attention to the cocoanut palms and made another search for fallen nuts, but without any success, though I sought the whole length of the beach beneath the trees. It became quite evident that to get the nuts I should have to climb for them. As the nut-bearing trees were from fifty to seventy-five feet high, without a branch on their cylindrical stems from the base up to the feathery crown, the climb was likely to prove a difficult if not a dangerous task. However, selecting a palm with plenty of nuts on it, I made the attempt to "shin" — as the sailors call it, — up the stem. It was hard work, and the heat was so oppressive that I had to stop several times and rest on the way up and was very glad when I found myself at the top. I broke off and threw down a score of the nuts in all stages of ripeness, and then descended in safety.

The fruit of the cocoanut palm grows in clusters of a dozen to twenty nuts in each bunch, which hang immediately under the crown of leaves. Upon the trees they by no means present the globular hard-shelled appearance which is familiar to our eyes. Each nut is encased in a thick fibrous rind or husk; exteriorly this husk is of a sub-triangular form, about twelve inches long and six inches broad. Of the fibre of this exterior husk the well-known cocoanut matting is made, and also the coarse yarn called cöir; it is also used for cordage.

I carried the nuts to a shady place and stripped off the husk by means of a pointed piece of rock set upright in the ground. The smaller ones not yet entirely ripe were full of a sweet liquid, and the meat was soft enough to have been scooped out with a spoon; the older ones were also very good, not nearly so dry and hard as we find them in our northern markets. For the first time since the shipwreck I ate until my hunger was fully appeased. What the result of a long-continued diet upon such food would be I could not of course forecast, but it seemed probable that I need not starve while the nuts were plentiful. Those which were left from this meal I carried to the landing-place and laid them on the chest, where the land crabs would probably not get at them.

With this ample supply of food, presumably nutritious and certainly quite palatable, my anxiety was greatly relieved. Animal food I could probably obtain from time to time as the island appeared to abound with birds of various kinds, if I could have time to contrive some method of ensnaring or killing them. Then too there were doubtless fish to be caught, and probably turtle. In some of the islands, I knew, there were wild pigs, as it was a common thing for the people of Martinique to come to these small isolated islands on pig-hunting expeditions. I sincerely hoped that these animals might be found on Key Seven; for I felt quite confident of my ability to think of some plan for killing or capturing them. But there was no immediate need to go fishing or hunting for birds or pigs.

I determined to find, if possible, some means of getting a supply of salt before I sought for flesh food of any kind. With this end in view, as the afternoon was still young, I began looking about for a suitable place to serve as a salt pan. I walked along the beach for a mile each way, but could find no suitable spot. The requirements were a shallow basin near the sea, with the bottom impervious to water, which should hold in a shallow depth at least five or ten barrels of water. There was plenty of rock of a coralline limestone variety, and an abundance of shells; and the idea occurred to me that I might burn a supply of lime and thus make a mortar or cement of slaked lime and sand. With this material it would be possible to construct just above high-water mark such a pan or cavity as I desired. If I used shells to make the lime, there would probably be no need of erecting a kiln, as heat enough could be attained in a large open fire, by building it of several alternate layers of dry wood and shells.

I immediately set about collecting shells with which the beach was most plentifully strewn in all directions. As I had nothing in which to carry them, I adopted the expedient of throwing them one at a time into heaps. This was very hard and fatiguing work, and it was four o'clock or later in the afternoon before I had gathered into about twenty different heaps the four or five bushels of shells which I thought enough for a burning. It still remained for me to collect the scattered heaps together, and gather the wood for fuel.

But it was high time now to stop work and prepare for the night. Some sort of sleeping-place must be contrived in the two or three hours of daylight that remained, for I had no fancy to try again the sort of couch I had last slept in. I went to the stream and drank a good draught of water, a welcome refreshment after my exertion in the hot sun. I then gathered a quantity of dry grass for a bed and carried it down to the sand near the landing-place, which seemed a sort of home to me, although I had resolved speedily thereafter to move my property nearer to the brook. The contents of the chest were now dry excepting the books, which presented a sad appearance. I gathered all of these things together and covered them up as well as I could with the focussing-cloth that belonged to the camera, piling stones around the edge to secure it. The empty chest I turned up on its side, hinges uppermost, and propped up the lid in a nearly horizontal position. This would afford me shelter for the upper portion of the body. Under the shelter thus improvised I piled the dry grass for a couch, and my sleeping-place was ready. I then gathered a fresh supply of fuel and built up a fire on the landward, which would presently be the leeward side of my shelter.

By the time these arrangements were all complete, the sun was setting. Tired out, I lay down and watched the fire, thinking over my situation and planning what to do and how to do it. No doubt, sooner or later some vessel would pass in sight or land on the island and take me off. It was not as though I were on a remote or inaccessible place; the native sloops and small vessels occasionally visited these islands for wood or turtle, or on pig-hunting expeditions, and I fancied it would not be long before an opportunity offered for my escape. In the meantime, while thus a prisoner, be the time long or short, it would be necessary to keep up my health and strength. For this purpose food and shelter were necessary, and occupation, too, that I might not brood over my situation and worry at the delay in my plans. There was likely to be plenty of occupation, however, in providing myself with the bare necessities of life. If there should be any spare time on my hands I would devote it to the construction of a boat, a raft, or a vessel of some other sort, with which to get away. But with only a pocket knife how could I expect ever to build a boat capable of navigating more than a hundred miles of sea? How could I carry fresh water enough to last during the voyage?

These problems were indeed difficult of solution. I ran over in my mind, as far as I could recollect them, all the different kinds of boats, canoes, kayaks, etc., known to primitive man. There was the ancient coracle, used by the old Britons, woven in basket fashion from willows and coated with clay or lined with a hide, — a thing good enough in an emergency to ferry one over a stream, but utterly useless to me. There was the canoe or pirogue, hollowed from a single tree-trunk, — called also the dugout. Possibly by the aid of fire I might with patience construct such a thing by months of hard work; and by adding an outrigger log or float, after the manner of the South-Sea islanders, such a canoe could possibly be rendered capable of navigating the sea in favorable weather. Then again there was the whole class of skin boats such as the Esquimaux use; the Greenlander's kayak made of skins stretched over a framework, and "decked over" like a modern canoe. But how could I build a boat without tools to work with?

I lay thus for an hour or two watching the embers and thinking over one plan after another, until I felt inclined to sleep. When I turned over with my back to the fire, I could see along the beach where the moonlight glinted and sparkled on the sand and shells and pebbles, tinging each wave with liquid silver, as it ran up in graceful curves upon the sand.

I was looking on this scene of magic beauty with the soft fingers of sleep just ready to press down my eyelids when I saw what I thought was a rock just in the wash of the breakers, begin slowly to move. Was this a fancy or was it a fact?

I roused myself and watched the object intently. Yes, it was slowly moving out of the water upon the sand. I realized instantly that it was a turtle making for the sand in order to lay her eggs. Here was a good supply of meat which could be kept an indefinite time, to be obtained by the simple process of turning the creature on its back.

I watched the creature crawl slowly up in the moonlight until it was four or five rods from the water, and waited a minute to see if it would go further. Then I quietly reached for a piece of wood which might be used as a lever to help me turn it over, and ran as swiftly as I could for about three hundred yards so as to get between it and the sea. But the turtle did not seem to comprehend the situation, at least it did not move until I ran close up to it and thrust the stick beneath it. Then it began to walk away, and as it did so it rose up on its fins to such a height that my lever slipped and turned, and I could get no purchase on it. I immediately made up my mind that turtle are not to be turned with a lever. So dropping the stick, I seized the shell with both hands and with a mighty effort heaved the creature over on its back as skilfully as though I had been a veteran turtle-turner.

As soon as I had regained my breath, I scraped away the stones and sand until there was a level space around the turtle, so that it could not possibly work itself over again, and then contemplated my prize. It was a magnificent specimen of the hawk's-bill variety of sea turtle, and would doubtless weigh one hundred and fifty pounds. Visions of turtle soup and steaks floated through my mind. But I could not afford to kill this great creature until I had salt with which to preserve the meat; otherwise I could not hope to consume a tenth of it before it would spoil.

Quite content with this piece of good-luck, I returned to my shelter and, lying down, kept watch for another such prize; but none came, and after an hour or two my eyelids grew heavy again, — and the glitter of the moonlight on the sand, and the ceaseless motion of the waves, seemed to mingle together in a swimming confusion, until I lost myself and the moonlit waves and shore together in a dreamless sleep.

CHAPTER III.

HOUSE-BUILDING.

BRIGHT and early the next morning I awoke to what I felt must be a busy day. A plunge in the sea, a good bath in the brook, and a frugal breakfast of cocoanuts consumed but a few minutes of the time, which, being now practically my sole capital, must be expended with due regard to economy. The turtle was lying safe on its back, and as the sun would soon be very hot, my first care was to break off some shrubs and erect a shade for the creature. I should have been glad to pour a few buckets of sea water over it, but buckets were not among my present conveniences.

The first work on hand was of course the lime-burning. I found a great piece of bark, which I loosened from a fallen and partially decayed log, and used as a sort of tray on which to carry the separate heaps of shells to the spot where the burning was to be done. To economize time and labor, I concluded to burn the lime at the spot where I should subsequently want it. I selected for this purpose a flat piece of smooth sand free of stones and just above high tide, where the waves could not in ordinary weather wash into it. With my hands and pieces of bark I scooped out a basin about ten feet square and a foot in depth, throwing the sand up all around in a low bank. In this basin I piled dry wood and the shells in layers until the pile was five or six feet high.

This took me until noon, working hard every minute, with the perspiration streaming from every pore. Then

I discovered that my fire was out. But I had no trouble to start another with the burning-glass, as the sun was shining fiercely and so directly overhead that I had to search for my shadow. Presently the great flames were roaring and leaping high in the air and casting out such a heat that I was glad to retire to the brook for a drink and a cocoanut lunch while waiting for the fuel to burn out.

As I rested in the shade, I employed myself in twisting or rudely spinning some cord out of the fibre of the cocoanut husks. I first pounded the husk between two stones until the fibre was reduced to a mass resembling coarse hemp, and then began to draw it out and twist it as one twists a hay band, only into a slenderer thread. As fast as it became twisted, I wound the thread on a short stick about six inches long and a quarter of an inch in diameter. With the cord wound smoothly on this stick, and a half-hitch taken around one end, I could roll the cord and stick between my hand and leg to give the twist necessary for the spinning operation, and at the same time use the other hand to manipulate the entangling fibres. By this simple process it was possible to produce the thread, or coïr, quite rapidly.

In about an hour and a half my great fire was burned to the ground, and as a result there lay in the shallow excavation a mingled mass of embers, ashes, lime, fragments of partly burned shells, wood, and charcoal. Of course the ground beneath was very hot, and I could not work among the embers and hot fragments. The tide was now beginning to come in, and I dug a trench from the pit to the sea, through which the water flowed till it quenched the fire and slaked the lime, and partly sinking in the porous sand, left a muddy compound of lime, ashes, and sand, all over the bottom of the pit. I filled and plastered up the trench except a narrow gateway, cleaned out the sticks and fragments, and sprinkled dry sand over the mud, raking it well in and smoothing the surface as much as possible with the aid of sticks and a great clam-shell. It now remained for me only to let the cement or mortar set and dry, and then, I hoped, it would prove impervious to water.

There were still some hours of daylight, which could not be better employed, I thought, than upon the construction of some better shelter than the upturned chest had afforded. All day I had been turning over in my mind a plan for a hut or shanty that I fancied might be quickly and easily built. There was no telling how long the fair weather, which had now lasted for several days, might continue, and the utter wretchedness of existence if a storm should find me without a shelter was not to be patiently contemplated.

In gathering fuel near the edge of the forest I had noticed a great quantity of dead stalks standing six or seven feet high, straight as an arrow and perhaps an inch and a half in diameter except where they tapered at the top. The plant looked like some species of hibiscus. Any quantity of these stalks was to be had, and they were light yet strong enough for my purpose.

I selected a nice level piece of dry sand near the stream and fifty yards or so from the sea as a site for my proposed house. The shadow from a clump of cocoanut palms fell upon the spot for a part of the day, and near by was a bit of rock where I had sat at noon spinning cöir. Two young palms grew there about eight feet apart, the trunks of which would serve for the main supports of the structure. I hunted about in the forest until I found a reasonably straight stick, that would reach from one of these trees to the other, to serve as a ridgepole, and lashed it firmly to them with some of my cocoanut cord, about eight feet from the ground. Then I brought hibiscus stalks, taking care to cut their butts diagonally. They were easily severed by a single blow. These stalks I set upright in the sand; as firmly as possible, for the four walls of the hut, each wall consisting of two rows, the inner row being planted close together and the outer row parallel to it at a distance of about an inch and a half, the stalks of the outer row being separated from one another three or four inches.

When they were set up, which did not take long as I made no effort to drive them very firmly in the sand, I cut off the tops of the stalks forming the end walls to the shape that the roof was subsequently to take, and reduced the side walls to a common level. In the side next the sea I left an opening for a doorway. The space between the rows of stalks it was my intention to fill with dry grass laid horizontally, and to lay in at intervals stalks of hibiscus, finishing off the top of the walls with a good stout stalk of the same, laid in all around and lashed to both rows with cord. This, I thought, would make a reasonably stout and weather-proof wall, and so it subsequently turned out. But as night came on at this stage of the work, I could not complete even the walls of my hut before dark, and was fain to content myself with my bed under the chest.

I was awakened from a sound sleep by something crawling over me. Forgetful of where I was, I sprang up erect, and my head, coming violently in contact with the chest, overturned it, while I fell back half stunned with the blow. The moon had gone down and the stars were shining brightly, but there was not light enough to see anything distinctly except on the water, where a phosphorescent gleam lighted up the breaking waves with a pale greenish glow which ran in streaks along the surface.

As soon as I could collect my scattered senses and get upon my feet, I began to grope around in search of the cause of the disturbance. Presently a loathsome, warty, tuberculous land crab scuttled over my naked foot, and I could then make out literally hundreds of shadowy forms sidling over the sand. There was no more sleep for me that night, and I was glad to think from the appearance of the sky that it was not more than two hours before the dawn. As I had already been sleeping for eight or ten hours I felt rested, but was faint with hunger. Cocoanut no longer had an attraction for me, but as there was nothing else at hand I forced myself to eat enough to relieve my faintness. A good cup of coffee or even a bowl of hot soup would have seemed a fortune to me then, but I was obliged to be satisfied with a deep draught of water, which lay in my stomach sensibly cold and heavy. It was evident that there was no time to lose in getting more nutritious food than cocoanuts, if I was to keep my strength. This determined me to kill the turtle that very morning, without waiting for the slow operation of the salt pan even if it proved ready to fill with sea water that day; for the evaporation of such an amount of water might take several days before the residue was salt enough for brine. I went to look at the captive and found it as I had left it the day before.

I watched the eastern horizon patiently for signs of dawn. Finally a gray pale glow lit up the sky and slowly changed to a tender pink and primrose, then suddenly the golden rim of the sun shot up and daylight as suddenly took the place of night. The streaks and wreaths of mist that lay sleeping in the hollows of the waves floated away and dissolved.

It did not take me long to kill and dress the turtle, and to pack the meat, both callipash and callipee, — as the two sorts composing a turtle's anatomy are termed, — into the upper shell and to cover it up with the breast plate. I now resolved to have some hot turtle soup.

Among the photographic apparatus were two shallow developing-trays, made of sheet iron and lined with porcelain. They were about an inch in depth and six by ten inches in their lateral dimensions. While these would serve well enough perhaps to stew or fry the meat in, they did not hold enough to make soup. There was, however, a large glass bottle holding a gallon, filled with a solution of hyposulphite of soda to be used as a fixing solution for photographic negatives. This I emptied and washed thoroughly with sand and water until it was perfectly clean. Cutting some of the meat into small fragments, I put them into the bottle until it was a third full, then filled it with equal parts of sea water and fresh water, as this proportion seemed to taste about salt enough. I then set the bottle in the hot ashes until the contents were warm, gradually moving it nearer and nearer the fire, until finally all was so hot that I no longer feared the heat would crack the glass; so, drawing out some embers, I set the bottle boldly upon them, where the water soon began to simmer and gently boil. In the mean time, I stewed some of the meat with sea water in a developing-tray for immediate consumption, and of this made a good breakfast.

After breakfast I examined the salt pan to see if the cement had set sufficiently, but found that the mortar was still somewhat friable and not hard though seemingly quite dry. I concluded, therefore, to let it harden for another twenty-four hours before putting it to the test; but to obtain a small supply of salt for immediate use I filled the two developing trays with sea water and set them on the fire to boil.

When these operations were fairly under way, I resumed the house-building. First I gathered a great quantity of coarse, dry grass in the bottom land of the creek and laid it in the walls in the manner already described. When this was completed to my satisfaction, I began the construction of the roof after the following fashion: From the ridgepole to the side walls I laid at intervals of six inches hibiscus-stalk rafters, securing them in place at both ends by hay bands twisted out of the dry, tough grass, the lower ends of the rafters projecting to form eaves. On these rafters and parallel to the ridgepole I tied in like manner other stalks, at intervals of six inches. Here was a light and reasonably strong framework ready to receive a thatching of grass or palm leaves, but I concluded that grass would be preferable as it would make a roof better calculated to resist the wind.

Night was now approaching, and as the weather seemed as settled as ever, the lack of the thatch would be no special hardship. I hurried therefore to drag my chest up to the house and arrange my bed of grass within the walls, guarding against another intrusion of the land crabs by means of a row of short hibiscus stalks across the doorway. The result of the day's boiling of sea water in my developing-trays was something over a tablespoonful of salt. The soup which had been simmering all day in the bottle was delicious, and I made a hearty supper of part of it and some of the boiled meat. With the photographic apparatus were two chemist's graduated glasses, one of eight and one of four ounces. These made capital drinking-cups. The larger one I used for that purpose, and into the smaller put the precious, hard-earned salt.

As I had no notion to go to bed with the sun, I cast about for something to occupy the two or three hours before bedtime, and concluded to fry up a store of turtle meat in my trays. By nine o'clock I had thus prepared fully twenty pounds of the meat, which I piled upon a pavement of clam-shells in one corner of the house. The land crabs being duly fenced out, I turned in and slept soundly all night.

In the morning I was up at break of day, and ate a breakfast of hot soup. Immediately after breakfast I began to thatch my roof. For this purpose I carefully cut bundles of the long, dry grass, and beginning at the eaves, laid a row, butts down, in a layer about three inches in thickness. On this, near the tops of the grass, I tied a stalk of the hibiscus; then another layer of grass, covering the first down two thirds of its length and covering also the hibiscus stalk; and so on, layer after layer, on both pitches of the roof, until the ridge-pole was reached. At the comb of the ridge I finished all by bending down the grass at each side and securing it with a couple of the stalks, one at each side. I then heaped up the sand around the bottom of the walls on the outside, to give greater stability to the structure, and dug a ditch to prevent the water from flooding the interior if it should come down faster than the sandy soil could absorb it.

The next thing to make was some sort of door, and the planning and fashioning of this gave me occasion for no little thought and trouble. Finally, after trying other methods unsuccessfully, I rigged up a sort of rolling blind out of the stalks by cutting a number of them of a length a little greater than the width of the doorway and tying them close together by a cord at each end and one in the middle, so that the whole would be flexible like a curtain. This I hung over the doorway and attached a loop at each lower corner to secure it when it was down. When the door was to be opened this curtain could be rolled up and held in position by pulling a cord, or could be swung aside when ingress or egress merely was desired. Along the walls inside I made some rude shelves of hibiscus stalks, so that I might have my small possessions handy and safe.

I intended as soon as convenient to spin a good supply of cord and make a hammock to swing from one of the palm pillars to the other. In the mean time, as a temporary expedient for a bed, I laid a platform of hibiscus stalks in one corner, and covered them with a thick layer of grass. For ventilation and light, I cut under the projecting eaves four openings, or windows, into which, so sheltered, the rain would not be likely to drive. The chest answered for a seat or table as occasion required.

Here was a reasonably comfortable dwelling where I should be safe from the rain. And, indeed, it was completed none too soon, for even as I was sitting in the house on the chest, resting and contemplating my work, I heard the wind rustling among the palm leaves and was sensible of a darkening of the sky, which betokened a storm. The swaying of the two young palms which held the ridgepole at once warned me that the motion was likely to rack and weaken the whole structure. The tops of these two trees must come off at once. By hauling out the chest and using it as a scaffolding, I could reach the palm trunks at a point above the ridgepole; but when I tried to cut the tree with my knife, I found it would take too long to sever it. Therefore, the only way was to climb the slender trunk and break off its branches. One of the trunks bent so under my weight as to break short off above the ridgepole, dropping me on the sand, but without harm. The other one I succeeded in denuding of its crown of leaves.

The storm was coming up grandly from the southeast.

The sea in that direction was of an indigo tint streaked with flashes of foam, and above hung a leaden mass of clouds with a touch of copper-color here and there, where the internal fires flashed and glowed. The wind sank to a perfect calm, and occasionally a great drop of rain fell warm as blood. I had brought all the contents of the chest up near the hut, and I now hurried to get them under the shelter. The fire was smouldering near by, and there was a good supply of wood piled near it. I hurriedly carried this into the house, and also four or five charred and ignited sticks, which I placed in the middle of the room on the sand together in such manner that they would smoulder slowly there and keep alight. The smoke might be an annoyance, but as soon as there was a draught of air, it would drift out through the ventilators, and I could keep to windward of it. Finally I ran out and dragged in my turtle shell with its store of meat, and put that also under shelter.

The calm still continued deathlike and dark. When all was under shelter and I had returned from the brook with my goblet filled with fresh water, I stood at the open door, looking at the sea. Suddenly, without any further warning, down came the rain in bucketfuls, falling in vertical lines, — such a shower as is rarely seen. The roof held tight, the water streaming from it like a cataract, but not a drop coming through to the interior. In about twenty minutes the rain as suddenly ceased. Looking out over the ocean, I saw on the surface a streak of blue-black water, parallel with the horizon and flecked with tiny streaks of white, advancing. The squall was coming. Hurriedly I unrolled my door-curtain and fastened it securely at the bottom. I was just in time. As the blast struck the house, the whole structure trembled and swayed, but held fast. I could hear the shrieking of the wind as it swept through the neighboring palms, and the occasional crash of a breaking stem mingled with the dashing rain which now drove violently against the roof and walls, and I thanked my good-fortune that this shelter was ready. This gale continued to blow until long after dark. Indeed it was still raging when I fell asleep, to dream of shipwrecks and hurricanes.

When I awoke early in the morning and looked out through the ventilator, I found that the wind had fallen to a moderate breeze and had veered around to the northeast, bringing a dense fog, and that a fine rain was falling with a settled appearance such as betokened a wet day. My first care was to look after my fire. It was almost out, and to rekindle it from the few smouldering sparks was a matter requiring very tender manipulation. But at last I had it going again, and my pans of turtle meat stewing and frying on a gentle blaze, that demanded to be watched constantly.

This was a good time to overhaul my stock of books to see what they were, and to find out whether the salt water had left them in condition for use. They were now perfectly dry, but the bindings were warped and loosened. The leaves were in many places stuck together, and yellow and brown leather stains had crept in about the margins. But they still held together and were legible. The books consisted of a dozen well-selected novels, a manual of photography, the United States Dispensatory, a student's manual of botany, a school geology, and a German word-book. Looking over these books while I lay on my couch, with an occasional glance at the cooking, I passed the time very pleasantly all the morning.

At noon the rain still continued; so, not to be idle,

I ran out and picked up some freshly fallen cocoanuts both to vary my diet and to obtain a supply of fibre for spinning. The whole afternoon was spent in preparing the fibre and spinning it into cord, and by night I had accumulated quite enough to make me a hammock. This, I resolved, should be my next task if the foul weather continued. The smoke from the smouldering fire was a source of great annoyance, by getting into my eyes. I determined to remedy this as soon as I could, by erecting a fireplace and chimney of some sort. But in the mean time I utilized this annoying guest as much as possible by hanging several sticks full of strips of the turtle meat in the peak of the roof, where the smoke collected thickest, that it might become partially cured. This, I hoped, would preserve it, as it had been lying in sea water in the shell; and so it proved. For after this smoking the meat dried without taint, and, as I subsequently found, made most excellent eating.

With melted turtle fat, a clam-shell, and a wick made of fibre, I improvised a light, and after it grew dark, fell to looking over my library until bedtime, the rain still pattering on the thatch when I retired. The next morning the weather was still boisterous, the rain driving and the heavy mists sweeping along the sea. The leaden clouds still hung low and dark. This day I spent indoors working at my hammock and varying the monotony by hanging up the last of the meat to smoke, looking over my books and wishing for fair weather. I finished the hammock, but could not use it on account of the smoke, and was obliged to sleep on my pallet as before. As the turtle fat was all gone and therefore no light was to be had, I turned in early and awoke in the morning at dawn. On going out I found the sky clear and the sun rising fair. All the foliage looked fresh and bright after the rain, and the birds were cheerfully singing in the forest. It was a glorious change, and my confinement in the house for two days gave added zest to it. This would be a good day for an exploring trip, and I thought I would spend it in such an expedition.

CHAPTER IV.

PIG-HUNTING.

AMONG the photographic appliances there was a sort of haversack or bag with a shoulder-strap, designed to contain plate-holders. This I emptied and stored with a supply of fried turtle meat and a small bottle of water.

About seven o'clock I started up the bed of the brook, as affording the easiest path by which to penetrate the forest that, coming down nearly to the beach, extended on each hand as far as I could see. To the south was a stretch of low land, perhaps twenty acres in extent, covered for the most part with grass, and in the lowest portion with reeds and rushes. Just as the brook emerged from the forest it was shadowed by a dense mass of tall canes. The grass I had used in the construction of my house was a coarse variety growing from two and a half to three feet in height. On the higher ground grew a slenderer variety with heavy seed heads, a sample of which I gathered as it seemed to resemble canary seed, and might serve as food. Great quantities of this grass grew thickly on the knolls and higher parts of the upland. The water deepened where I waded through the canebrake, and ran with a sluggish current. I gathered a great bundle of rushes, and laid them on the bank, intending to pick them up on my return. They would be useful in weaving me a substitute for a hat, a convenience which I lacked at that time.

Just at the farther border of the canebrake, there was a muddy place where pigs had evidently been wallowing, for I found thousands of tracks about. Here was a favorite resort for them, not above a quarter of a mile from my house; but I wasted no time then hunting for this game, as I had formed no plan for its capture.

One thing I wanted to find was a bed of clay, which could be put to many valuable uses, especially the building of a fireplace and chimney. There was reason to believe that plenty was to be had on the island, which was of volcanic formation, and moreover the water of the brook, swollen by the recent rain, was stained as though with clay.

As I neared the line of cliff and rocks that formed the central ridge or back-bone of the island, the course of the stream bent to the north, and the forest was interspersed with small open glades where the great butterflies floated across through the sunshine, the metallic satiny blue of their lustrous wings glancing in the light. A flock of parrots with green, red, and blue plumage were chattering and screaming noisily in the bordering trees, and an occasional little green lizard would dash along the fallen trunks or over the rocks like a flash of emerald light. In one of these glades I found a quantity of shrubs growing about ten feet high and loaded with berries about the size of pepper-corns. The outside of these berries seemed covered with a greenish white wax. The leaf was somewhat like the myrtle. A sample of this, and of several other varieties of vegetation which were strange to me, I gathered to take home for identification in my manual of botany. I may here state that this berry-bearing shrub turned out to be the wax myrtle (*Myrica cerifera* of the botanists), and that the waxy coating of the berries was what is known as bay-berry tallow. This wax can be readily collected by boiling the drupes and skimming it off as it rises to the surface of the water; and a bushel of the berries will yield from four to five pounds of the wax, which can be employed to make excellent candles.

Near the cliffs I came upon a fine bed of clay, and I was so delighted with this discovery that I immediately began casting about for means of transporting a good supply to my house. The bed was distant from the house, as nearly as I could judge, about two miles, and the labor of carrying such heavy material would be very great. The best plan would be to knock together a raft of dry wood and float the clay down stream as a cargo. Vines and creepers to serve as cordage to tie the dead wood together were abundant, nor did it take me long to collect the wood and fashion the raft. Indeed, the harder task proved to be the digging out of the tough clay, as the only implements I had for this purpose were pointed sticks. But I finally cut a sharp, heavy stake of hard wood, and by driving this into the clay, was able to pry off large chunks, and soon had a load ready. On the raft I laid some broad leaves and pieces of bark to serve as a deck, and on this placed the clay in a great heap, as much as the raft would carry in the shallow water. Tying a long creeper to the raft, by which to pull, guide, or hold it back, as the navigation might require, I started it off into the current, and wading in the shallow stream, followed it down, holding on to the line as it floated away. Barring an occasional grounding in the shallow places, my raft floated serenely along at a good pace, and soon reached port, where I unloaded the clay and drew out the raft to serve as firewood.

This was a good job well done, and I more than once regretted the time I had wasted in the lime-burning task, for had I found this clay sooner, a much better salt pan could have been made with it than with the mortar. This thought caused me to go and examine the salt pan. I found the mortar on the bottom dry and hard, so I opened the gate that the sea water might flow in at the next tide and fill it.

The first use to be made of the clay was in the building of a fireplace and chimney for the house. My plan was to build up the structure of sticks, cob-house fashion, and then chink and plaster it with a good coating of clay. Before this could be done, however, it would be necessary to put the clay through some pugging process by which it could be rendered soft and plastic. This I accomplished by trampling the clay with my naked feet, adding a sprinkling of water now and then, until I had a mass of soft, mortar-like consistency. Then on the outside of the house I built up the fireplace close against the wall, and carried the chimney up about a foot above the highest part of the roof, plastering the sticks inside thoroughly with the soft clay. When this was done I cut through the wall to the fireplace, and plastered clay on the jambs to make all tight. The hearth I formed of harder clay, well pounded down and mixed with the sand. If no wind came until the structure was dry, it would become hard and strong enough to resist anything short of a hurricane. That the drying might be more rapid, I immediately built a good fire in it, and was rejoiced to find the draught excellent and the effect of the bright firelight upon the interior quite pleasant and homelike. This work occupied the whole day.

In the evening I brought a good supply of clay into the house, and using the chest as a work-bench, busied myself until bedtime with moulding several vessels of different shapes and sizes for use in cooking and about the house. I fashioned a rude pot capable of holding about five gallons; a smaller one to hold a gallon or thereabouts; a water-jar with two handles by which it might be swung with a cord from the ridgepole, to contain drinking-water; and others of various shapes and sizes. All these I dusted over inside and out with dry sand and set aside where they might dry ready for burning.

That night I slept for the first time in my hammock, and the change was a comfortable one, though in the early morning hours I felt the need of some warm covering. For however hot the days might be, the nights on the island were always cool. However, when it got chilly I turned out and heaped the dry grass of my former bed into the hammock, and was soon warm enough.

In the morning, after setting my vessels out in the sun, I turned to the careful examination of all the samples of vegetation which I had collected, carefully looking them up in the Botany to find their names and properties, and also in the Dispensatory. The seed-bearing grass was undoubtedly canary grass. Besides this and the wax-bearing myrtle, the only other notable sample was a species of india-rubber-bearing artocarpus. As the canary grass was ripe, I thought I could not do better than to harvest a good supply of it at once. The whole of that day and the next were spent in gathering it and stacking it up near the house. The labor was very great, as my knife was a poor substitute for a sickle; but the necessity of some sort of farinaceous food spurred me on. I gathered in all a great stack ten feet in diameter and twelve feet high at the peak. This I thatched with grass, just as I had seen grain stacks thatched at home, that it might be protected from the wet. Great flocks of small birds were feeding upon this seed where it grew, and I trapped a dozen or more by unhinging the chest lid and using it propped up with a stick as a trap.

To try the character of the seed as food, I parched a

pint of it over the fire and then crushed it in a great bivalve shell with a round stone into a coarse meal. This meal I mixed with water and salt, and it made a very good sort of cold gruel. This, with the birds broiled on the coals, made quite the best meal I had so far eaten on the island. The salt pan had already begun to yield salt, which was crystallizing along the edges as the water evaporated. The smoked turtle meat continued good, and I relished it very much. The weather remained fine from day to day, and I had strong hopes that a vessel might heave in sight at any moment. As a preparation for such a chance I laid a pile of wood ready to make a signal fire, and as a permanent signal selected an isolated palm-tree and denuding it of its leaves, tied a great stick across it near the top, — an arrangement which, I hoped, might attract the attention of a passing vessel should I fail to see it. Of material to make a flag I had nothing to spare except the square of black focussing-cloth belonging to the camera, — and this I needed every night as a covering, as it was all I had for that purpose.

As soon as my pots and other vessels were thoroughly dry I built a great pile of dry wood over them and set fire to it. I greatly feared some of them might crack with the heat, but fortunately they all came out in a serviceable condition though by no means very hard. Now that I had a large vessel in which water could be boiled, I bethought me of the wax berries and made several trips to gather a store of them. These I boiled in my large pot, and skimmed off the wax until I had collected fully forty pounds of it, the product of about ten bushels of the berries. Of this wax I made candles, or rather rushlights, by dipping dry rushes into the melted wax and letting it cool on them. When one coat of wax set I would dip the rush again, and so on, until each rush had four good coats. One of these candles would burn about four hours and give a good steady light without sputtering or guttering, though the rush wick required occasional snuffing. These lights were a great comfort to me at night, for I could read and do light work until bedtime without the necessity of keeping up a hot fire.

It was by candle-light that I made me a hat out of rushes as follows: Selecting about fifty of the cleanest and slenderest I could find, and all of about equal length, I tied them firmly together by a cord wound tightly around near the butts. Then I interwove stalks of the tough, heavy grass, spreading the rushes out into a conical shape until large enough to fit comfortably on my head. This was the body of the hat. The brim was produced in the same manner by bending out the ends of the rushes to a common horizontal plane and then interweaving the grass as before, finishing the edge of the brim with a grass selvage. This made a light, cool structure, sufficient to keep the sun off my head, and far more comfortable than the handkerchief I had worn wound about it as my sole head-covering up to this time.

Now that the salt pan was doing its work, and a supply of salt within a few days was considerably more than a mere possibility, I felt justified in endeavoring to obtain a store of meat. My mind turned to the turtle and the pigs, especially the latter; for if I could by any means capture a pig, there would be several weeks' rations, at least, of fresh, salted, and smoked pork. Visions of broiled ham and bacon troubled my dreams. I made an effort to capture another turtle, watching the beach for the good part of a night; but I saw none. The next morning, I determined to go upon a regularly organized pig-hunt. The only method of capturing them was by means of a lasso or the bolas. The forty-foot line that came ashore around the chest would make an excellent lasso, and I rigged it at once with a slip noose. I also cut a hard-wood pole about eight feet in length, charred the end in the fire to harden it, and made it sharp for use as a lance. A bolas was contrived out of two stones tied, one at each end, to a stout cord six feet long. Thus accoutred, I struck off from the creek and made a détour through the dense jungle so as to force the game into the stream, or at least to be upon higher ground if they should prove to be in the mud, as I hoped would be the case. The labor of penetrating the dense scrub was very great, and the heat intense; not a breath of air could reach these fastnesses, and perspiration poured from me as though I were in a Turkish bath.

After a two-hours struggle I found myself nearing the place, and it became necessary to move with the greatest caution. Every few minutes I would stop and listen. Presently I could hear the murmur of the brook, and crawling along cautiously, I came to a fallen tree, the trunk of which reached quite to the stream. By following this down carefully, I came to a point where I could see the wallowing-place. There, sure enough, were the pigs, a score or more in number, mostly lying asleep and half buried in the mud. I studied the whole situation rapidly but thoroughly. It seemed probable from the lay of the ground that if something could frighten the animals from the other side, they would naturally rush under the fallen tree just below me. Indeed, there was a well-beaten track at this place going under the trunk, which was at this point about five feet from the ground, and the stream, the canebrake, and the dense jungle made this by far the easiest route for the pigs.

My plan was made instantly, thus: I would throw

the bolas at a half-grown pig that was rooting about near the jungle on the farther side of the group, and take my chance of the herd coming this way when they broke. I unrolled my lasso and laid it ready for instant use, placed my lance where it could be grasped, and cautiously rising, that I might have free play, swung the bolas around twice and let it fly. Gyrating like twin planets, the stones sped fairly through the air, true to the mark; one passed under the pig, and the other swung behind him, wrapping the cords around the hind-quarters and legs, and bowling him over like a ten-pin. The little fellow set up a squeal, and then, whoof! whoof! with a grunt and a squeal, the whole herd sprang up, looked around, saw their overturned and struggling companion, and started directly toward my place of concealment. In the mean time I had crouched down out of view, and spread my noose ready for business. Underneath they ran squealing and snorting in great panic, and I let them pass as I had my eye on a great boar who was very deliberate in his movements and appeared to disdain undignified flight. He slowly advanced, however, champing his tusks until they frothed, and shaking his great head. I thought it best, in view of his great size and weight, to take a turn of the lasso around a limb and give it a hitch as a holdfast, as my own strength would not be enough to stop the brute. I had scarcely done this when his head came under the tree, and I swung the noose deftly over it as he emerged, and then hauled in the slack. The astonished beast sprang forward with a great bound and jerked the rope from my hands with such violence that I was thrown to the ground.

When I scrambled up I saw the rope tighten until it sung in the air like a bowstring, and then slacken again. I could not see the boar, as he was hidden in the long grass; but I seized my sharpened stick lance and ran toward where he ought to be. Suddenly the great brute emerged from the grass, facing me, and charged toward me, evidently bent on mischief, the flakes of froth flying from his tusks. There was no time to get out of the way, nor even get the lance around into position, and I thought I should speedily feel his sharp tusks. He was almost upon me before I could realize the situation. Just at this critical juncture I felt the lasso fly up under my feet, throwing me over backward, and I caught a glimpse of the boar as he turned a half-somersault and plunged down on his side. When he fell he was not two feet from me. The lasso had been doubled around a bush and had thus brought the desperate creature up just in time to save me. The lance was still in my grasp, and I got to my feet before my enemy could recover. Now it was my turn. Knowing he could not reach me on this side, I came close up to him as he was making the dirt fly with his legs in a vain endeavor to get up, and drove the sharpened stick with all my force and weight into his side, just back of the shoulder.

This ended the battle as the stick went half-way through him. Panting for breath and with the perspiration fairly running into my eyes, I turned away and left him to die in peace, and went to look after the pig, thinking I had been a great fool to tackle the boar at all. I found the pig still struggling with the bolas wrapped around him. I immediately determined to keep this one alive. To do this, I must get my lasso loose from the dying boar. When I went back I found him just kicking his last. With the lasso I secured the pig in such manner that he could not get away, and then removed the bolas and let him up, giving him very little rope as I had no mind to let him run into the brush and entangle himself. I then proceeded to flay the boar, cutting off the hams and choicer parts, and securing as much of the lard and fat as I was able. I carried this down the bed of the creek to the house. I then went back for the pig and endeavored to get him home alive; but I found it utterly impossible to do so, as the vicious, obstinate brute could not be made to go in any but the wrong direction. So I was finally obliged to haul him tight up against a tree and kill him.

I now had a great store of pork, and the next thing was to cure it. Salt was now the important thing, and I went to my salt pan to see what the prospect was. To my great satisfaction, I found the water all dried up, leaving a fine layer of glistening salt, thickest in the lower part of the basin and gradually thinning away to a mere frosting at the edges. It was quite dry and caked, so that there was no trouble to get it up from the bottom, and when I had heaped it together in the centre, there were, I should judge, over fifty pounds. This precious commodity I carried at once to the house so that it might be under shelter from the dew and rain.

I turned to at once to "dry-salt" the pork, rubbing each piece thoroughly on all sides, and piling the whole up in the now empty turtle shell with the breast plate weighed down on it with heavy stones. The only place where I could store this meat was in the single room of my house. But I determined to remedy this by building as soon as possible a lean-to at the back of the house, which I could use first as a smoke-house, and then as a storeroom for my provisions. The turtle meat, now perfectly cured, I stored temporarily in the chest.

That night I lay in my hammock in position to see the starlit ocean through one of the ventilators, and thought over my situation. I could not now complain of lack of food, for there was a supply sufficient to last me two months at least, and there was reason to suppose that it would not be at all difficult to replenish the store. In my porous earthen jar, slung at the head of my hammock in the cool air-current, and by its slow evaporation cooling the liquid contents, was pure, cool, sweet water to drink, and outside was a running brook from which to fill it as often as required. I could safely hope to support myself here as long as might be necessary. But as I had no desire to remain indefinitely a prisoner on this island, I began to turn my thoughts persistently upon the problem of building a boat to get away in. If in the mean time a vessel of some sort should heave in sight I was prepared to take advantage of the chance ; and if none came I would still have my work started and no time unnecessarily lost.

Before I went to sleep that night I had planned a method of building a boat which I thought would be within the possibility of accomplishment, and had determined to begin work on the morrow.

CHAPTER V.

BOAT-BUILDING.

WHEN I roused the next morning the first thought that came to me was about the building of the boat. It would be necessary to have a shed to work under, large enough to contain a boat, both for shelter from the rain and for shade from the pitiless tropical sun. The building of such a shed was therefore the first task. As a suitable shipyard I selected the side of the stream on the sands of the sea-beach, and far enough above tide to be safe from a possible storm. Here I put up eight posts in the sand. To get these posts (for they had to be hunted for among the fallen wood), to carry them one or two at a time for a distance ranging from half a mile to a mile and a half, and to set them up in holes dug at the proper distances apart, was a whole day's work, and left me only time to overhaul my dry-salting before bed-time. I went over each piece of meat, rubbing it again with salt, and turning it the other side up, and finished by putting the weights on again as before. This salting and turning every day would be necessary for about two weeks, and then the meat would be ready for the smoke-house, which I would endeavor in the meantime to get ready to receive it.

The next day I spent getting poles for rafters, and lashing them together to form the roof of my workshop. Then a rain storm set in and lasted three days, during which I was practically confined to the house, and busied myself indoors with making an easy chair out of a dry stick of cedar that split readily into straight pieces. It was a pleasure to work in this soft, straight-grained, fragrant wood, and I made a good, strong, comfortable arm-chair, dowelling and cording the parts together, and framing a sort of base for it so that it would stand firm on the sand floor. I could now sit and read with comfort, or look at the gray, rainy sea as it stretched its misty plane away before my door. It was at this time that I began to keep an irregular sort of journal, entering my thoughts and doings from time to time as the enforced semi-idleness of rainy weather prompted me. Besides pencils and pens there was paper enough in my stock, wet and stained and wrinkled though it had been, to last me indefinitely.

As soon as the rain was over I took the first day to construct my provision and smoke-house, in order that I might store the meat in it. A doorway was cut from my living-room into this store-room, and I purposed fitting a tight door into it before smoking my pork. I busied myself after that on my work-shed until it was finished. This roof I covered with palm-leaves, — not leaves of the cocoanut-palm, but of the great, spreading fan-palm, a single one of which was often three or four feet in diameter. I had used these leaves in making my storehouse roof, and had secured a giant specimen in a horizontal position over my front door as a sort of porch, and to keep the sun out of the house when the door was open.

The work-shed when finished was about twenty-four feet long by ten feet wide, with a shed or single-pitch roof, at the upper side about eight feet, and at the lower side — which was toward the sea — about five feet from the ground. Underneath was the clean sand of the beach. I was now ready to begin the actual work of boat-building, and my first need was a supply of clay, — so great a quantity, in fact, as would take me several days of hard work to raft down the stream to the boat-shed.

You will see as I proceed what part this material was to play. After a great deal of labor, wading up and down the creek, digging, loading, rafting, and unloading, I at last accumulated a sufficient amount for my purpose in a great heap close to the boat-shed. I next proceeded to smooth the sand beneath the shed, and to compact it into a smooth, hard floor as follows: I took of perfectly dry clay several bushels in fragments, and crushed these to a fine dust; this dust I sprinkled evenly all over the sand floor to the depth of an inch or more, sprinkling and wetting the dust and the sand liberally with a bough dipped in the sea water. As the mixture grew dry I trampled it with my naked feet until it was smooth and firm, sprinkling a little dry sand on the surface and trampling it in. The result was a dustless, dry floor, hard enough to support my weight readily, and smooth enough for my purpose.

On this floor, with a stretched cord rubbed with charcoal, I marked, as carpenters do with a chalk line, a straight line twenty-one feet long or thereabouts; this was to be the length of the boat, and its centre line from stem to stern. Using the cord as a measure, I laid off at each side of this centre line, the horizontal outline of my proposed boat. The greatest breadth of beam I made about six feet, and tapered both the stem and the stern alike, after the manner of a whaleboat. At each end of the centre line I drove a stake upright, and notched the top to carry a guide line stretched from one to the other directly over the centre line. Then, with tempered clay, I marked the outline of the boat by building up a little wall about three inches in breadth and as many in height all around from stem to stern on both sides. The space inside this wall I filled with sand, sprinkled and compacted until it was level with the top of the wall. Then I added to the wall another course of clay and filled in again; and so kept on adding and filling and sloping in the wall, until I had a mound of clay-coated sand, shaped like a boat turned upside down.

This labor, simple as it sounds in statement, took me over a week, and before it was done I was interrupted by the necessity for setting my smoke-house in order for curing the hams and bacon. I built for the smoking a slow fire of bark, which required attention only once or twice each day. The clay form under the boat-shed I left to get dry and hard. It was my design, as I have no doubt you have already guessed, to use this clay form as a core or groundwork, upon which to shape my boat.

The next step was a most serious task; I had to procure a piece of timber for a keel, and shape it and fit to it two pieces, one at the stem, and one at the stern. The timber must be new and strong. There was absolutely no way to get this timber except by felling a tree which must be at least a foot in diameter. I could not hope to do this with a pocket knife except by an appalling amount of labor, and at the continual risk of breaking the blade; and, moreover, I did not want to subject this valuable instrument to any more wear than was absolutely necessary. I now carried it on my person tied securely to a lanyard as my most highly prized possession. But I thought I could manage to get down a tree by the aid of fire. Having selected the tree, I plastered the trunk with wet clay all around for a height of five or six feet, excepting a space of about two feet next the ground; then piled up dry fuel on the windward side and set fire to it. After an hour or two the trunk caught fire and slowly burned. I kept checking the fire from eating upward by dabbing wet clay on, until finally the tree burned through and fell. It was a much less difficult task to burn it in two at the proper length after it was once down.

This done, the next thing was to reduce the stick to the correct lateral dimensions, which should be ten inches by three or thereabouts. As there was no saw, adze, or axe to be had, this reduction could be done in no other way so easily as by splitting the trunk with hard-wood wedges. I made several and charred them in the fire, then sharpened them and drove four of them in a line into the wood of the trunk at equal distances apart. By judicious management, driving them little by little, one after another, the trunk was riven asunder, and a second split produced a piece of the right size when a little had been split off from each edge. The plank was not as smooth as if turned out by a saw mill; but it was strong and was smooth enough for my purpose. I dragged it down to the boat-shed, and went back to the log and split off in like manner a piece of suitable size to make the stem and stern posts. I set the keel timber up on edge on the clay mould, securing it temporarily with some lumps of clay until I could mark the correct length. The stem and stern posts I cut and halved on to the keel, pinning them on by pins.

The drill by means of which I bored the holes for the pins was fashioned by inserting a piece of sharp chalcedony splinter into a split stick and securely wrapping the stick with a piece of cord. This stick or shank, which was about two feet in length, carried a ball of dry clay of three or more pounds in weight, and mounted about six inches from the chalcedony point. Through the upper end of the shank was a hole passing through which was a cord secured at each end to a loose cross-stick about a foot long. By twisting this cord around the shank the movement up and down of the loose cross-stick would cause the drill to revolve first in one direction and then in the other, the momentum of the whirling ball of clay causing the apparatus to continue its motion far enough to rewind the cord. This device is much used by primitive peoples, and it certainly proved a most effective instrument to me; for without renewing the drill point I bored five holes at each end, through the keel piece and the uprights.

The gunwale I made by splitting cane into long, thin strips half an inch in width, and laying these in a bundle tied securely round every three or four inches with a wrapping of cord. By this means I produced a sort of stiff, untwisted cable. I secured the ends of these gunwale cables firmly to the stem and stern uprights by cord passed through holes. I next got a great store of a sort of long, slender-stemmed creeper, which I fancy must have been a species of climbing palm, though I am not sure; for there was no description of it in my books. The wood of this creeper was tough and exceedingly fibrous. Of it I proposed to make the ribs of the boat, setting them about three inches apart along the whole length of the boat. The creepers which I chose for this purpose were about half an inch in diameter, and smooth and uniform in size. Holes drilled through the keel piece close to the clay mould permitted the passage of these ribs over the mould from gunwale to gunwale, where they were fastened by being inserted in the mass of cane splints and securely tied there with several wrappings of coïr. Of course I had to stop this work from time to time to manufacture the necessary supply of coïr.

Such interruptions were a relief to me, and I would sit in the shade of the palms spinning away and thinking of my Mohawk Valley home, or gazing out upon the broad sea, where the perfect shading from deep blue to faint cobalt and fainter green, the long swell, and the transparent, curling breakers, the restless sea fowl, and the serene, cloud-flecked sky, formed a view of which I never tired. It is a mistake, it seems to me, to speak of the sea as a lonesome thing. Its ceaseless motion, its constant change of color and of mood, never exactly alike and yet never entirely unlike, all lend to it an indefinable charm. It may, indeed, be filled with solitude, but it also is filled with companionship for the solitary, as I learned then to realize.

The island was the home of an astonishing number of species of small birds; several different varieties of the parrot family flew from tree to tree in flocks; different kinds of finches, many of bright plumage, in great numbers haunted the bushes about the stream; larks, flycatchers, gorgeous scarlet tanagers, little wrens, and tiny humming-birds were very numerous. The bird that I took most interest in was a daring little fellow, perhaps some sort of wren, of a brownish color, specked with pearly white spots. This self-contained and self-satisfied little fowl had a habit of carrying his tail stuck straight up in the air and cocking his head to one side in a most comical manner. This species seemed quite fearless of me, and I often saw them come hopping up on the ground near to where I sat, as though bent on ascertaining what sort of creature I was. Scarcely bigger than a walnut, with a tiny "chirp, chirp," these dainty creatures seemed to be introducing themselves politely to me, and deprecating any possible unfriendliness that might have arisen, or might thereafter arise between us on account of an occasional seed stolen from my stack. At one time I had the notion to capture one or more of these little birds and train them as pets; but their courage and confidence utterly disarmed me.

When all the vine ribs had been fitted to the boat the next thing was to apply an exterior sheathing. This also I constructed of the long smooth creepers, uniform in size and laid close together each piece extending the whole length of the boat. I secured the ends of these vines to the stem and stern pieces by setting them into a groove or rebate, and dowelling a piece of wood down firmly upon them. At intervals I sewed or tied the rib and plank vines together with strong thin cord. When this was done I had the form of a boat, but of course it would leak like a sieve, and moreover would be crank as a basket. The next thing was to procure some sort of gum or resin, with which to coat the whole structure and thus bind it all together and strengthen it, as well as to make it water-tight.

There were trees of the pine or fir species growing on the island, high on the rocky backbone. I could see them distinctly, and had little doubt that they would furnish me with at least some of the ingredients for a sort of pitch, that might be made to answer my purpose. Up to this time I had never ascended the precipitous rocks and cliffs which formed a miniature mountain-range running north and south through the centre of the island. Now I resolved to make the attempt and to ascertain definitely what could be found there in the way of pitch or resin, among the several species of evergreens. To ascend these cliffs and rocks through the thickets and tangled vines was no easy task. Giant beds of fern, fallen tree-trunks, jungles of thorny bush, barred the way apparently at all points. The most feasible route seemed to be up a chasm through which came a tinkling rivulet to join the stream, with many a fall and leap, boiling now, and now dashing in spray over the fern-embowered rocks. It was a hard, hot climb. The humming-birds, like flying jewels, — rubies, topazes, amethysts, lapis lazuli, — darted to and fro in a dozen varieties, pausing to hover over the deep, scarlet chalices of the trumpet flower. Far above in the clear, deep blue of heaven slowly swung a circling vulture on motionless wing, a mere speck against the light.

At last I reached the top, a sort of broken rocky plateau covered with trees among which were numerous evergreens. After a brief rest to recover breath, I examined some of the trees, and found to my great delight a species of pitch pine among them. The scaly, reddish bark was bedewed with tears of gum which I knew would with a little boiling or drying be converted into a hard resin. Without losing any time I went to work with my knife upon the trees. I bared a place of its bark on each of a dozen trunks, about three feet in height and six inches in width, and cut a notch at the bottom to collect the gum, scoring the bared place with cross cuts at intervals of a few inches. This occupied me until it was within two hours of sunset, and I dared stay no longer that day, for fear of being benighted on the way home.

Early next morning I returned with my lasso, an earthenware vessel, and my burning-glass. The wounded trees had already begun to yield a supply of sticky sap or gum, which I scraped down and collected in the earthen pot, until it was quite full. I placed this to melt and boil over a slow fire and proceeded to wound about a dozen more trees. That night I slept on the summit, and worked hard all next day collecting and boiling the resin, so that when I went the next night to the house I was able to carry with me twenty-five or thirty pounds of the material, — a hard, dark resin.

At this labor I spent about a week longer, sometimes going home at night, and sometimes sleeping on the rocks, until I had got together, as I thought, sufficient for my purpose. Now I wanted some grease to mix with the resin, and concluded to kill a pig for this purpose. I had to wait two days to find the herd, but finally succeeded in capturing a fine young porker, which yielded a good store of lard and fat, much more indeed than I needed for the pitch kettle, as well as a fine supply of fresh pork-chops and some meat for the smoke-house.

I melted the resin in my five-gallon pot, and added to it sufficient melted pig-fat, so that the pitch when cold would be quite stiff and hard, but not brittle. With this hot, tenacious pitch I payed the whole exterior of the boat with a good thick coat, penetrating and filling all the interstices. When this was hard and cold I tried to lift the boat from the clay core in order to turn it over. To my disgust I found that the pitch had stuck it fast to the core in a thousand places, so that it could not be moved. There was nothing to do, therefore, except to undermine the whole structure, dig the sand out, and take out the dry, hard clay from below, piece by piece, — an immense labor, as you may well conceive. But this was finally accomplished without injury to the boat. I found that the structure was entirely too flexible for practical navigation, and that it would be necessary to deck over the greater part, if for no other reason than to stiffen it. I decided to make an airtight compartment at each end, extending about three feet, and carry a deck fore and aft over the entire boat, excepting a well hole in the middle, six feet long by three feet wide, which was to be surrounded by a washboard, or raised edge, about six inches in height. Having cleared away the débris, I turned my boat right side up.

I was very anxious to get this boat completed, and had been working hard at it every day for over a month. I wanted to know if it would at least float properly, and therefore labored from early dawn to dark without cessation. One night I had been restless and wakeful, and got up without appetite for parched seed and smoked meat. Fancying this was merely from excitement about the work, and from want of variety in diet, I concluded that the next day I would knock off work for a time and go fishing. But when I went down to the shed and got to work I felt tired and languid. There was a great pain in my head, chilly sensations ran up and down my back, and pains in the limbs and a general depression of spirits warned me of an approaching illness. Fearing a collapse I started for the house, when suddenly I grew faint and fell on the sand, and lay there for several hours, a fierce fever raging through me. An intense thirst stimulated my feeble energies to make one or two attempts to reach the house; but I failed and crawled back to the shed. Once I managed to reach the creek and get a drink, but it was preferable to suffer thirst, I thought, rather than make the attempt again. About sundown the fever left me, and though much weakened I felt well enough to get to the house, light a candle from the last sparks of my neglected fire, and turn into my hammock.

Evidently I was seized with some malarious disorder. Anxious to know what I could do for myself in the way of medicine, I got the Dispensatory and began a search for febrifuges. I could not hope to find Peruvian bark on the island as this region was, I conceived, out of its habitat. However, I made pencil notes of everything I could find mentioned as a febrifuge. Among other things I noted that it was customary in the Campagna near Rome for the fever-stricken inhabitants to make a sort of tea of sliced lemons, which was said to cure the Campagna fever. Now I remembered to have seen wild limes growing along the upper part of the creek, and thought if I could get strength enough to gather some the next day I would try an infusion of them.

That night I slept pretty well, and in the morning got up feeling fairly well. But warned by yesterday's experience, I dreaded a recurrence of the chill and fever, either that day or the next. So I went immediately and gathered a quantity of the ripest of the limes. These I sliced thin with my knife and poured boiling water over them in a small vessel, and set them aside to steep. As soon as the infusion was cold I took a small sip to see what the effect would be. I found no bad consequences, and in an hour took another larger sip. This I kept up every hour all day, and did some work on the boat. That night I drank about a quart of hot water, and buried myself in a bed of dry grass in the house, with a small fire going. I was soon in a profuse perspiration, and after a while fell sound asleep and awoke in the morning hungry. Whether the lime tea checked the fever, or whether the attack was no more than a passing biliousness, I do not know. At any rate I soon recovered, and was not ill again while on the island.

I now resumed work persistently on the boat, and finally the air-tight compartments and decking, made like the rest of the vessel of vines coated with pitch, were done. I got some rollers under the boat and pushed it into the creek, where it floated true and buoyant as I could desire. Mooring it securely I got on board and found it stanch, and every way much better than I had hoped. To my great joy it did not leak a drop, though I had expected to have a great deal of patching to do.

My next task was to rig a mast and sail. The mast I had already brought down from the heights, in the form of a slender evergreen, trimmed and peeled of its bark. Nor was I long in stepping and rigging it with the necessary stays. The making of the sail was a much longer matter. I had given this question a great deal of thought, and while at work on the boat had carefully weighed several different devices, but had been unable to hit upon a feasible plan. Therefore I deferred it until the very last thing, fitting on a rudder and even making and burning a water jar and a cover for it to contain a supply of fresh water on board, before regularly beginning work on the sail. Finally, however, all was finished except the sail, and I was forced to the task. The best thing I could think of for the purpose was strips of bark woven on cord after the fashion in which some window blinds are made from wooden slats and cord; and as this could best be used with what I believe is termed a latteen rig, that is to say a single short mast in the centre of the boat, with a long yard suspended at its top and inclined upward from the bow aft, upon which the sail is hung, I changed my mast and stepped it to suit such a rig. Then I procured a long, slender, tapering pole for a yard. I found a tree with a smooth, flexible inner bark, and after a great deal of labor secured a sufficient quantity, cut in strips one and a half inches in width, and some of it as long as the boom. Then I spun a great quantity of cord, and tied doubled lengths of it to the boom at intervals of a foot. Then laying the boom down on the beach I placed a strip of the bark alongside it and tied it there with all the cords; by the side of that I added another a little shorter and tied it, and so on until I had built up a triangular sail of the bark strips attached to the boom by the cords, the strips running parallel with the boom. In order to make it hold the wind better, I punched holes in the edges of the bark strips, and tied the edges of adjacent strips together.

When I had this sail complete and rigged to the mast the wind was blowing away from the shore, and I had to wait until the next day to give it a trial. But I made everything ready, including food and water and a ballasting of stones, and on the next morning, the wind blowing quietly on shore, I went on board, cast off, and poled the craft out of the creek, watching a good chance to push her through the breakers at the bar. I got safely out, and hoisted the sail. For a moment she fell off and rose and sunk with the swell, but taking the wind fair, presently leaned down until the lee gunwale was nearly buried in the green water, and began to forge ahead rapidly, fairly sliding through the water, with the wake running away behind and a white curl of foam racing from the bow. I tried her on all tacks, on and off the wind, ratching and running before it, and found that the best point of sailing was on the wind. This was entirely satisfactory. So delighted was I with the operation of the boat that I tacked away in stretches of two or three miles until I had beat up a good league from the island, and then turned and ran before the wind straight for the creek, where I arrived safe, and moored the boat securely in her snug harbor.

The building of this boat had taken me three months; but it was at last finished, and offered me a means, at the first fair wind, of sailing away for Martinique or some adjacent island, a port which I could fairly expect to make in two or three days at farthest. I went to bed that night in a happier and more contented frame of mind than I had theretofore experienced on the island.

CHAPTER VI.

"DUKE 2D, PROPERTY OF H. SENLIS."

AS the wind next day was in the wrong quarter, I set deliberately about lading my new boat, as far as my means went, with all the provisions and appliances that seemed necessary for the voyage. This was all done by noon, and I sat down idly to wait for a wind that should promise settled weather, and be in the right direction. The first, second, and third days passed without any prospect of change, and I grew very impatient. Things seemed to have lost their interest for me. The one idea of getting away drove all else out of mind. I walked to and fro along the beach like a caged animal, overhauled my cargo, added to it, changed the water in my storage jar, and did a hundred useless things. Still the breeze blew softly and steadily from the south of east, — a head wind, which would oblige me to ratch all the way to Martinique.

On the third night, as I was sitting out on the beach in the moonlight, I bethought me of the ancient rhyme of the mariner who, cursed by everlasting head winds, toiled on day by day only to be blown back night after night. There was plenty of time now to plan what I should do when I reached Martinique. Up to this time I had not thought it out very carefully. So to pass the dreary hours I began to go over the whole programme mentally. The more I thought about it, however, the less prospect could I see of getting at Martinique what appliances and assistance I wanted, even if

I had possessed money enough. I should have to go clear back to New York to get another diving apparatus, and that of itself would consume the greater part of my funds.

When this conviction forced itself on my mind, I was aghast. Must I give up the search for the treasure-ship merely for lack of funds, after all my trouble and expense? I sprang up and began walking up and down the sand at the very edge of the breakers, like a wild man. Abandon my enterprise? Never, never! I would rather stay and die on the island than do that. Why not, indeed, stay on the island and take my chances. I had built a boat out of nothing, and why could I not contrive some means for at least finding the sunken galleon and locating it accurately? Then, with something definite in prospect, it would surely not be difficult to go to Martinique and there interest somebody else to furnish the necessary funds for the enterprise, and divide the proceeds. There seemed to be wisdom in this course, and I resolved to adopt it forthwith.

Even as I made this resolution a heavy cloud passed over the moon, a faint breeze stirred through the rattling palm-leaves, and putting up a moistened finger I found the wind had changed to the southwest; soon it began to increase, and in an hour there was a fine steady breeze blowing exactly from the best quarter for my voyage, if I had chosen to take advantage of it. I was thankful at that moment that it had not come sooner. I looked long and musingly upon the darkening water and it must have been nearly midnight when, after seeing carefully to the security of my boat, I turned into the hammock with a contented mind, and buoyed up by a firm resolve to succeed.

In the morning, as I was going down to the stream, I saw approaching along the sands a dog. Nothing could have been more astonishing to me than this sight. What could a dog be doing on this island? When and how did he get here? Where dogs are, there also are men. This dog could never have come here alone. The animal saw me as soon as I saw him, and came running up wagging his tail in the most friendly way, running around in half-circles, and barking with delight. I called him up and stroked his head. He was a fine black Gordon setter, with an intelligent high-bred appearance. Around his neck a chain collar bore a plate engraved "Duke 2d, property of H. Senlis." "Duke, good Duke," said I, "where is your master?" But the only answer Duke could make was a series of delighted contortions, jumps, and short barks. I went to the house and got some dried turtle-meat, which he ate voraciously, and seemed to call for more. When I had fed him all he seemed to demand he curled up on the sand as contentedly as though this was a long sought resting-place. With his head over one paw and one eye occasionally opening to look at me, he was the very picture of contentment and satisfaction.

As I sat eating my breakfast of parched-seed gruel and broiled bacon, and looking at the dog curled up on the sandy floor of my house, I speculated on the method of his arrival on the island. Was he shipwrecked like myself, or left by some hunting party? Was he here alone, or were those to whom he belonged still on the island; and if so where were they? The whole island was not above six or seven miles in length, and three or four in breadth. Yet the dense forest growth, the jungles and cane-brakes, the central ridge of precipitous rocks could easily conceal the presence of other people, especially if they were on the other side. At any rate I thought it high time for me to take a careful survey of the entire domain, and this, if for no other purpose, to satisfy my curiosity aroused by the startling advent of Duke 2d.

When I first saw the dog he was coming up apparently from the southern end of the island, and I concluded to start in that direction down the beach, and go as far as possible along the sea, — quite around the whole island if that were practicable. With this view I packed my haversack with provisions, and filled my large bottle with fresh water, and swung it by a cord under my arm. Taking my lasso and lance and burning-glass, I started down the beach. Duke followed or ran on before, as much pleased apparently as though we were on a gunning expedition. The beach extended south from my house for a distance of about three miles, and then terminated in a low, rocky shore covered with cactus and thorny shrubs. Beyond this the southern-most extremity of the island extended in a rocky headland, and there were some low rocks detached from the shore and covered at high tide, forming dangerous breakers, to which a navigator rounding the southern cape would wish to give a wide berth.

In the sand and among the rocks where the cactus grew I captured an armadillo. This harmless little creature, about the size of a sucking pig, was called to my attention by the dog, which had discovered it and seemingly did not know what to make of such a strange customer, covered with its curious, horny armor. Duke was sniffing and jumping back and barking, when I caught sight of the hindquarters of the armadillo just disappearing in the sand. The animal was burrowing itself out of sight with astonishing rapidity in the loose soil. At first I could not conceive what it was, as it appeared from the view I had more like some sort of a reptile than an animal. But I speedily recognized it, and pulled it bodily out of the tunnel it was excavating.

The little fellow did not attempt to run away, but curled itself up into a ball with its head and feet tucked out of sight. Duke went up to it and turned it several times over with his paw, but evidently could have inflicted no injury upon it had he been minded to make the attempt. However, as roast armadillo is noted as a savory dish I speedily put an end to its life by inserting my knife blade between the joints of its armor, and it was added to our larder at once.

We now crossed over through the rocks to the west shore, which was formed, so far as I could see, of rocks and cliffs, which rose bolder and higher toward the north. The travelling along these cliffs was very bad, and at a break I descended to the narrow margin of sand and rocks at their feet, left bare by the receding tide. Here the walking was fairly good, and we made our way along at a good pace for a mile. Now the shore rose boldly up in a sheer cliff nearly a hundred feet in height, and the beach was little more than a mass of fallen rock. In a shallow indentation or bay we, or rather the dog, discovered bubbling up through the sand a spring of cold, pure water which must have been under the sea at high tide. There was also an abundance of small oysters attached to the rocks, and I ate of them for my lunch.

At this spring I refilled my water bottle and sat down to rest in the shade of the rocks. The dog seemed very uneasy for some reason, and thinking there might be some animal about, I got up and looked around. To my great alarm I soon discovered that the tide had risen so far as partly to submerge some of the rocks that were dry when I had passed a half-hour before. It would be no trifling matter to be caught in this place by the tide; but whether it were best to go on or go back I could not tell. However, as I knew the road behind me I determined to retrace my steps. I had not gone a quarter of a mile before I found that it would be impossible to pass in that direction. Whether it would be practicable to proceed in the other I could not foresee; it was so doubtful that I had no time to lose. So I hurried back again to the spring, where a margin of sand was still uncovered by the rising waves. Here I soon found that advance as well as retreat along the water was cut off. Above me frowned the perpendicular cliffs. The situation seemed full of desperate peril, and was grave enough in all reason.

I felt much as one might fancy a rat feels when the door of the trap snaps on him, and breathless he circles about and finds no exit. Duke was crouched down and shivering as with an instinct of apprehension. There was a sense of numb despair with it all — a sickening sense of giving up the fight, as though it were useless to strive against brutal ill fortune. Why did I ever come into this rat-trap? Now a man should not waste any time or thought on vain repinings, self indignation or accusation, under such circumstances, but turn his attention to the real question, and keep his eye fixed firmly and singly on the main chance. But it is not always easy to think when and of what you ought. Indeed, I found myself speculating as to how the end would come. Inch by inch the water would creep up. Duke would first be swept under, unless I chose to support him for a while. Then little by little I would be submerged, knees, middle, chest, shoulders, neck, chin, lips, — and then the final struggle. I cast my eyes up to see how far above my height the water would rise. The marks of high water were there plain on the cliff, and I calculated that I should be submerged at least eight feet at high water.

All along, the rock rose sheer up without a break to

the very top. There was one place, however, where the cliff, undermined by the waves, had split off and fallen down, making a ledge about twenty-five or thirty feet above the water's edge; but there seemed to be no way of climbing up to this ledge, — indeed it overhung the base. Upon it grew two or three small trees, and one of them leaned out over the sea. When my faculties once more began to assert themselves, it occurred to me that it might be possible to cast the end of my lasso over this projecting tree-trunk and thus perhaps haul myself up to the ledge hand over hand.

The conception of this idea was almost equivalent to its execution; I felt that I was saved. To one end of the lasso I tied a stone, and secured the other end firmly around the body of the dog. This stone I cast easily over the tree trunk, and swung the rope in such a manner that the weighted end would twist several times around the body of the rope. I pulled and tested it with my weight, and it held firm. Casting my lance up on the ledge, I climbed hand over hand up the rope, occasionally steadying myself with feet against the rock, until I had a firm grasp on the trunk and was safely on the platform. Leaning over I called to the dog, and when he came up close to the rock I spoke to him kindly to allay his fears, and then hauled him up. The platform was at least ten feet wide at the middle part, perhaps forty feet long, and tapered away to a mere ledge at each end. There was plenty of dry dead sticks and wood which had fallen down from above, and, as the afternoon sun shone hot and bright in the western sky, it was not long before I had kindled a fire with my burning-glass, and had spitted the armadillo for a roast.

I now sat and watched the sea rise and wash in breakers on the base of the cliff, and shuddered to think what would have been my fate but for the lasso and the timely aid it afforded me. I watched a glorious sunset wherein long bars of purple cloud edged with molten gold, and fleecy flakes of burning vermilion melted on a sky of gray-green light, over an ocean of dark blue shot with violet, and here and there tinted and gilded with crimson and gold from the red, flaming ball that was just dipping to the horizon. And far into the night I sat awaiting the rising of the moon, the novelty of the situation driving all inclination for sleep from me. Duke was a good companion, and inclined to sit out the company. He lay with his head on my knee, occasionally looking up into my face in a truly sociable and friendly manner.

About nine o'clock at night, there being then a dead calm, I heard distinctly the beat of a screw propeller, accompanied by the regular blowing at slow intervals of escaping steam. I looked all about for the vessel, and presently made out her mast-head light, like a star quivering on the horizon. Gradually it lifted above the water in the southern sky, and I knew it would pass me quite near at hand unless its course were changed. There were still some embers of my fire alight, and nothing would have been easier than to make a signal which doubtless would have been seen on board. But though I gathered the embers together instinctively, I took no step toward making the signal. She drew nearer and nearer, and finally passed along the coast not half a mile distant, trailing a long plume of smoke. So near was she at one time that in the starlight and upon the light of the sea I could distinguish her form and build, and conjectured that she was some ocean tramp, sliding along stern deep down, and nose cocked out of the water, looking for a cargo from port to port, — an iron steamer, such as are sent out by thousands now-a-days to wander over all the seas and oceans, and which, going from port to port, finally return to the home port, perhaps when it is time to lay their sides and ribs into the junk heap for old iron.

When the moon rose the steamer was a pale, gray spot at the end of a long stain of dark smoke far in the northern horizon. It finally disappeared, the smoke fading away and mingling with the faint mist-wreaths that stole up from the sea under the moonlight. I went to bed on the rock with Duke coiled up beside me, and slept until broad day. I found the water still too high for me to descend safely to the sand; the tide had apparently gone out and was coming in again. I did not much like the idea of descending again to the foot of the cliff if it could be avoided, because there was no telling whether I could safely proceed farther to the north; nor was I yet ready to go back home, for I intended, if possible, to make the complete circuit of the island.

Therefore I turned my attention to that portion of the cliff that rose above my ledge. After a careful scrutiny I concluded it would be possible to reach the top by climbing a tree that grew close to the rock. A narrow ledge could be reached from the upper limbs, and it led along the face of the rocks for a few steps to a sort of crack or chasm up which one might easily clamber to the top. I climbed down to the beach as soon as the water was low enough, and filled my bottle anew at the spring, Duke howling and barking all the time, as though in great distress at being deserted. I returned to the ledge, fastened the end of the lasso around the dog, and climbed up the tree with my lance, haversack, and water bottle. With some difficulty I reached the chasm safely, and proceeded to haul up the dog. From there the climbing was not difficult to the top.

Here was a considerable forest, similar to the growth on the central mountainous plateau of the island where I went for pitch. Indeed, as well as I could then see, and as afterward I found to be the case, this line of cliffs was connected with the central plateau by a ridge running east and west. There was a valley between the cliffs and the plateau, divided into two parts by this transverse ridge. The travelling through the woods on the cliff was not difficult, as there was very little undergrowth.

I made a discovery in this wood of several lofty trees which bore nuts of the triangular variety known as Brazil nuts. They grow enclosed in a hard outer casing like a small cannon-ball. One of these fell as I passed beneath the tree. If it had struck Duke or me there is no estimating the hurt that would have been occasioned. It fell fairly on a projecting root, and burst open, scattering the loose nuts about. I gathered a haversack full and filled my shirt and pockets, casting uneasy glances the while up into the trees in fear of a possible bombardment from above; nor did we linger long under those dangerous limbs.

Pushing along, as near the edge of the cliffs as possible, we came, near the middle of the island, north and south, to a well beaten path leading down toward the sea through a break in the cliffs. Duke immediately bounded down this path, and I followed him anxiously; for it did not look as though made by pigs, but rather as if trodden by human feet. The narrow gorge speedily widened out into a little bowl-shaped valley, open to the sea on one side, and on three sides walled in by the cliffs, which were hung with luxuriant vegetation, — a most lovely spot. A gently sloping sward extended nearly to the pebbly beach, and a little stream of clear water, which came frothing in haste down the glen, paused in a quiet sweep and curve through the meadow, the long grass bending over its narrow course, and dipping into the limpid surface, till finally it flowed down over a bed of bright-colored pebbles to the little bay in front. Here and there a wide-spreading tree cast a broad, purple shadow, and many flowers sent forth fragrance to the pure, warm air. It was truly a sylvan paradise.

What specially interested me, however, was the white gleam of canvas shining through the foliage. A tent was pitched near the stream. I called out to announce my presence, but nobody appeared, and going up to the structure, I found it vacant and deserted. The tent was made of a huge mainsail, stretched over a pole and secured to the ground by pegs. It evidently had been long deserted, perhaps a month; the rains had washed the ashes of a fire nearly all away. In the trunk of an adjacent tree stuck an axe, buried to the helve as though by a powerful hand. The metal was all covered with red rust, and so firmly imbedded in the gash that I could not release it until I had pounded it out with a stone. A further search disclosed a dish broken in half, a rusty case-knife, a hand-saw, an iron kettle, a frying-pan, which lay in the tent, and fragments of old newspapers and letters strewed about. In one corner were two blankets rolled loosely together and somewhat mildewed. I hauled these blankets and also an old topsail out of the tent, and spread them in the sun to dry.

Then I wandered about seeking some clew as to who had been here and how long since; but conjecture was idle. At the mouth of the creek there was a tree with the marks on it of a mooring line; and the trace of the line was still faintly visible on the earthy bank. The most probable supposition was that a party of pig-hunters had landed here, and for some reason had been suddenly called away. That they had left hurriedly was evident both from the standing tent and its contents, and also from the fact that a garden had been planted, which was now grown up to rank luxuriance. In this garden was a great quantity of yams and sweet potatoes, most of them just in a condition to be gathered; also peas and beans quite dry and ripe, and some Indian corn, the last still green. A rusty shovel and hoe were lying there just as they had been left. I made no scruple to help myself to what I wanted of this abundant harvest that chance had placed in my hand. It was not long before I had a fire built and the kettle on, and some of the yams and sweet potatoes boiling. These vegetables eaten hot, with salt and bacon, were to my unaccustomed palate more delicious than I can describe. Duke also ate of them ravenously.

About two o'clock in the afternoon, after packing up the new-found property in the tent as securely as I could, I hurried away to the north along the cliffs, anxious to reach home in order to get my boat and return for these treasures; for treasures indeed would this abundant supply of food as well as the other things be to me. About a quarter of a mile north of this little haven, which I named "Farm Haven," the cliffs ran back from the sea, leaving a broad, smooth beach which gave an excellent road quite to the northern extremity of the island, excepting at one place where I was obliged to wade waist deep across the mouth of a deep indenting cove. At the northern end were isolated rocks, one of which rose boldly up to a height of fifty or sixty feet and was surrounded by the water even at low tide. After clambering over the rocks for an eighth of a mile I struck again the smooth, incurving beach that margined the eastern shore, and before dark reached home.

Everything about the house was just as I had left

it, and the boat was gently heaving to the modified swell that penetrated in gentle undulations to its safe harbor in the creek. I sat long that evening enjoying the cool air, and speculating on the events of my journey. I had not found Duke's master, but could account at least in some measure for his presence on the island; for he had been undoubtedly forgotten in the hurried departure of the party whose camp I had just visited.

CHAPTER VII.

THE WATER-GLASS.

THE morning broke fair with a gentle breeze from the west, which would enable me to make the run easily in a couple of hours. I put on board two light poles which might, if necessary, serve for oars, and rigged a couple of loops on the washboard at each side, through which to thrust them when they were to be used. After taking on board a supply of water, and food enough for several days in case I should chance to be blown out to sea, and not forgetting my lasso and burning-glass, I called Duke on board, hoisted the sail, and cast off. Out through the creek mouth, over the bar, and through its breakers slid the little craft, and as soon as we were fairly outside I bore up and ran straight for the north cape, with a fair beam wind. The fresh morning air, the dew still wet on the boat, the sun scarce a span above the sea, the cool, blue water sliding by, the breaking of the surf as it ran angling along the strand, all acted like a cordial to my spirits. Duke sat up in the bottom of the boat eyeing the whole proceeding with a critical air, hardly willing to yield an entirely unqualified approval, and yet not ready to advance any positive objection. I fairly burst into a laugh at his quizzical expression. He sprang up wagging his tail and came to me and laid his head on my knee, as much as to say, "It is all right, I see."

Before reaching the cape I eased off a little with the intention of running approximately over the region where the sunken galleon was supposed to lie. The spot, according to the admiral's account, was about a mile east of north from the rocky point, and I wanted to sound as far out in this direction as my forty-foot line would allow, if, as I hoped, there should chance to be any shallow that would allow me to reach bottom at all near the shore. The yellowish color of the water off the cape gave token of an extensive shoal in this direction, as did also the peculiar action of the swell, which seemed half inclined to break as it passed. With a stone tied to the line, I sounded as soon as I passed the cape, and found at two hundred yards from shore not over twenty feet of water. This depth increased very gradually until the full length of the line, forty feet or thereabouts, ran out at a distance of an eighth of a mile from the shore, showing that there was a long shoal or submerged spit extending out from the north end of the island.

As soon as I left the immediate vicinity of the shore, where the breakers stirred up the bottom, the water became beautifully clear and transparent, so that at my last sounding I saw, or fancied I saw, the gleam of the bright sand shining up from below. I now lowered the sail to test if there was any current running, but beyond a slight movement, I could detect nothing. I was now far enough from the cape so that I could take a slant to the southwest and easily clear the rocks. So I hauled up the sail and brought her head around. Soon we were spinning along the western shore, and in an hour were off the "Farm Haven," toward which I turned, and running into the mouth of the little stream moored the boat safely and landed.

There was a busy day before me, and I lost no time in beginning work. First of all, I threw the ballast overboard to make room for a cargo of yams and potatoes. I next wove out of willow branches a rough basket, or rather a sort of shallow tray, to carry them to the boat. I dug and loaded fully five bushels of fine, clean sweet potatoes and a number of large yams, and the supply remaining in the ground would have filled my boat a half-dozen times. I next turned my attention to the dry peas and beans, and gathered about a bushel of each, besides a number of great scarlet pepper-pods. Then I took down the tent and put it aboard, as well as the axe, the shovel, the hoe, and the sail and blankets. I boiled a lot of yams for dinner, and this being over at about three in the afternoon, I called Duke and went up the gully path to the top and looked about a little to see what prospect there might be for a path over the island to the other side. In a straight east and west line the distance could not be over three and a half to four miles.

There was a ridge running back from the cliff to the central plateau, which I thought might afford an easy path, and I knew that once on this central plateau I could descend to the stream and so reach home. Having seen this much I returned to the boat, and casting off poled out as far as possible to get an offing. By short tacks I managed finally to get far enough to venture on my northern slant. But the sun was almost down when I rounded the north cape and started down the other shore.

Just as I came opposite the mouth of the creek, the wind died away, and I hastened to get out my rude poles and row into the harbor. This was a terrible task, and if the wind had not gone down I much doubt whether I could have done it at all until the tide turned. But at last we made the creek and moored the boat safely with its precious cargo. I was too tired that night to do more than unload the tools, blankets, canvas, and cooking utensils, leaving the vegetables on board till morning. That night being oppressively warm, I swung my hammock under the open workshed, and lulled by the music of the breakers, slept soundly until broad day.

The first work on hand was the care of my cargo of potatoes. These with the beans and peas I carried up to the dark, dry store-room. Some of the potatoes I buried in the dry sand, to test its preservative properties. As a future provision I turned up with the spade a little patch of soil near the creek and planted half a dozen hills of yams and potatoes in a favorable spot, and a row of the beans and peas, guarding the latter from the birds with a layer of brush. This occupied the greater part of the day.

In the afternoon I drew a wire nail out of the chest, with which to make a fish-hook. The back of the axe formed a good anvil, and the shank of the hoe, the wooden handle being removed, did fairly well for a hammer. With these tools I fashioned the red-hot nail into hook form, using for tongs a pair of clam shells. I drew the point out sharp, bent the hook, and cut a barb over the edge of the axe. The head of the nail was left intact to secure the line. As this was my first effort at blacksmithing the hook was not perhaps as elegant as it might have been, but it looked as though it might work satisfactorily. For a line, I unlaid and retwisted some pieces of hempen rope that had formed reef points on the sail of the tent, and coated them well with candle-berry wax. I made a wooden float for a bob and fitted a stone for a sinker, so that by bed-time, my fishing-tackle was finished, together with a good hundred feet of stout line.

That night a rain set in, and it continued steadily for

three days without ceasing, varying only between a violent downpour and a fine, driving mist from the northeast. I could not work out of doors in such weather; so, gathering a great quantity of cocoanut husks, I busied myself hour after hour spinning cöir. I wanted to make a good, strong, sounding-line at least a hundred fathoms long, and a line of equal length by which to anchor a buoy as a guide in the submarine search operations. Thus the time was by no means lost, though the confinement was exceedingly irksome. Duke made an occasional dash out into the wet, and once returned carrying in his mouth an armadillo rolled up tight in a ball, which afforded us a variation in diet.

But the sky finally cleared and I hastened out to try my fishing-tackle. Anchoring the boat just beyond the breakers at the mouth of the creek, I baited my hook with a shell-fish and cast it over, letting the line run slowly out as the hook sank toward the bottom, and then hauling it up and repeating the operation. Presently I got a tremendous bite, and drew in a fish that weighed about fifteen pounds. It was a red snapper, and proved most excellent eating. This was fishing enough for once, and I pulled to shore and set about cooking part of my prize. Soon the air was redolent with the odor of fried fish, and both Duke and I regaled ourselves with fish and potatoes, washing them down with pure, sweet water cool from the porous water-jar.

I now set about the construction of an apparatus by the aid of which I hoped to be able to make a reconnaissance of the bottom of the shallow sea, where the sunken galleon was supposed to lie. I went out with my axe to the upland and cut down a fine cedar tree. This I split until I procured four rough but slight slabs, an inch thick and about a foot in width, sawing them to a length of about three feet. I pinned these securely together in the form of a rectangular tube a foot in diameter and three feet long, and in one end of the tube fitted a tight cedar bottom. In this bottom I cut an aperture just large enough to receive one of my glass photograph plates, five inches by seven, and after cleaning off the sensitive gelatine coating securely fitted it in place like a window. With melted pitch I payed freely all the joints and seams, so that the structure was perfectly water-tight, and then blackened the wood on the inside with a mixture of pulverized charcoal and hot wax, so that it would reflect no light.

Before this was finished the rains set in again and continued for a whole week. I concluded that the annual rainy season must now be at hand. For though the sky would occasionally clear for a day or part of a day, the showers were so frequent that the house grew damp and unwholesome, and I was obliged to air it every day with a rousing fire in the fireplace, the heat of which drove me to seek shelter under the workshed. The weather was so uncertain that I did not dare to venture out in the boat further than a few hundred feet, and then with a line fast to the shore; this I occasionally did for the purpose of fishing, and always with good luck, catching the red snappers, rock cod, and various other varieties, all of which found their way to the larder.

It was on one of these occasions that I tried my new-made contrivance, the water-glass. When the closed end of this was submerged over the side of the boat, by looking in at the open upper end I could plainly see the bottom and the fish swimming about my hook. Of course I was very anxious to try the apparatus in deeper water to ascertain how far the vision could penetrate. But the weather would not render it possible without too great risk. The value of such a device would depend entirely upon the clearness and depth of the water. I knew from written accounts that the sponge fishers use a similar contrivance, — frequently a wooden bucket with a pane of glass in the bottom, which they call a "sponge glass," and with which they search for sponges and conch shells in the Bermudas, employing it with perfect success, in clear water, even at a considerable depth. The sponge glass enables the operator to overcome the surface agitation and reflection of the water, just as a thin transparent sheet of ice sometimes renders the bottom of a deep pond visible to a skater.

One morning, when there was an almost perfect calm, I noticed on the surface of the sea a long streak extending from a point about half a mile from shore away toward the eastern horizon until it was lost in the distance. This appearance was so curious and inexplicable that after gazing at it for a while, both from the beach and from the top of a palm, I finally rowed the boat out to it, and found that it was muddy water, with leaves, grass, and vegetation floating in it, and a great number of cocoanuts bobbing about among the other fragments and detritus. It looked precisely as though the contents of some slack water lagoon connecting with the sea had been suddenly swept out by a freshet or some extraordinary current. Among the floating matter were innumerable sea beans, as they are called, — a sort of nut or seed that is sometimes used as an ornament for watch chains, — also little scarlet, egg-shaped seeds, like those that are picked up in such quantities on the Florida beaches. But there was no sea-weed with the other detritus. This mass of matter slowly travelled along the surface and by the next day was out of sight. I suppose to a more skilled observer the phenomenon might have proven a valuable aid in determining the set of the currents, or other natural facts worthy of note.

While out on this excursion I several times tried the water-glass, but found the sea so charged with matter and so cloudy and milky that I could see but indistinctly and to no great depth. This, however, did not discourage me, as I knew the water was likely to change in this respect from week to week.

There came upon the island at this time great numbers of pelicans. They would light on the beach in large flocks, and sit there for hours, apparently resting from a long flight; then all together, as by a concerted signal, they would rise and in an irregular body wing their way to the south. Duke took great delight in hunting these birds, and would watch by the hour for their arrival. As soon as a flock appeared in the northern sky he would prick up his ears, all attention, and wait until, circling about, they alighted. Then he would begin a deliberate attempt to stalk them, creeping along, belly to the ground, until nearly up to them, then making a bold rush, but always without success, the birds on such occasions merely rising and circling to another resting-place. He would come in after this sport wet with the rain and panting with exertion, and appeared to look with reproach at my lack of interest in the game, as though he would say, "Where is your gun, you idle fellow?" But I had no use for pelicans. Indeed, I still had too vivid a remembrance of the peculiar flavor of gull meat to hanker after fish-eating birds of any sort, as food. The white crane, or heron, and the beautiful pink and white ibis also made their appearance occasionally in flocks; but they were so shy and difficult to approach that I could never get within a hundred yards of them.

Penetrating one morning, in spite of the drizzling rain, to a part of the forest just under the rocky plateau, I came upon some trees about thirty or forty feet in height having flowers variegated with purple, yellow, green, and red, and bearing at the same time fruit in the form of great gourds. This I found was what is known as the calabash tree (*Crescentia cujete*). I collected a number, of different sizes, and carried them home through the rain. The hard, wood-like shells could readily be cut with the knife and saw, yet they were strong and tough. With this raw material, already partially shaped to hand, I set about making various kinds of vessels, — domestic and culinary utensils, a water-bottle to carry on my tramps and excursions, etc. With four great gourds lashed together I constructed a buoy for subsequent use in my marine explorations, and with a number of small ones I made a life-preserver as a part of my boat equipment. It was a great comfort to have a dish to eat from once more. Indeed, I had often regretted that I did not bring with me the two halves of the broken dish which I had seen at the "Farm Haven." My two developing-trays with their deep sides had proved but inconvenient substitutes; besides, they were generally kept for other uses. Taken altogether there was no single vegetable product of the island that contributed more to my comfort than the calabash tree.

As I now had plenty of canvas I concluded to rig my boat anew and change it from the awkward latteen rig to that of a sloop with mainsail and jib. The want of a needle and thread to sew the sails was a great drawback, but I made shift to use an awl made out of a leg of a compass belonging to my drawing instruments, and for thread a slender cord made of cöir. I rigged the jib with a traverse so that it needed no special attention except to be hauled aft when I went about, and the mainsail with a gaff and throat halliards, that it might be lowered by the run upon emergency; I also provided both jib and mainsail with three rows of reef points, that I might show little or much canvas, as the state of the wind should require. With axe and saw and knife I fashioned a good pair of cedar oars, light and strong, and fitted thole-pins in the gunwales to receive them; I put a pair of thole-pins in the stern for sculling, and had a spare oar for use in case of breakage.

The weather continued stormy, with rain nearly every day, and frequently for several days together without cessation. I passed most of the time under the boat-shed, and generally slept there at night, as the climate was very mild and warm notwithstanding the rains. Moreover, I had now two blankets to sleep in at night, and lay quite warm and comfortable in my hammock. The house I used as a kitchen, dining-room, store-room, and library. It was quite impossible to read elsewhere at night, for the candle could not be kept alight in the open-sided shed. I read all the books through deliberately, including the German Word-book. I would lie in my swinging hammock by the hour during the daytime and read even the Dispensatory faithfully through while the rain pattered on the roof, with an occasional "swish, swish," as the eddying wind drove it with greater or less violence against the house. That I should find the dry details of a Dispensatory sufficiently interesting to make the continuous reading of them even endurable expresses well the desperate dulness of my lonesome surroundings. Duke slept much, and I envied him his capacity for slumber. He would lie in a dry spot and snooze for fifteen minutes at a time, get up and gape and stretch, then lie down and shiver and drop to sleep with one eye open, and so alternating pass the day. Sometimes I would practice on him with German words from the Word-book, which he understood, so far as I could see, quite as well as English. At any rate, when I spoke he wagged his tail, and thus demonstrated that he was a good fellow and not disposed in any degree to criticise or find fault with the personal peculiarities or the language of a friend.

At last one clear, bright morning, when the birds were noisily rejoicing and the butterflies were out in their gala dresses, I undertook an expedition by land to the "Farm Haven." The creek was swollen deep with the rains, so that I could not conveniently travel up the bed. Therefore I made my way north along the beach for a mile, and struck west through the jungle at the most open place I saw. By an occasional use of the axe I forced a path through to the rocks, which happened here to be low, and speedily gained the central plateau. At the point where I mounted the rocks I found great quantities of ripe whortleberries growing on low bushes, and of large size and exquisite flavor. I ate my fill of these and pressed on along the plateau looking for the connecting ridge. The walking was not bad on this upland, as there was no tangled mass of undergrowth, and the trees grew well apart. The ridge was not difficult to find and proved easily passable, so that I made shift to reach the cliffs long before noon.

Being near them I went to the Brazil-nut trees and gathered a peck or more of the nuts, filling my haversack quite full as well as my pockets. Duke here chased a little animal which I fancied must be what is called an agouti; but as he did not catch him I could not know positively. However, this persistent hunter soon after managed to tree an animal which I had no difficulty in recognizing as the familiar raccoon. I had no idea until I saw this specimen that this plantigrade was to be found in the Caribbean islands. There was, however, no mistaking the identity of the species. It was undoubtedly a genuine "coon." The silver-tipped fur, the pointed snout, the barred tail all spoke in favor of a true descent and a perfect relationship with the animal which I had so often hunted on moonlight nights in the woods at home. It was an undoubted "case of coon." When I found him he was in a slender sapling, with Duke barking below. I laid the axe to the trunk and speedily felled it to the ground. Duke seized his victim before he could recover, and shook him as a terrier would a rat. Running to his assistance I speedily put an end to the combat with my knife, and bagged the game. Here was material for a feast, for I well knew by experience that roast coon is a morsel fit for an epicure.

Farm Haven looked beautifully fresh from the rains. I found the garden still more choked with weeds, and the potatoes mostly gone to seed. I gathered a few to roast in the embers for my dinner, but most of them had begun to decay. The Indian corn was ripe, and I took this occasion to gather it all, a good heap of perhaps ten bushels, which I carried little by little to a sheltered nook under the rocks and piled up without removing the husks. I started a good fire to roast some corn and potatoes. After dressing the coon I swung it by a cord in front of the fire where it was slowly turned by the twist of the cord first in one direction and then in the other, requiring only an occasional twirl to keep it going.

While the dinner was cooking, Duke and I looked about the valley to see what could be found. We went over to the north of the mouth of the rivulet among some willows, to gather a few wands for basket-making. As soon as we reached the other side of the stream I noticed a strong stench as of decayed animal matter.

The source of this smell was soon disclosed in a great heap of oysters. Great bivalves, some of them eight or more inches across, lay rotting in a pile on the pebbly shore. All about were heaps of open shells and decayed shell-fish. It occurred to me at once that I had chanced upon the headquarters of a pearl fishery; and this accounted most satisfactorily for the encampment, but not for the hurried departure of the campers. There was at least a ton of unopened oysters lying in the rotting drying-heap, and I determined to examine them as soon as we had finished dinner.

CHAPTER VIII.

BREAD-MAKING.

THERE was a wooden tub lying near the oyster heap, which I conjectured was for holding water in which to open and separate the oysters in the examination for pearls. I filled this tub at the stream and set it in the shade of the willows. Then, with bared arms, and nostrils plugged with leaves, I began the disgusting task of examining the oysters carefully one by one. The second oyster I opened contained fifteen little seed pearls not much larger than a grain of mustard seed. Then I drew blank after blank in the lottery, until I had opened perhaps fifty shells. Then a great prize came out in the shape of a beautiful pear-shaped pearl of the size of a small hazel-nut, rainbow tinted and lustrous as a moon-lit cloud. Thus it went with varying fortune all the afternoon, until the heap was exhausted and I had collected two hundred and fifty seed pearls, ninety-seven small pearls, and a hundred and sixteen larger ones, some of them of great lustre and beauty. What the value of these pearls would prove to be I had no means of estimating, but it doubtless would be considerable. I tied them carefully in my handkerchief and put them in my pocket. The smell of the decayed shell-fish is something frightful to remember, and after I had finished and washed myself thoroughly in the stream it still seemed to cling to me and to permeate everything in the neighborhood. Why I had not noticed this awful stench on my first visit was strange to me, and must have been due to the course of the wind at that time.

When I had finished this loathsome task it was so late that I concluded to stay all night at the cove instead of trying to go home. If the weather kept clear there would be no great hardship in sleeping on the grass for one night. The sun set, however, with an angry red glow amid a mass of heavy clouds portending foul weather. Moreover, as the night fell there was an oppressive calm, and the heat was intense. So threatening was the aspect of the weather that had I been at all sure of being able to find my way in the darkness, I should have certainly attempted to get home even after the sun had set. There was no shelter if it should rain, and I was at my wits' end how to contrive a place to pass the night. What a fool I had been not to notice the approaching storm in time to get to my comfortable house. The best provision I was able to make was to gather some grass and willow-boughs and take them under an overhanging rock, where I cut with the axe in the dark some limbs and boughs and made a sort of lean-to. This I supplemented with the tub turned up toward the quarter whence the rain would most probably come, and Duke and I crept into this sorry nest to await events.

One event came without waiting, and that was a powerful stench from the unlucky tub. But as I had endured this already for nearly half a day, I concluded it would, by familiarity, become less and less offensive. I could not go to sleep, but lay there turning and tossing on my uncomfortable couch and watching the weather.

The calm continued until near midnight, when a cool breeze sprang up and swept down the gorge and out to sea. I thought this indicated that the storm was about to pass around and away; but the heavy rumble of thunder out at sea, growing louder and sharper, and becoming almost continuous, and the constant play of lightning, quickly dissipated this notion. I looked out with awe at this tremendous electric display.

The breeze fell presently, and I looked out and saw coming in from the sea a coppery red mass of cloud glowing as though it contained a furnace. Instinctively I crouched down behind the rock beside the dog, who was shivering with fear, and grasped the corners of a huge fallen fragment. With a dreadful, screeching roar, mingled with a din of thunder such as I am utterly unable to describe, and can liken to nothing I ever heard before or since, the hurricane burst upon the island. There was no rain, but at first I thought there was, for the spray from the ocean beat in my face and drenched me to the skin. It was not rain, for it was salt to the taste. My shelter of boughs, and also the high-smelling tub were blown away instantly, and with the dog under me I fairly had all I could do to hold on. Above the roar of the wind, the rattling of stones, and the din of the thunder, I could hear the crash of falling trees and breaking boughs. Nor did the awful wind let up for nearly half an hour, and I was quite worn out with the apprehension and the struggle. If I lifted my face for an instant the spray and sand and pebbles whipped with such violence against it that I was glad to bury it close to the ground. Such awful storms I had heard of, and even been witness to their effects after the event; but never could I have had an adequate idea of the terrible reality without this experience.

During the entire passage of the hurricane not a drop of rain fell, so far as I could judge, though, as before stated, I was drenched with spray. Gradually, with an occasional renewal of the blast, the wind went down, and in an hour the stars were shining pure and serene in the dark vault above.

The temperature had now fallen many degrees, and there was a cool, steady wind from the north that chilled me through to the bone. Of course I had no fire, and no means of procuring one, and the only relief obtainable was such exercise as I could get by stamping about and thrashing my arms until the blood was in rapid circulation. Sitting back against the rock I dozed a little now and then, and waited impatiently for the break of day, which seemed as though it never would come.

As soon as it was fairly light we started for home. The effects of the hurricane were visible on every hand. Trees broken off, blown over, and uprooted, green branches scattered here and there, the silvery under sides of the leaves showing, and giving an air of disorder and destruction by their unaccustomed appearance and tint, all marked the hand of the destroyer. The central plateau seemed to have suffered most. Here several great trees had been twisted until the trunks were a mass of splinters, indicating that they had successively occupied the very eye and centre of the rotary wind. Hurrying along rapidly we came down to the lower land, and I was glad to observe much fewer signs of destruction here. We came upon a dead pig, killed by a huge fallen limb, and I pulled him out, as we were now nearly home, and dragged him along with me for food.

When we reached the open beach I found plenty of evidence of the mighty wind in the scattered palm leaves, boughs, and branches strewn along the strand. In the distance I could see the ruins of my work-shed. The roof was off, and lying down the beach a hundred yards or more in a heap at the water's edge. The boat, for which I felt specially anxious, was hidden from view by a clump of water bushes that grew on the hither bank of the creek. The mast I could see, and noted that an unnatural tilt had been given to it. Dragging the dead pig I slowly made my way along the sand. The house stood intact, my hammock still swung to the frame-work of the shed. The top of a cocoanut palm, twisted off by the wind and carried through the air, had brought up against the frame of the shed and lodged there, while the nuts growing on it were scattered about the ground, some of them as far as the water's edge.

I went immediately to the boat and found it careened and sunk in the shallow water of the creek, the upper gunwale just above the surface. At the house the only damage done was a hole in the northeast corner of the wall, caused by the end of a bough which had been driven through it and was still sticking in the gap. The first thing I did was to build a rousing fire in the chimney; then hanging my damp clothing up in front of it to dry I went down for a bath in the creek, and to examine more minutely the boat. When she was righted up and baled out with a gourd I found she had suffered no injury whatever, being as tight as a bottle. Nor would she have sunk except for an extra amount of ballast that happened to be on board, as the air-tight compartments held perfectly. But the sinking was doubtless the best thing that could have happened.

As soon as I could dress and get something for breakfast, I cut up the pig and put part of it in salt, and then turned to with a will upon the work of repairing the shed. The larger part of the material of the roof was uninjured, and as the weather fortunately remained clear, by the following night I had the roof on again in good shape and much stronger than before, as with the aid of the axe I was able to cut a great number of stout poles to add to the structure. When I had patched up the hole in the wall of my house and cleared away the litter, most of the signs of the hurricane had disappeared from my neighborhood.

The dampness of my house in wet weather, which was due to the walls getting wet and soaking through with the driving rain, led me now to undertake a new task. The clay used in the building of the boat would, I thought, be sufficient in quantity to give the floor and the walls inside and out a good coat, and this when once dry would make the structure like an adobe building. I intended, moreover, to add an extra thickness of thatch, put in a row of glass photograph plates toward the sea for windows, make a good cedar door, to be hung on wooden hinges, and add a wide veranda to the front, under which I might sit in the evening.

The rain still came every day or two now, though evidently the dry season was fast approaching. The weather was too uncertain to venture out any distance in the boat, and I therefore had plenty of time on my hands to attend to my building and other schemes for domestic comfort. As planned, I daubed the whole house, inside and outside, with a good thick coat of the clay smoothed with the back of the shovel. On the outside, to give a workmanlike finish, I lined the soft clay into blocks and pointed the joints neatly. Then, with dry, pulverized clay and sand, which I sprinkled with water, trampled with the feet and smoothed by beating with the shovel, I produced a hard, smooth floor like that under the shed. All around the edge of this floor I fitted a single row of clam shells, and inside of this a second row of pink-mouthed tiger shells, which formed a handsome border. I put in a narrow horizontal window, of six panes side by side, at each side of the doorway, and constructed a good door of split cedar, pinned together and hung on wooden hinges to swing outward, and provided it with a latch. I then doubled the thatch all over the house and put up a light porch in front thatched with palm leaves, and built a floor for it the same as in the house. At one end of this porch I constructed a little low shed with walls and roof for the dog.

As there was still a great quantity of clay left I built an oven near the house, as follows: upon a raised platform of poles erected about three feet above the ground, and about three by four feet in extent, I put a layer of sand and clay about four inches thick. This was the floor of the oven. All around this floor I laid a wall of adobe bricks, made of sand and clay partly dried. I then filled the interior with sand heaped up in the form of an arch, and laid the adobe bricks over it, daubing and plastering all the cracks. At the rear was a small clay chimney, and at the front an opening for a doorway. When the clay had well set and partly hardened, I raked out the sand through the doorway and left the hollow clay structure standing. I then constructed an adobe slab with which to close the doorway. In this oven I built a hot fire of dry wood and kept it going all day, by which means the clay was partly burned and the construction made entirely proof against the wet, — though, for that matter, the adobe would have stood without such treatment.

To utilize the heat left in the walls from the burning I had put a pot full of beans on to boil, with a good chunk of salt pork. At night I put the beans and pork in an earthen dish and set them in the oven, which was still hot, and closed it up tight, covering the chimney and luting the door slab with wet clay. In the morning, when I opened it, there gushed out a delicious vapor, and the dish of beans and pork, brown and crisp came forth hot and fit for a king.

One article I needed very badly was soap. I had tried to wash my clothing several times, but it was quite filthy notwithstanding these attempts. My entire wardrobe consisted of a heavy woollen shirt, a pair of tough moleskin pantaloons, a home-made hat, and a stout pair of shoes. Socks I had none, as the single pair I brought on shore were entirely worn out. Latterly I had made a practice of going barefoot, except on extended excursions through the jungle and over the rocks. With plenty of wood ashes and pig fat at hand why should I not make soap? I rigged up a leaching apparatus thus: in the bottom of a huge gourd I pierced several holes, and laid over them a layer of grass so that the ashes would not stop them up; then I filled the gourd with alternate layers of grass and ashes to the top, and poured in fresh water as long as it would absorb any. In a little while the lye began to drip out of the holes into a vessel placed beneath to receive it. By changing and renewing the ashes several times I finally collected a kettle full of the lye. This I placed over the fire and boiled until it had lost two thirds of its volume. Then I put into the boiling lye strips and pieces of fat pork until it would dissolve no more, keeping up the boiling slowly all the time. The result was a good article of light colored soap of a jelly-like consistency. Its use both upon my clothing and myself was a luxury indeed.

One day I burned some lime and mixed a whitewash, which with a cocoa-husk swab I applied to the interior walls of the house, changing them to a dazzling white and rendering the whole interior light and cheerful; which was a great comfort on dark days when I was confined there. Moreover, it gave the place an air of wholesomeness and neatness that was very home-like. As a further improvement I made a bed of soil at each end of the porch and transplanted some flowering vines and creepers of several varieties; I also made a half-dozen hills in front of the house, carrying and filling in these spots a quantity of rich muck, and planted sweet potatoes that they might spread their vines over the sand. The garden which I had made before the rains set in was now in thriving condition, all the peas and beans being up and the potato-vines in blossom.

My diet was now varied and healthful enough; but I lacked one article of food that I longed for and felt the need of more and more every day, — and that was bread, the staff of life. Parched-seed gruel was a very poor substitute indeed, and at last I got so hungry for a taste of bread that I determined to make some out of the Indian corn.

So one day I made a basket and started across the island to bring home a supply of the corn. All the way over I kept a good lookout for a suitable gritty stone, that could be used to grind the corn, and found several that I thought might answer the purpose fairly well; but one sample — being a slab of grit-stone having a rough, pocked surface with small hard bits of chalcedony interspersed throughout — was so superior in quality to all the rest that I concluded I could do no better if I sought the island over. This slab, which was quite as much as I could carry, I laid against a tree where I could easily find it, and went on my way to "Farm Cove." I had not been here since the great storm, and was surprised to see how quickly and fully all traces of the hurricane had disappeared. The corn was all right, the husks had fully dried, and the heap lying on the rocks had not suffered from the rains. I filled my basket, — a good bushel, — and immediately came home, returning forthwith for the slab of grit-stone. Duke treed another raccoon, which we captured by cutting down the tree, and then with our plunder and the stone we managed to get home at nightfall.

The next day it began again to rain in intermittent showers; raining and shining alternately, as in the April weather of northern latitudes. After building a fire and heating up the oven and putting in the raccoon to bake, with some yams for dinner, I went to work on my stone slab. First I broke off a good piece the full width of the slab in length, and about six inches in width to use as a grinder. With the back of the axe I hammered and dressed this as smooth as I could. Then I went at the slab itself, pounding it with the axe and breaking it at the edges until it was formed into a reasonably smooth, rectangular shape two feet long by one foot in width. I now sprinkled the face of the slab with wet sand and water, and placing it in an inclined position, rubbed the grinder up and down upon it, feeding on fresh sand and water from time to time, as it lost its cutting properties.

This was slow, hard, tedious work, and the progress made was so gradual that it called for all my will to keep at it. Perseverance, however, will finally conquer most obstacles, and this was a mere question of muscle and will-power struggling against a hard grit-stone. The stone was fated finally to yield; but it took me two days of hard work to get it into the right shape. All this for a piece of corn bread, and the bread not yet forthcoming.

When finished the slab had a smooth, gritty surface slightly incurved from end to end, and the grinder designed to lie across it had its corners rounded smoothly off.

I set to work now to grind my corn as follows: The

slab was propped up at a slight angle on a piece of canvas; on this slab the corn, a handful at a time, was sprinkled and then ground by rubbing the grinder up and down over it. As it became pulverized the meal would gradually drift down on to the canvas, the coarser particles rolling away to the edge of the heap, only to to be scraped up and ground over again. This was, as you may imagine, tedious work. When I had accumulated about four quarts of meal, I felt that I had enough of grinding for once.

Now commenced the first act of bread-making proper. In a gourd I mixed about a pint of the meal with warm water and a little salt, and set it in a warm place over night, that it might have a chance to ferment. This was to be my yeast. In the morning the contents of the gourd were in a state of incipient fermentation, and I went out and fired up the oven to be ready for the grand final act. While the oven was heating I mixed up the rest of the meal with salt and water, and added the fermented meal to it, mixing the whole to a consistency such that it could readily be stirred. This I set near the fire in an earthen pan, and watched it from time to time. In about two hours it began to rise slightly, and the oven being fully ready I clapped the pan in and closed it up to bake. In an hour I opened the oven and took out a fragrant panful of nicely browned, light, and crumbling corn bread, as a reward for all my labors. Perhaps it was not so good as a skilled bread-maker might have produced, but it was sweet and delightful to me, and well repaid all my trouble, and both Duke and I rejoiced over it with our broiled bacon.

After this experiment bread-making was a regular thing. Sometimes I simply stirred up the raw meal with a little salt and water and baked it on the back of a shovel before the open fire, — hoe-cake fashion, — to be eaten brown and hot; but I generally made raised bread by the process which I have described, sometimes adding a modicum of pork fat for shortening.

CHAPTER IX.

THE GALLEON FOUND.

THE severe rains gradually ceased, until sunshine was the rule and rain the exception. I did not expect a season of absolute dryness, for in this locality rain prevails to some extent throughout the whole year, so that the vegetation rarely suffers from drought.

One morning, the sky being clear and a gentle breeze blowing from the southwest, Duke and I went aboard the boat, — which by the way, I had named the "Mohawk" — and started for a trial of the water-glass. We were soon on the ground, a mile to the north of the cape. Lowering the sails I put the glass over the side, with very little hope of success as the water seemed to have a cloudy appearance. It proved to be in such a condition that I could not see the bottom at all. I then put up the sail and ran in nearer the shore to where the depth was about thirty feet. Here I could see the sand and rocks and shells on the bottom very distinctly, and noted that there were streaks and veins of the murky water running through the more transparent portion.

Finding that nothing could be done in the way of investigation until the water became clearer, I stood out to the west until by a single tack I could make Farm Cove, intending to bring back a cargo of corn and some yams and potatoes. I found a few bushels of yams still in good condition, and noted with pleasure that many of the potatoes left in the ground had sprouted and the vines had already acquired quite a growth. With spade and shovel I turned to heartily, and cleared away the luxuriant growth of weeds which threatened to choke this volunteer crop. Then I loaded in my corn and started back, reaching home in time for supper.

The next two days I devoted to planting a patch of corn, hardly expecting to remain long enough upon the island to enjoy it, but thinking it wise to provide for an uncertain future. On the third day I went out again to try the water-glass, but the water was still lacking in transparency and there was nothing to do except to wait.

But while returning I thought of a thing that would be very useful to me in future expeditions, and that was to set up on the northern cape something which might serve as a guide to me in future operations. I had no compass and was obliged to guess the direction blindly by the sun. Now the Spanish admiral, when he reported that the galleon bore east of north from the point of rocks, and about a mile therefrom, probably spoke, as to direction at least, from actual observation of the compass, as a sailor would; for nobody knows better than a sailor the impossibility of guessing at direction without a guide. Indeed, the sailor, when he comes on deck, turns instinctively to the compass to orient himself and correct his sense of direction, because the course of the vessel may have changed half a dozen times during a watch below, without his knowledge. To one on board a vessel the parts fore and aft, starboard and port, below and aloft, have a fixed relation to each other, and one is apt to get a set impression as to direction from this fixed relation of familiar objects. Thus I have heard of an old sailing-master who was on board the same vessel for twenty years, and who declared that, no matter where the ship might be or upon what course, it always seemed to him that the head of his bunk lay to the north; that when at sea the most distressing thing to him was that the sun never rose in the same quarter two mornings in succession; and that it never rose in the east except on Long Island, where he was born.

As to the accuracy of the estimated distance — one mile — that, to be sure, was a much more uncertain quantity; though officers of war vessels are, and were then, well trained to estimate distances on the water, as otherwise they could not determine the range of their cannon and arms. Altogether I had every reason to suppose, barring variations in the compass and individual errors, that the location assigned was reasonably accurate. At any rate I decided to start my investigation with the assumption that the assigned location was accurate, and to work from the designated point as a centre; it would then be easy, as I proceeded, to allow for error in all directions without the chance of multiplying it in any particular direction.

In my little box of drawing-tools was a small brass protractor — a semi-circle divided into one hundred and eighty degrees, with half-degree marks. This would be convenient in the work I was about to do, though not absolutely necessary, as in its absence I could have easily constructed one that would answer my purpose. The first thing to do was to establish a true north and south line. That night the stars shone brightly, and I easily found the pole star by the pointers in the Great Bear, or "Dipper." In the sand at the north cape I drove an upright stake made of a stout cane. Then taking another straight piece I placed it in a notch on top of the upright and sighted along its length adjusting it until it pointed straight at the north star. To secure it in this position I drove a short notched stake at the butt of the inclined cane and tied the cane firmly to both. I was now sure that the two uprights were in a true north and south direction from each other, and the work for that night was finished, as the remainder could be better done by daylight.

The next thing I wanted was a standard of measurement; unfortunately my drawing instruments did not contain the usual ivory rule. But this did not occasion me much uneasiness, as I hoped to be able to deduce the standard inch by a comparison of my belongings. If I once got the true inch it would be easy to get from that the foot, the yard, the rod, the mile. I had my photograph plates as one guide; these I had every reason to suppose were cut quite accurately to the dimensions of five inches by seven. Then there was the brass protractor. It is true there were no inches marked on this; but the workman who made it would naturally follow some standard, and the chances were very great that the diameter of this instrument would be found to be an exact multiple of the inch, and as I conjectured, exactly four inches. To test this matter I laid the protractor on the short side of one of the plates, and taking the difference between the two found, as I had expected, that this difference was one fifth of the width of the plate, and one seventh of its length. This proved satisfactorily to my mind that the plate was accurate in dimensions, that is to say, five by seven inches, and that the difference between the length of the straight side of the protractor and the width of the plate was the standard inch. From this starting-point I constructed a foot measure, and cut me a light pole exactly a rod in length.

Returning now to the cape where my north and south direction rod was fixed, I proceeded to set a peg, which to avoid confusion we will designate as A, in the sand in a prolongation of the line, and with the protractor got the true east by north, marking this line by a second peg. Then I turned about and marked a line which made an angle of one hundred and twenty degrees with the east by north line, and which would lead down the beach.

I now proceeded to plant in the sand three poles about fifteen feet in height: one at the central point A, one in a prolongation of the east by north line, which pole we will call B, and the third in a prolongation of the angle line down the beach, which latter pole we will call C. The next thing was the measurement of a base line from the pole A, through C down the beach for a mile. This I did as accurately as I could with my rod measure; but it was a sort of work highly conducive, as you may imagine, to the backache, especially as I went over it three times to eliminate as much error as possible, taking the average of the three measurements. Nor was the third measurement completed much before it was time to go home.

Only one thing now remained to be done, and this I did the next morning. At the end of the mile line on the beach I erected a tall pole, which we will call D, and from it as a centre laid off a line thirty degrees from the base to intersect the east-by-north line or its prolongation, and marked the direction by a second tall pole which we will call E. Now, according to a simple problem in trigonometry, it will be seen that if I should sail out in my boat east of north from the cape, guiding myself by the two poles A and B, when I had brought the poles D and E into line having A and B in line at the same time, I should be a mile away from A in a true east-of-north direction.

Although I now went out every day to try the water,

it did not grow clear. Finding the guide-poles barely visible, especially the more distant pair, I mounted a gourd on the top of each one, after which I had no further difficulty in seeing them. As it was some little trouble to take the bearings constantly, I rigged a buoy and anchored it at the spot where theoretically the galleon lay. I found the water about sixty feet deep; and the buoy — a large gourd attached to a line with a stone for an anchor — floated easily on the swell, with eighty feet of line. After this buoy was anchored I took down the guide-poles, marking their places with pegs, in case I should require to use them again. This I did out of a superabundance of caution, not that I believed any one else than myself — had there been any one else — could have read the riddle they told to me.

Every day for three weeks I went out to the shoal near the buoy and examined the water. It was getting gradually clearer; but had it not been for my recollection of the first visit made, before I had the water-glass, and of the appearance of the water at that time, I should have doubtless given up the attempt in despair. The remembrance, however, of the clear water, and the gleam through it of yellow sand, was not to be forgotten, and it kept up my hopes to the last.

The weather grew oppressively hot, and there came on one day a terrific thunder-storm followed by a gale of wind from the northeast which lasted two days and was followed in turn by fair weather, with a gentle southwest wind. When I went out again I found the water quite clear. I was very impatient to test the glass, so much so that I would not wait to make any trials until I had reached the neighborhood of the buoy. Here I lowered the sails and put the glass over.

I could see the bottom quite plainly. It was of

clean sand and strewed with shells. Here and there was a fragment of sea-weed, sponge, or other ocean growth. A shoal of silver-sided mackerel dashed by, and numerous strange fishes came into view. One sort there was with long streamers extending from the tail, and a body banded with rainbow hues. I looked long and intently at the strange panorama unfolded to my view, and found when I raised my head that the boat had drifted half a mile to the northeast of the buoy. Then I hoisted the sail and ratched back beyond the buoy, and drifted again, with the glass over the side, watching the bottom for signs of the galleon. This manoeuvre I repeated as long as there was light enough to see. I found that I could not see the bottom after four in the afternoon, nor before nine in the morning.

I spent three days at this work without any success, and then found that I was going at times over ground that I had already searched, for I began to identify objects as having been already seen. Especially did I recognize a huge conch-shell with a clam-shell wedged in the mouth. It was necessary therefore to devise some systematic method of search, or I should simply be hunting over and over the same ground. So I adopted the plan of gridironing, so to speak, a territory of a mile square, after the following fashion : I made me an extra buoy and anchored it at an arbitrary point about a half-mile south of the centre buoy. Taking this as a starting-point I drifted a mile before the wind to the northeast; then ratching back to the starting-point I lifted the buoy and carried it a hundred feet to the northwest, and drifted again down another parallel line, and so on.

The wind held steadily in the southwest, fortunately, day after day, and after a week's hard work I came nearly on a line with the central buoy; but no signs of a wreck, or even a mound where one might be buried in the sand. On the eighth day of this systematic search the weather seemed about to change. A huge bank of clouds lay low in the southwest, and I hardly knew whether to venture out or not. But as it would in all probability take some hours for the storm to brew, I set forth and made one drift with my usual success, then returned and started for the second.

When I was about half-way down on the second drift I found the wreck. There was no doubt about it. The hulk lay there very slightly buried in the sand, a great, black mass careened a little to port, and the bows somewhat higher than the stern. Strange to say, it was not further than twenty rods from my central marking buoy, and about due north from it. I immediately dropped overboard my reserve buoy, composed of four large gourds attached to a strong line, and having a hundred-pound rock for an anchor, and watched to see that the anchoring-stone dropped just beside the hull.

At last I had found it! Here beneath me in sixty feet of water lay the Spanish galleon, exactly where the admiral so long ago had reported her to have sunk. His report being so far verified, it would also prove true in respect to the treasure contained within her ancient ribs.

A darkening of the sea and sky warned me that there was no time to waste in dreaming over my discovery. The storm which had been coming would now soon be here. I therefore hoisted sail and turned my back on the galleon. It was none too soon. Indeed, before I made the creek the wind had risen to such a height that I had to lower the sails and double reef them, and then went into the creek gunwale under, with the white spume and froth flying clear over the boat. But a miss is as good as a mile. I got safely in and cooked me a noble dinner of corn bread and baked pork and beans in honor of the day's glorious event.

Duke and I sat in the open porch that afternoon, sheltered from the wind and rain, resting contentedly after the long strain of hard work which had kept me on the keen jump every day from dawn until dark since the search began. The wind blew strongly, with occasional gusts of driving rain, and I feared the storm might shift my buoys, or tear them loose and carry them away; but I could locate the central buoy again by the sights already taken, if it should go, and from that the spot could easily be found. But I hoped for better results, as the main buoy, which marked the wreck, had plenty of line, and moreover, was strong and buoyant. I wished this one might last, for with the anchor lying close beside the sunken hull, it seemed to me a sort of claim stake. I determined, as soon as the weather would permit, to rig a buoy which would outride the storms, and anchor it securely over the wreck. As is usual with the heavier winds and gales in this locality, the wind before nightfall began to veer around to another quarter, getting before sunset quite around into the north, and by nine o'clock settling down in the northeast, exactly the opposite quarter from its starting-point, with fine rain and mist.

Having located the galleon, I had now done all I had intended to do before leaving the island, except to mark the location more securely, if that proved necessary; and I was therefore impatient to get away in my boat for Martinique or some other civilized port where I could get the necessary assistance and diving-apparatus. Of course I must now wait for settled weather and a favorable wind as I had once before had to do. But this time I hoped most sincerely that I should not be kept waiting as long as before, for with little to do the time would hang heavily on my hands. The bare thought of getting back once more to civilization made my heart beat faster, and stirred my very soul.

The northerly wind was chill, and the air so moist that I built a cheerful fire in the chimney and drew my chair up in front of it, closed the door, lighted a candle, and tried to read, Duke snoozing on the floor at my feet in front of the hearth.

But although I sat thus until midnight, I could not read. I watched the embers fall and die away hour after hour, thinking over the days spent on the island, the trials and the labor, the mistakes and the successes, and the strange outcome. That I should have actually found the galleon seemed now upon cool reflection little less than a miracle. That some of the hundreds of professional wreckers and divers who make a regular business of seeking out such things on the faintest clues should not have run across the Spanish admiral's report and sought and found the wreck and removed the treasure seemed a strange thing to me now. Why had not the Spanish government done this long ago? Then the horrible idea entered my mind that perhaps they had already done so. Or if not, perhaps an expedition designed for that purpose might even now be on its way, and might arrive when I had left the island. If so, they would speedily pick up my buoy, and I should return to find the treasure gone.

All these and a thousand such distempered fancies tortured me into a state bordering on frenzy. To have the treasure almost in sight and yet to lose it would be too much for human nature to bear. I would remove my buoy, erase every mark and take my chances of picking up the clue. But after all, how foolish that would be. The treasure lies there safe, and has lain there many, many years, and this frantic fear coming at so late a day is the height of folly.

Then my mind would wander away to plans for conducting my negotiations: how I should seek out a man whom I could trust, and how I should present matters to secure his aid and co-operation. How should I get the money? Ah, there were the pearls! I would sell them and possibly raise money enough myself. But would I dare offer these pearls for sale? Would not their possession excite the cupidity of others and cause them to follow me back to the island and come upon me in the midst of the work of securing the treasure?

And so my fancies came and went, until at last, overpowered by fatigue, I fell fast asleep in my chair, and was wakened an hour or two before break of day by Duke's cold nose against my hand. Whereupon I sensibly went to bed and to sleep.

CHAPTER X.

THE CASTAWAYS.

IT was now the month of May and I had been about nine months a prisoner on the island. If all went as well as I hoped, I might be at home before the end of a year with money enough to redeem the dear old farm.

The morning was gray and gloomy, the wind still driving gusts of rain from the northeast, and the breakers yellow with sand rolling in on the beach, and dashing up fragments of weed and long streamers of bladder plant. There was a strong salt smell in the nostrils that such weather brings on the seashore; the gray, leaden clouds hung low and heavy over a dark, indigo sea, whitened far and near with foaming crests, like manes of racing steeds; the foliage gleamed silvery gray as the leaves were swept by the wind; and the willows along the creek bent until they dipped their slender branches in the stream. Occasionally a parrot or other long-tailed bird could be seen tossed and buffeted in an attempt to fly from one tree to another, frequently giving up the struggle and fairly drifting away to be lost among the foliage.

Notwithstanding the wet, I went about getting stores into the boat and preparing for the voyage. I filled half a dozen two-gallon gourds with water, and stopped them with well waxed wooden plugs, stowing them carefully in the bottom of the boat with due regard to her trim. Then I put on board the remainder of the dried turtle-meat, and set a ham on the fire to boil. I made two pans of bread, and put them, with pork, beans, yams, and potatoes, in the oven to bake. This food would all keep well. In addition I parched and ground up two or three quarts of seed for cold gruel. Everything was stowed away, and the boat in readiness by three o'clock in the afternoon.

There was but little sign of an abatement or change in the weather. I felt curious to know if my buoy still held, and as there was yet time before dark to go up to the north cape by way of the beach and return, I called Duke and started along the strand. About half-way there we came upon the carcass of a magnificent silver-sided tarpon, — a huge fish somewhat like a sea-bass, — that would have weighed probably two hundred pounds. It was dead when cast ashore, and so of course unfit for food. A flock of gulls were quarrelling and fighting over it, and as we approached they arose and filled the air in a great cloud. After we passed by they circled around, wind-buffeted, and settled again on their food, covering the beach, and hovering in a seething, hungry, struggling crowd about the fish, which must have been a rare feast for them.

I picked up a beautiful and perfect specimen of the fragile shell of the pearly nautilus, thin as paper, fluted and corrugated with lovely regularity, and tinted like the shaded petals of a blush rose. Rarely beautiful, divinely perfect, this sample of nature's handiwork, cast up by the foaming, angry breakers amid the brown tangle of the shore and the foul-smelling ocean-weeds, seemed like a poem, a hymn in praise of nature's God. I put the delicate and perfect structure carefully in my bosom to carry away as a memento of my island home.

We reached the cape, and I clambered up the highest rock from which I could obtain a clear outlook, and found my buoy all right, rising and falling with the swell, now submerged, and now reappearing, evidently tugging at its anchor-rope, and securely held thereby.

I thought how peacefully slept the ancient hulk beneath all this turbulence. Undisturbed by wind or wave it lay there slowly changing its tough timbers of Andalusian oak back into the elements from which they sprang. I thought, too, of the indestructible gold that lay buried there, waiting the fulness of time for its reappearance in the active life of man; how long the years had been since it had felt the grip of avarice or slid freely from the fingers of charity.

Suddenly I saw away upon the rim of the sea in the northeast, in the very eye of the wind, the white glint of a small sail. The mist, the waves, and the changing rain hid it momently, and then it would gleam out again a white spark among the gray. I watched it intently for a quarter of an hour, and made out that it must be a small schooner-rigged boat hove to with jib and close reefed mainsail, drifting bodily before the wind, and rolling in a frightful manner. The mainmast had been broken off at the top, and on the foremast, half-masted, fluttered a red flag. I made out clearly, presently, that the craft was merely a half-decked boat similar to my own, though perhaps of somewhat larger size, and I thought I could see somebody on board, but could not distinguish clearly. But of course, if it was hove to, there would be some one on board, as such a condition of the canvas would not be likely to occur by accident in a boat fortuitously adrift. If the wind held in the present quarter, the boat was certain to drift on to the island, and that too in a short time. It would not take above two hours and a half for it to reach the breakers, unless it could run before the wind and thus make a course to avoid the island. Very soon indeed, the island would be a lee shore, and an exceedingly dangerous one. I marvelled greatly that they did not seem to see this danger.

There was but one thing I could do, and that was the preparation of beacon-fires to guide them into the creek mouth, the only harbor on the east coast of the island. With this in view I hurried as fast as possible down the beach to the house, and laid two fires, one on each side of the creek mouth, heaping up the dry wood from my store in such a manner that it would make a great blaze, and getting all in readiness to light as soon as the sun went down. The wind was appreciably less, and I believed was gradually decreasing. Moreover, it had now stopped raining, and I could see the boat more distinctly.

An hour before sunset I thought it would be possible to go out with my own boat under double-reefed canvas, and intercept the stranger. Something was undoubtedly wrong on board of her, otherwise she would not be allowed thus to drift to leeward without control, with the island in plain sight. If there should prove to be no one on board, I might possibly be able to save the boat, which could hardly fail to prove better than my own. On the other hand, should there be some one on board, I might render valuable assistance. I determined forthwith to make the attempt. So I lighted my fires and got on board.

It was no easy matter to run my boat out over the bar in the teeth of a half-gale of wind; and I did not accomplish it without getting completely wet through, as I was obliged to tail on behind and push her out through the breakers until I was immersed to my neck in salt water, and then clamber in over the stern and haul aft the main sheet with the sail flapping and thundering as though determined to burst loose. However,

I soon got her under control and was gliding along close hauled on the starboard tack, with the spray, as she pitched nose down, flying as high as the gaff, and raining down on the deck in bucketfuls.

The sun was about an hour high as I left the creek, and the strange boat in plain sight about a mile and a half dead to windward. I could easily get to windward of her in a single tack, by standing well off shore on the first slant.

When I came up near enough to hail I did so, and got no response. Getting to windward I wore and ran down quite to the boat, and letting both sheets go, loosened the halliards and lowered the mainsail, and brought my own boat close up along side. For the moment my own sail hid the vessel and I could not see what was before me. But now I looked and saw lying in the stern sheets what seemed to be the corpse of an old, gray-haired man of perhaps seventy years, the head held by a girl of eighteen or thereabouts.

I never shall forget the look that was on her face. Pale, drawn, with dishevelled hair, and dark circles around her beautiful eyes, she gazed at me without a word.

"Do you know," cried I, "that you are drifting on to the beach and will be among the breakers in half an hour?"

For answer she pointed to her dry lips.

"Is it water you want?"

She nodded. I hastily cast a line on board and lashed the two vessels together, where grinding they rose and fell with the waves, and then seizing a gourd of water made my way to the girl. She would not drink herself until after I had poured some water into the mouth of the old man, who though perfectly helpless was still alive, and swallowed the water as fast as I gave it to him.

Then I held the mouth of the heavy gourd to her own lips until I thought she had drunk enough. She gripped it with both hands, and I had to force it away from her. It was a pitiful sight.

But there was no time to lose, for we were fast drifting into the breakers, and it was absolutely necessary to get the boats before the wind and get steerage way on, or we should be on shore and dashed to pieces by the rollers. I sprang forward and loosened the main sheet of the strange boat, unlashed the helm which was tied amidships, and she paid off at once handsomely.

The sun was now quite down, but my two beacon-fires burned brightly, and I steered straight for them. Finding my own boat alongside had a tendency to bring us around to the wind, I put the helm into the girl's hand and bade her hold it just so, and jumping on to my own boat lowered the jib, that was still set, cast off the lashing, and hitching a line forward made her fast to tow. I then hauled up and got on board the other boat again, and let my own boat drop behind us. Now I found no difficulty in steering, though my own boat would yaw and pull a little, first one way and then the other.

We were soon close to the bar, and I felt no little apprehension as to what might happen when we actually encountered the huge roller which broke every few moments there. But there was no help for it; we must take our chances, one of which — and not the least probable — was that the first boat might ground and the one in tow come crashing in on top of us. Fortunately, — for it was pure good-luck, — we struck a roller just at the right moment which lifted us over the bar as it broke. The tow-line snapped in twain as we were on the crest, and my own boat shot alongside like a water-fowl and passed us, both boats riding into the creek alongside of each other, the red glare of the beacon-fires at either hand lighting up the scene like the last act of a sensational drama.

As soon as we were fairly in the creek I jumped overboard, the water not being above my chest, and beached both the boats safely. The girl still sat holding the old man's head, and had not spoken a word. But she followed my motions with her eyes, and I could easily read therein that she was grateful enough for my exertions, and appreciated the danger we had escaped.

The old man could apparently neither speak nor move. An ashen pallor lay on his countenance, and one side of his face, especially one corner of his mouth, was drawn down and distorted, — a sufficient indication, had I understood it, that he was suffering from a stroke of paralysis. From his clothing, which was soaked with spray, I could easily see that he was a clergyman.

I helped the girl out, partly carrying her as she could scarcely stand, and then attempted to lift out the old man. He was a heavy, strongly built man, weighing all of two hundred and fifty pounds. A heavy, helpless man is about as awkward a burden as one can imagine. Limp and yielding he could not be picked up except by the middle, and he was so lying in the boat that it was impossible for me to get a good hold of him in such position as to exert my strength. His clothing, all soaked with rain and salt water, clung to him, and must have chilled his poor helpless body through. If he was to live at all it was absolutely necessary to get him warm and dry right speedily.

Meantime the poor girl stood shivering in her equally wet garments, looking on anxiously at my efforts. Finally she spoke: "I think if you will turn him across the boat, you may be able to lift his head and shoulders up here," — placing her hand on the gunwale. "Have courage, dear father, he will be gentle with you."

A wan flicker, somewhat like the wrecked ghost of a smile, seemed to pass over the old man's distorted face at the words of the girl, the first I had heard her utter. It was idle to expect any help from her, as she could scarcely stand, and was in fact partly supporting herself with her hands on the boat. Following the daughter's suggestion, I moved her father around until he lay thwartships, and then placing my feet on the gunwale and seizing him under the arms pulled him bodily up until his head and shoulders were out of the boat. Then jumping overboard I managed to get him fairly on my back, his back to my own with my two hands under his armpits. Though I accounted myself pretty strong, and the hardy life on the island had by no means diminished my muscular power, this lift was the very limit of my strength. With bare feet fairly gripping the yielding sand, and the water above my knees, I managed to stagger through it to the shore and up to the work-shed, where I sank on my knees and lowered him to the ground. The girl followed us. I turned to her as soon as my breath came, and said, "Go and stand by the fire, you are chilled almost to death. I shall be able to get your father into the house and into a warm, dry bed, where I can change these wet clothes."

"I can be of some help, can I not?" said she with a piteous look. "Oh, sir, be careful and gentle with him, I beseech you."

"No, I can manage better alone, and you need to warm yourself," said I, and without waiting longer I stooped to the old man again, and now with much greater ease managed, by putting my arms around him, to lift him and carry him to the house, where I laid him down on the floor, and immediately went to the beacon-fire near which the girl was seated. I secured two half-burned pieces of wood, and returning to the house built a rousing good fire in the chimney, and lighted a candle. Then as rapidly as I could do so I stripped off his clothes and rolled him in a dry blanket on a couch of grass.

"Are you more comfortable now?"

For answer came the abortive flicker, as of a throttled smile, and he closed and opened his eyes once or twice as though assenting.

"Can't you speak at all?"

A sort of struggle seemed to come over his face; then he closed his eyes and held them shut for a moment. It then dawned upon me that the man was suffering from a paralytic stroke. Up to this time, without giving the matter any particular attention, I had thought that perhaps he was merely suffering from chill and exhaustion, and several times during my tremendous struggle with his weight it had been on my tongue to urge him to exert himself for his own sake. Now the awful nature of his condition, his utter helplessness, the mental torture he must have endured and be yet enduring, came upon me and must have shown itself in my face; for as he looked at me he closed his eyes again in the same manner as before. There he lay swathed in the blanket, his intelligence intact, perfectly able to see all that went on around him, and to realize his situation and condition, doubtless also fully alive, so far as sensation went, to every pain and discomfort, and yet utterly unable to stir hand or foot or speak a word. Even distorted as his face was, there was the stamp of a noble, generous nature upon it, and a venerable benevolence yet shone forth from every feature. What a terrible fate was this. I was moved to deepest pity by the contemplation of it.

I placed my hand upon his forehead and said gently,

"Be assured and rest easy now. I will go and bring your daughter here and see that she is made comfortable. Here are food and shelter for you both, and you are most heartily welcome to it and to my best assistance."

I found the daughter sitting on the sand before the fire, her wet garments already steaming from the heat. I told her that her father was as comfortable as it was possible to make him, and that she had better go to him and see if she could not get off some of her wet garments. In the mean time I would get some food warm for them both.

"For pity's sake," said she in a tremulous and vibrant voice, "let me have some water. We have been three days without water except what you gave us."

Without waiting to reproach myself for not doing sooner what I should have known from personal experience was the thing to do, I ran to my boat and got a gourd full and held it for her to drink. I then went with her to the house and gave the old man a long drink.

The girl then said to me that on board there was a trunk containing her clothing, and that she would be glad if she could have it; that as there were several chests and trunks stowed under the deck forward, I would know hers by such and such marks and peculiarities. I went down and got the trunk, and moreover took out a chest and another trunk, which I put under the work-shed, bringing her trunk up to the house. I had afterward to be again called to get it open for her, as the key could not be turned by her slender fingers.

Getting out of my boat a pan of baked pork and beans, I proceeded to extemporize a hot soup by mashing up some of the beans and adding half of a pepper-pod and some water, and setting the preparation on the fire to come to a boil. This made a good hot porridge soup, and did not take long in preparation. When it was ready I went up to the house with the kettle and knocked at the door; it was opened by the girl, her dress changed for a dry one and much of the distress seemingly gone from her pale, beautiful face.

"Here," said I, "is some hot bean porridge for your father and you; and here are a couple of cocoanut-shells from which to eat it. I will take some for myself down at the shed."

"But," replied she, "we cannot drive you out of your house, sir; why do you not come here and eat with us?"

"Very well, if you like," said I. "There will be some corn-bread also and plenty of water to drink."

We ate heartily of the soup and bread, the old man taking only the soup.

I then brought up my hammock and swung it as low down as possible for the girl, and took back the mainsail, that had once formed a tent at Farm Cove, to use for my own bed at the shed. I explained as well as I could how she should sleep in the hammock, and gave her one of the blankets. She assured me she had often slept in a hammock and thought she could manage it. She was then about to explain how she and her father came to be adrift in the boat; but I stopped her by saying, "No, let us wait until to-morrow. You are both exhausted and need sleep and rest. You shall tell me all about it in the morning." And then I wished them both good-night.

"Good-night, and God bless you, sir, for your kindness," answered the girl.

When I reached the shed, built up a fire close by, and lay down it was after nine o'clock, and as the wind had gone down, and the rain was over, it was not so chilly as to make wet garments especially dangerous, though sufficiently disagreeable. However, rolled up in the sail with my feet to the fire, I soon felt warm enough to sleep. The rescue of the two people on the island seemed likely to prove at least a temporary hindrance to the execution of my plans; for I could not see how it was possible, for a few days at least, to leave the island, as the old man was in no condition to undertake such a voyage in an open boat, and probably would not survive it. Indeed, that the hardships which he had already undergone had not killed him was a sufficient matter for wonder. No, I could not leave these people now, and at present, for days and perhaps for weeks, it would be impracticable and cruel to attempt to carry him away either in my boat or his own. Doubtless, if I were to suggest departure, they would agree to it, and undertake the voyage; but I saw it would be little less than murder. However, if he should be no better in a week or two, then, provided he still retained his present vitality, it might be wise to attempt to get him where a physician could see him.

It was no use repining over this enforced delay. Humanity, and the commonest sense of duty to my fellows, demanded that I should stand by these helpless ones so long as they stood so absolutely in need of my aid. The food question, which had long since ceased to trouble me, might now, by reason of the increase in the number of mouths to fill, become something to require considerable exertion, planning, and thought. The weak spot in the larder was likely to be the supply of breadstuffs and vegetables. There would be no lack of pork and fish. Judging from the appearance of several boxes and gunny sacks on board the strangers' boat, there was a supply of food there which might be relied upon to tide over any present necessity that might arise, though my own supply was still considerable.

Then too I must rig up as soon as possible in the house, perhaps by hanging a curtain which could be temporarily drawn at night, a place of privacy for the girl. At night the old man would require somebody to watch him more or less, or at least be near him. I could not expect his daughter to take this all upon herself, as that would be physically impossible. How to manage about this puzzled me considerably. For a short stay of a week or two I did not like to go to the considerable trouble of enlarging my house, and yet the requirements of the situation seemed actually to demand three separate rooms.

At last, as a compromise, I hit upon the idea of cutting down the back wall of the house, between the house proper and the lean-to addition wherein my provisions were stored, and which had been used upon occasion as a smoke house. The provisions could be stored if necessary on board the boats, or under the work-shed. And a wide doorway cut between the two compartments would, with a curtain dividing the larger one, give me the necessary room. I myself would take as my sleeping-place the added room, and by arranging a couple of bunks, the thing would be done.

CHAPTER XI.

ALICE AND HER FATHER.

THE next morning, when shortly after dawn I awoke from a sound, refreshing sleep, my clothes were dried upon me, the storm had passed, and there was promise of a calm, clear day. Raking together the few coals that remained, I soon had my fire burning brightly, and then went down to look at the two boats lying in the creek. The stranger I found had the name "Alice" painted on either bow. The "Alice" proved upon closer examination a much larger boat than the "Mohawk." She was fully four feet longer, and much broader and deeper. A flush deck extended aft from the bows about one third of her whole length, and as in my own boat, was carried clear aft at each side of a well which was protected by an upright washboard. She was provided with an iron centre-board, hinged at the forward end on a pivot. A very considerable rise or sheer fore and aft indicated that she would be pretty safe in heavy weather and high seas. There was a good boat's-compass swung in gimballs, and mounted near the after part of the well, where it would be in sight of the steersman, and an extinguished lantern lying near it, as though to be used when needed, for a binnacle light. The boat was very strongly built, and evidently intended as a sea-going craft. An oiled tarpaulin, buttoned over pins on the washboard, partly covered the well-hole forward, and evidently could be drawn over the whole opening in case of heavy seas.

Of course I was much interested in the examination of the boat, and in the minutest detail of her construction and condition, as I expected when I came to leave the island to use her instead of my own boat, an exchange of vessels greatly to my advantage. On the deck just forward of the foremast a water cask had been lashed. The two hollowed skids nailed to the deck were still there in place. There was a ringbolt let into the deck at each side originally, designed to take the cask lashings. One of these ringbolts was pulled through the deck and the water cask was gone. This condition told the story almost as plainly as words. A heavy sea had struck the port bow and coming on board had washed away the cask, tearing out the bolt. The tarpaulin had saved the vessel from filling.

I looked to the mooring-lines to see that both boats were secure, and then waded over the creek to a place above the willows, where there was a clear, bright-bottomed pool, sheltered from view and well adapted for the fresh-water bath which I needed. Here, too, was a gourd of soap, placed there on former occasions for the bath.

I was in the very midst of the soap-and-water refreshment when I saw on a log at the bank and among the leaves what I took for the head of a huge python or boa constrictor. A hideous head, thrust out toward me through the foliage, bright eyes gleaming like jewels, a wrinkled, pouchy throat, — the unmistakable reptilian characteristics, — caused a shiver of horror to pass through me for a moment. My first impulse was to fly and leave my clothing on the bank. Up to this time I had not seen a single snake, great or small, venomous or harmless, on the island. Backing and edging slowly away, I soon reached a point where I could plainly see that my terrible snake had feet. Ah! it was nothing more nor less than an iguana, a great, harmless species of lizard that loves to haunt the banks of the streams; not only harmless but edible, a delicate morsel for an epicure, hunted as zealously as the Marylanders seek for diamond-back terrapin.

Instantly from fancying myself the hunted I became the hunter. I had tasted iguana-stew at Martinique, and had a distinct recollection of the delicate white meat, with a flavor apparently compounded of those of spring chicken, green turtle, and frogs' legs.

The reptile remained perfectly motionless, with the exception of a sort of regular waving of the folds of the pouched throat. I quietly lowered myself into the water and went a few rods down stream to the boats, where I got a strong cord and a stout ten-foot cane pole. I made a running noose in the cord and hung it upon the pole. With this apparatus I returned and found the lizard still pumping slowly away with his throat, in precisely the same place and attitude. Slowly and cautiously I waded up at one side, until I was distant the length of the pole, and then by infinite degrees advanced the noose, watching the pumping in the wrinkled throat, until the loop was fairly over the head, but of course without touching the reptile.

Just then the pumping action abruptly stopped. But I did not wait for him to be off. On the contrary, I hauled aft on my line like lightning, the noose closed around the ugly neck and jerked a fifty-pound iguana splashing into the creek. As I had no mind to feel his sharp claws, I drove the end of the pole into his mouth and thus between cord and pole held him firmly in the water. He swam like a fish, but he was too securely caught to get away. I dragged him up to the bank where my clothing lay, and getting hold of my knife dispatched him; then I hurriedly clothed myself and cleaned the iguana, taking off the skin and cutting him up ready for the pot. And in fifteen minutes a good portion of him was in my iron kettle and on the fire.

Though snaring big lizards is not perhaps within the strict limits of what may properly be called true sport, still I must say that for real excitement, eager earnestness of pursuit, and genuine pleasure at the capture, I have never experienced before nor since anything approaching the hunter's joy excited by this morning's pot hunt for an iguana.

As I stood by the fire the door of the house opened, and the girl came out. She had on some sort of light dress, and all trace of the bedraggled condition of the previous evening was gone; her brown hair was smoothly swept back from a face still pale, and a bit of bright ribbon at the neck gave the effect of a flower. She came down toward me with a kindly smile and a good-morning greeting, which I returned. Somehow a senseless, foolish embarrassment came over me, which like an idiot I attributed to the fact that I did not know her name. Actuated by a ridiculous impulse, I pulled out my pocketbook and extracted therefrom a stained and withered visiting-card, whereon in the most *recherché* style of the copperplate engraver's art appeared my name, "William Morgan." This precious document I handed to her with a deliberate bow, hat in hand. A smile ran over her countenance as she bent to receive it, so very expressive that I could not fail to understand it. She was undoubtedly laughing at me. Like a flash the full absurdity and incongruity of my act came over me. I pictured my own appearance, — barefoot, clad in pantaloons of moleskin stained to a thousand tints of autumn brown and rolled up half-way to the knee, a blue flannel shirt with sleeves rolled up and throat open, and a hat of bungling rushes; my skin, where exposed, tanned and peeled; a great bush and shock of hair, the growth of nine months, tangled and unkempt, faded by the sun at the ends, and reaching down to my shoulders; the cavalier air; the limp, red-stained, dirty visiting card. I felt the hot blood surge for a moment into my face, and then the absurdity of it all overpowered me and I laughed aloud. She also, after a little struggle, and looking at me again to see, perhaps, whether I was hurt, joined in the chorus, my visiting-card in her hand.

"Mr. Morgan," said she presently, "both my father and I are deeply grateful to you. You saved our lives, and your kindness and tenderness to a helpless old man I shall never forget. I thank you for him and for myself. My father's name," here there was a faint indication of a return of the smile, "is Caleb Millward, and mine is Alice."

I asked her how her father had passed the night, and was informed that he had slept almost continuously, and was still slumbering peacefully. Then I told her that I thought her father was suffering from paralysis, produced, probably, by cerebral hemorrhage; that some small blood vessel had burst in the brain, and that if this could become absorbed in a reasonably short period he would probably recover the use of his faculties either wholly or partially; that we could only await results, keeping him warm, well nourished and quiet; that I believed this was all the best of doctors could do for him, and that we must put our trust in his good constitution and the favor of the Almighty, and hope for the best.

I learned from her account that her father, Caleb Millward, was a missionary, whose work for the past five years had been among the coolie laborers, of whom large numbers from Hindostan and the lower provinces of China had been imported into various of the West India Islands, under what has been known as the contract-labor system, only another name for slavery. Her mother had died several years before, during a yellow fever epidemic, and since her death the Rev. Mr. Millward had broken up his permanent home station, and had travelled in a regular circuit from point to point in his little schooner, making a complete round in a period of about six months. It was on one of these trips, while sailing from one small island to another, that the series of mishaps took place which resulted in their being cast away. There was on board only her father, herself, and a young Jamaican of English descent, who was employed to help sail the boat, and to take care of the vessel when in port. The voyage they were at the time engaged upon, was a traverse of about twenty miles. The wind was fair with no appearance of bad weather. Suddenly a tremendous wave was seen approaching, not parallel with the swell but at an angle thereto. All three saw it coming down. Her father called out to the Jamaican to lower some sail, and the Jamaican was forward at this work, when the sea struck the boat with tremendous force and dashed him overboard, and also tore loose the water cask and carried it away. The Jamaican never rose to the surface. Her father, she said, appeared to be wonderfully affected by the accident, and soon grew faint and half stupid. Presently partially recovering, he set the sails so that the boat was hove to under the sail that she subsequently bore, then almost immediately sank down unconscious. He remained thus all day breathing heavily, and then came to, but was unable to move. So they drifted without water, until the storm came and they were drenched with spray. After a long period of suffering they were rescued as we have seen.

This was the story of their disaster. Leaving Miss Millward to watch the stew, I went up to the house, and finding the old man now awake gave him a thorough rubbing with my hands, — a sort of massage treatment, — until the circulation of the blood was evident on the surface. This seemed to do him good. Then I put on his clothes, now dry, and returned to the fire.

Miss Millward had gone down to the "Alice" and rummaged out some spoons and knives and forks, a small tablecloth, some salt and some black pepper, three bowls, three plates, and some glass tumblers, and had them at the fire in a hand basket, and the kettle containing the stew had been removed from the fire.

"Now, Mr. Morgan," said she, as I came up, "Let us understand each other. I intend while we stay here to make myself useful. I have been taught to work, and the cooking and housekeeping are woman's work. You will let me do that work as far as I am able, will you not?"

"Certainly I will, Miss Millward. There will be plenty of work for both of us. It will relieve me, and frankly, I think you will be better contented and happier for it."

"Very well, then. Please give me a lift with this kettle to the house. Our breakfast is ready as soon as the cloth can be laid."

That breakfast of delicious iguana-stew, toasted pilot-bread, and cool, pure water sparkling in glass, set on a clean, white cloth, and eaten from real dishes with the table implements of civilization, will linger long in my memory. I picture the scene before me even now; the cool white interior, the old man stretched on the couch, the table presenting to my long unaccustomed eyes an appearance of elegance, though plain and common enough in reality, the savory fragrance of the stew, the beautiful girl seated opposite me, the open doorway, and the glimpse through it of the sunlit sea, — all return to me as a happy, pleasant dream. It seemed to me then like a dream, and as though it all might fade away on awakening.

Heretofore I had eaten my food in a perfunctory fashion, spending no unnecessary time over it, with no special enjoyment except the satisfaction due to hunger allayed. Now all was different. Meals were about to become, I foresaw, delightful domestic episodes, enlivened by talk and rendered social by companionship. This was life, and not a mere struggle for existence.

We discussed the proposed changes to be made in the interior by cutting an enlarged opening through to the store-room, the hanging of a sail-cloth curtain, and the building of bunks. I explained how I was cast upon the island, and my experiences since then, But I did not mention the purpose of my voyage nor say anything about the wreck of the galleon.

When finally we had finished, and I had reluctantly risen, she said: "Mr. Morgan, I should like it very much if you would get me a broom."

"Nothing will be easier, Miss Housekeeper," replied I, and immediately brought in a cedar-bough. This she eyed ruefully, but accepted as the only available substitute for the familiar domestic weapon.

All that day I devoted to the work of clearing out the store-house, cutting the opening, rigging up the curtain, and building a bunk for myself in the new apartment. I did not build the second bunk, as I had intended, for a new plan had occurred to me; namely, to construct a movable couch for Mr. Millward to lie upon, and on which I could convey him on occasion out into the sun or on the porch, and upon which he might be propped up in a sitting posture. But before the day was over I had arranged some shelving at each side of the fireplace for Miss Millward's dishes and domestic appliances. It was simply delightful to be called to a dinner that I had no hand in preparing, and to witness the air of homelike comfort given to the little house by this girl. The whole atmosphere seemed changed. Not that one could note any great or marked alteration; but in little details here and there, were evidences of a woman's hand, — a bit of white cloth disposed over the windows as a curtain, my nautilus shell set on the mantel-shelf with a spray of flowers, and a hundred similar trifles; perhaps most of all, the unaccustomed presence of others, the sound of a woman's voice, her light footstep, and the rustle of her garments. I did not attempt to analyze my feelings, but at any rate the place seemed like a home, and I began in advance to regret the day of leaving it.

That night I slept again at the shed. Before I retired, however, Miss Millward asked me to wait until she read a chapter in the Bible to her father. And when this was done she gently lifted the old man's helpless hands together in an attitude of prayer, and then prayed aloud herself, in such a pathetic and tender manner that the tears came to my eyes in spite of myself.

The next day, after getting a stock of cedar, I started to fashion the couch for Mr. Millward. This with the making of another armchair occupied two days. The couch I made like a great chair, with a back pivoted to fold down or prop up, and wove an upholstery of rushes. It occurred to me that I could easily saw some wheels out of a round limb and mount them as rollers on which to move the couch more easily over the smooth floor; and this improvement I added. When the couch was finished there was then a bunk for each of the well ones and the couch for the invalid, and I therefore took up my quarters in the house, which I was glad to do, as I could then give Miss Millward a needed relief in helping watch the sick man at night. By wheeling his couch beside my own this was an easy matter.

In the morning we wheeled the old gentleman out upon the porch and propped him up for a rest, until he would sign with his eyes to be lowered again. I kept up the rubbing daily. At the end of about a week I noticed that he could move the fingers of his right hand. This was a most promising sign; and I then began to rub him regularly three times a day. In the course of two days more he could use this hand and arm quite freely, and recovered some power in the muscles of his neck so that he could turn his head. But though he could utter some unintelligible sounds he could not yet articulate anything. He kept making signs as though he wanted something, which I could not understand. I got out a pencil and some paper, which he took and attempted to write, but I could not read the characters. His daughter, however, coming out just then, was able to comprehend his wants at once, and going in to where his coat hung, brought out his spectacles and placed them on his eyes. The old man then wrote plainly the word "Bible," and the book was brought to him. Propped up on his couch he turned the leaves and began to read with an air of perfect contentment. The distorted appearance of his face had gradually been passing away, and when his daughter gave him the book his countenance was lighted up with a singularly sweet smile.

In the present condition of the old man I felt that if he could have a little generous wine, as port or Madeira, to drink it would be a benefit to him. Some alcoholic stimulant in small amount was evidently what he needed. But such a thing could not be had. Why should I not make whiskey? I remembered that the negroes frequently made what they called palm wine from the juice of the cocoanut palm. And I had drunk both the sweetish, fresh preparation and the same in the sour, fermented stage, the latter being quite alcoholic in its nature. Moreover, I knew the whole process of obtaining this drink; for I had watched the negro boys climb the palms at Martinique, bind and cut the unopened flower spathes, and attach the small gourds or little earthen chatties to catch the juice as it trickled out.

Without explaining my purpose either to the old man or his daughter, I climbed six palms that evening, bound the flower spathes to prevent them from opening, tied them in a bent position, and cut off the point, attaching to each spathe a gourd to receive the liquid drippings. The next morning I collected from these trees nearly two gallons of sweet sap, and cutting each spathe to a fresh surface left them to flow again. When I brought the sap down it was already beginning to ferment, and had somewhat the taste of sweet cider with a slight sparkle. I put half a pint of it in a bottle, corked it tight, and tied the cork. Some of it I set in an open gourd in the shade; and about a gallon I set on the fire in a pan, intending to boil this latter portion down into syrup, or into "jaggery," as the gummy, sweet preparation is called. In about three hours after collecting it that portion which was left in the open gourd had changed to such condition as to have a sharp, subacid taste, something like hock. I immediately drank a tumbler full of it, and found in a few minutes that it had indeed already developed sufficient alcohol to make that amount all that a person of sober habits would care to imbibe at one time. It was pleasant to the taste and very refreshing, and had a sparkle and a slight hum like new ale, when poured into the glass. I gave the old man a tumbler full, and also his daughter, and for company's sake took an additional half-tumbler myself. It did him good, apparently, at least he seemed greatly to relish it, and held out his glass to be filled again.

"Why, this is like wine!" exclaimed Miss Millward, "where did you get it?"

"We have wine trees on our island, Miss Millward, and I have been tapping them, as you will see," pointing to the suspended gourds, some of which could be seen from the porch where we sat in the shade. I then explained to her the whole process, and my purpose in making the wine. I showed her the pan of boiling sap, and she at once undertook to attend to the treacle-making. That evening at supper I opened the bottle which I had filled, and the cork flew out with a report like a pistol, the wine bubbling and frothing like champagne. This the invalid drank alone. The sap left in the open gourd turned quite sour, like vinegar; but I did not have any use for it in that condition and so poured it out. The result of the boiling was about a pint of thick, dark-colored sweet syrup, or treacle, of a rather pleasant taste. By carrying the boiling still farther it could of course be reduced to the condition of the sugar called jaggery. But it was more convenient for use in its treacly state.

The unusual and remarkable rapidity of the fermentative change in this palm-sap had the attendant inconvenience that it would require to be gathered fresh every day, if used for wine. I therefore concluded that I would make a still and distil a brandy from the fermented sap, which I could subsequently use as a check to the fermentation in the wine, after the manner that port-wine, sherry, Madeira, and other similar wines are prepared. I took a large earthen jar which would hold three or four gallons, and luted to the mouth of it with clay a gourd cut with an opening to correspond with the jar mouth. I then procured a long, straight cane about three inches in diameter at the butt, tapering in a length of twenty feet to less than an inch. I split this cane throughout the whole length and cut away the septum or partition which occurs at each joint. I then joined the two split halves together, pitched the joint, and wound the whole length with cord to hold it solid, and afterwards wound over all a grass rope of rather loose texture. In the neck of the gourd I inserted the butt of this cane tube and luted the joint with clay, but so that it could be removed. The cane tube led away in a nearly horizontal direction, having a slight fall from the gourd outward.

I now collected palm-sap enough to fill the jar, and when it had undergone a full fermentation, and just before it turned sour, I set it on in the still to boil over a fire. The gourd and tube were in place and the joints well luted. Then as soon as the fermented sap began to boil and throw off vapor, I wet the grass rope that surrounded the tube, and set a vessel to receive what came dripping from the end of the tube in drops. Very soon the brandy began to come over in a warm, thin, trickling stream. When I had collected a little over a quart I stopped the process for fear of getting some other product over. It was good, strong brandy, and had no disagreeable flavor, being quite clear, with a slight yellow tint.

I had now what I needed for my wine-making, and made use of it in the following manner: I collected a fresh supply of the sap and permitted fermentation to proceed in it until it was, as I thought, at the precise point where it had the best sub-acid flavor. I then added some of the palm syrup to sweeten it a little, and also enough of the brandy — about half a pint to the gallon — to stop the further fermentation. The wine so prepared had a rough resemblance to port. It was quite pleasant to the taste, and would keep any length of time. Having now a supply of about two gallons I made no more, as there was enough for the invalid, and nobody else needed it, or cared particularly for it.

CHAPTER XII.

THE PROBLEM.

DAY by day the old man slowly improved in condition, until at the end of three weeks he was able to sit in the armchair with comfort. He startled us one morning by uttering his daughter's name, and little by little recovered the use of his tongue. He was not yet able to stand or walk, and it was still doubtful whether he would recover the use of his lower limbs. I felt reasonably confident, however, that he would do so ultimately.

As soon as he could talk, almost his first words were a request to me to get the Jamaican sailor's chest from the boat and use the clothing for myself. I was glad enough to do this, as almost any sort of change was acceptable. I found in the chest a number of good shirts, both woollen and cotton, a good, serviceable suit of dark tweed, and two complete suits of white duck; also socks and underwear, and a good straw hat. These things fitted me very well, but a pair of dancing pumps were so small that I could not get them on my feet; however, my own shoes were still very good. The kind-hearted old man then said that if I wished it he would cut my hair; he thought he could use his daughter's scissors well enough. But I did not fancy having him clipping about my ears with uncertain fingers. and resolutely declined. My hair, which now reached to my shoulders, was as long as it was likely to grow. The ends, exposed freely, would naturally wear and fray away as fast as it grew, and I concluded to let it go as it was until I reached civilization.

Thinking about my plans one day, it occurred to me that it would not be a bad idea to plant a garden for use when I should return to the island. Potatoes and yams, and fresh green corn would not be a bad provision to have ready at hand in plenty while working at the sunken galleon. There was a patch of good, rich soil near the creek, now covered with dry grass, beneath which the new grass had sprung since the rains. By burning it over the ground might be readily cleared for a couple of acres in extent. I put fire to it at several places on the windward side and it was soon black and bare. I began at once with the shovel to break up the soil in spots, and to make hills for the potatoes and yams, and to form a place in which to plant the corn. With the hoe I could subsequently go over the ground between the hills and cut up the grass when it started. After I had been working a couple of days at this severe labor, Mr. Millward asked me why I thought it necessary to prepare to plant so extensively, as we should soon be leaving the island.

"I shall be well enough in a week or two longer to go. You are making provision there as though you expected we were all to remain here for six months longer," said he.

I looked at him a moment before answering, debating with myself what reply to make. At last I said, "Mr. Millward, I expect to return to this island after we have reached Martinique."

"And why should you do that?" he asked, with an air of surprise.

"I may tell you the reason why, and think perhaps I shall," I answered, and continued after a pause, "I believe I may trust you, and that you will not betray me. It is now a secret known only to me."

The old man said no more, and we changed the subject of conversation.

That afternoon while at work in the new garden I considered carefully the propriety of telling the Millwards about the galleon. It would be a great comfort to have some one to talk to and advise with concerning the matter, and I already knew enough of these people to feel confident they would not betray me. On the other hand was it best to tell any one of my secret? But I finally decided to give them my confidence. And that evening, as we sat in front of the fire, — a chill rain having set in, — I told to the father and the daughter the whole story of my coming to the island, the search for the wreck, the successful location of the sunken hulk, and also what my plans for the future were. Mr. Millward after listening to it all said, " Now, Mr. Morgan, I am better able to appreciate the sacrifice you are making in remaining here with us, and the great inconvenience to which we are putting you. Is it not better that you should start at once? I think I shall now be able to stand the voyage."

" As soon as you are strong enough to stand the voyage, Mr. Millward," said I, " we will start; but not before that time."

Mr. Millward now asked to see the pearls of which I had told him in the course of my statement. When I had handed them to him, he said, " These pearls are highly valuable. I am sufficiently familiar with the value of such gems to be able to assure you that you have ten thousand dollars' worth here, at a very low estimate, and perhaps double that amount in value."

I asked him where I could find a market for them. He thought that it would not be wise to attempt to sell them anywhere in the islands, unless at Havana, but that Havana would probably prove as good a market as I could find anywhere. He further told me that he had heard a rumor of a valuable pearl fishery having been found and secretly worked somewhere among the islands. No doubt this island was the place. If so we might expect the pearl fishers to return at any time. Now this was a prospect which was very far from pleasant to contemplate; not because they might lay claim to my pearls, — I had no fear of that, — nor because I could not substantiate my right to the abandoned property, or if necessary give them up without a murmur. The situation was more serious than that. These pearl fishers, if they came, would be out in their boats and prowling about, and would be sure to find out what I was doing. Moreover, they would doubtless be a well armed, lawless, and adventurous set. If they found us on the island, and knew that we had discovered their secret, there was no telling what they might do. It made me feel very uneasy. If by any accident they should run across my buoy, the first thing would be to send a diver down and my own secret would be disclosed.

"I shall go to-morrow morning and remove that buoy," said I.

The old man agreed with me that this would be advisable.

That night I slept very little till toward morning. All night I lay thinking about the galleon and the treasure that it contained. If I only had a diving-apparatus I could see my way clear. The old man and his daughter would be all the help I should need. I began to dislike the idea of leaving the island even temporarily, until I had secured the treasure. But probably I could not procure a submarine helmet and diver's dress, with air-tubes and pump, short of Kingston, Jamaica, or Havana in Cuba, and possibly not nearer than New York. Ah! the loss of my diving-apparatus was a vexing misfortune. It might, and probably would be more than six months before I could get back with these appliances. This line of cogitation finally brought me around to the thought that possibly I might be able to make a diving-apparatus myself which would answer my purpose. Why not? There must be some way to do it. And why shall I not find that way? I began to think it over by fairly stating the problem to myself, and before I went to sleep I had convinced myself that I could make all the needed apparatus except the air-pump. But this was a device I could see no way to supply. "Never mind," thought I, "it will suggest itself as I go along, if I keep my mind upon it. I will stay and try it." With this resolve I felt better contented, and soon dropped to sleep.

At dawn I was up, and immediately took out my boat and went to the buoy. The wind was light and I had no difficulty in getting fast to it. Instead of taking up the buoy, as I had at first intended, I merely shortened the anchor line so that the buoy was held under water about two feet. I knew that the gourds would remain in this condition for a long time, and with my sights on shore would enable me to find the neighborhood, while they would not be likely to be seen by others not looking for them.

When this was done I sailed back to the creek in time for breakfast, congratulating myself on the additional peace of mind this act had brought me. Now nobody would be likely to stumble on the galleon, and I could give my thoughts to the problem before me.

As I rounded into the creek before the wind, I saw the graceful figure of Alice Millward, who was coming down from the house to look after her fire for breakfast.

When I came up I found her lamenting that not a single spark could be found alight, and that the breakfast must needs be late, or cold. But the sun was already well up above the sea, — at least an hour and a half high, — and I found no difficulty in procuring a blaze with the burning-glass, and the fire was soon burning bravely.

I sat down in the shade of the shed, while she busied herself with the simple cookery, and thought as I looked on, what a beautiful girl this was, with her clean-cut profile, her floating tendrils of silken, brown hair, her well rounded form, the graceful poise of her shapely head, the elastic step, the sweet voice humming bits of song, the cheerful, musical laugh. She was fair indeed, and more than that I knew she was pure and true in everything, a lovely and lovable woman. I then and there confessed to myself that she had become a part of my life. I was in love, and the strange delight of her presence thrilled my heart with new emotion. Up to this time my thoughts had been bent solely on getting a treasure buried in the sea; I now realized that here was a treasure recovered from the sea, which if I could hope to call it my own, would far exceed in value all the gold and jewels ever carried by the richest fleet that ever floated on the Spanish seas. It was all so new and strange and sudden to me that I was afraid to stay longer near her, lest I might be obliged to speak to her, and thus betray myself. So I got up and wandered away to the edge of the forest. But the leaves trembling in the gentle morning breeze seemed to whisper my secret; the rasping locust, which had been noisily droning all night long, seemed to play it in every trill; the birds sang it.

So this was love, — love that makes the world go round; that comes once at least into each life, and fills it with light and sweetness, or with gloom and sorrow. When did I begin to love this girl? I could not tell. Yesterday I did not know it, but it must be that I loved her then as now; and before that and ever since I had first seen her. And even before I had seen her had not my heart been waiting for her? But now I felt that somehow our relations had changed. Could I have again the sense of comradeship that I had felt toward her? Would she not see a change in me? I could not analyze this new sensation nor predict what would happen. A dreadful doubt and uncertainty oppressed my heart simultaneously with its new-born gladness. Could I hope that this sweet maid would ever find anything to love in me?

A hot, despairing wave of self-depreciation came over me. I looked at myself in imagination, — my great hulking frame, my tanned skin, my bearded face, my long, unkempt hair. Oh, William Morgan, what a poor fool you are to fall in love with this fair vision of beauty, this domestic goddess, this Hebe, this sum of grace and loveliness. And then a tender desire welled up and filled my heart to love and cherish and protect this helpless waif that had floated in to me from the wild sea.

After a little I plucked a spray of orchids that hung from a half-rotten limb, — one of those strange, rare flowers that seem rather the dreamy vagary of a flower painter than a natural production. They were white, but beautifully marked with spots of rich purple and ribs of golden yellow. This spray I carried to the house, and gave it to her. Such an act could have no particular significance, but to my distempered fancy it seemed a homage paid, a tribute given, a declaration of fealty.

At the breakfast table I broached the subject of the

galleon, and stated that I had almost determined to remain upon the island and to undertake the recovery of the treasure by aid of such apparatus as could be made here, provided they were willing to delay their departure a sufficient time. The truth was that since the last hour my mind was fully made up to stay if possible, and the presence of Alice Millward was doubtless a moving cause for that determination. I felt very anxious that they should both fall in with my plan.

"I think," said I to the old man, "that if you go on improving as you have done, you will soon be able yourself to give me the aid I need. And remember, in that case there will probably be treasure enough for all. In the mean time, while you are getting well your daughter and I can be making preparations for the work. There is a great deal to be done. Now what do you say?"

"But let me know exactly your plan of work," replied he, "in order that I may be better able to judge of its feasibility."

Thereupon I detailed my proposed scheme, so far as it was formulated in my mind, confessing that I had as yet thought of no practical method of making an air-pump. "Still," said I, "there is no doubt in my mind that some method of supplying that deficiency will occur to me."

"Well, Mr. Morgan, let me think this over for a little while. There is no hurry required of me in making up my mind, for I should not like to leave the island for a week or so anyhow. Give me, say three days; but during this time there is no reason why you should be idle. If in the mean time some practicable method of completing the apparatus should occur to you I am free to say that fact would have great weight in determining my course of action."

After breakfast we all went out on the porch and sat down, Duke lying in the sun at the old man's feet. We discussed at great length the whole art and mystery of wrecking and diving, and the apparatus for such work.

In this discussion Alice Millward took an active part. She seemed so anxious to learn and know all about it that I went over, for her benefit, all the book knowledge I had pertaining to the subject. While this was not very extensive, the brief descriptions of apparatus familiar to me helped us all wonderfully to get a clearer idea of the problem before us. There was one method of raising sunken vessels about which I had read somewhere that was specially interesting and suggestive. This method is to attach to the hull barges partly filled with water, and pump the water out of the barges little by little, until by reason of their rise in the water the hull is lifted clear of the ground. Then barges and hull are towed into shallower water and the operation is repeated until finally the shore is reached. But this operation would require diving-apparatus for attaching the hawsers or ropes to the sunken hulk, and it brought us, therefore, no nearer a complete solution of the problem.

The talk was interesting and animated, and was kept up until the old man gave signs of weariness. Finally, in the midst of a discussion as to the best method of making an air-tube, he dropped to sleep. The practical benefit which I derived from this conversation was the familiarity obtained by holding up before the mind all the conditions and necessities of the problem, in the effort to make others understand these requirements. It is by steady and continuous thought that all problems are solved, and the first requisite of every solution is this very faculty of holding all the conditions without effort simultaneously in the mind. By continued effort mental process becomes finally so far a matter of mere habit, in any particular case, that the mind is left wholly free to act. It is a familiar saying with regard to mathematics, that a problem clearly stated is already half solved. This is true with regard to everything depending upon human thought. But problems are not solved by a mere effort of the will. The mind of man does not so operate. One must jostle various thoughts about in the brain, until finally by an unconscious process of selection the fitting thought is found, and its fitness perceived. One thing suggests another and that a third, link by link in a continuous chain, until the mind finally sees in the procession the needed thing, and immediately seizing upon it ignores all else.

I wanted to be alone that I might, by revolving the riddle over and over, finally seize the key and unlock it.

CHAPTER XIII.

THE ABANDONED PLANTATION.

CALLING Duke I took my lasso and the axe, and started out for a long tramp to the woods, where I might think undisturbed.

That the walk might not be wholly aimless, I decided to go up the beach to the north a little way, and then strike over to that part of the creek which ran down parallel with the beach and follow it up to its headwaters. Poor Duke thought this was a hunting expedition pure and simple. His delight was extravagant to witness. For each foot I travelled he went at least six. Forward and back, ranging to and fro into every nook and corner, with his sensitive nose investigating everything, he made the most of his holiday. The gulls were out as usual, but Duke ignored them completely. He had already learned that this fowl was not game, and as he measured all things by that single standard, these birds had sunk to a point in his estimation that was beneath the contempt of a well-bred dog. We routed up an armadillo just after we crossed the creek, and captured it. Being so near home, I carried it back and instructed Miss Alice how to bake it in the oven, in the afternoon, for supper, and filled the oven with wood for her to light at the proper time. Then telling her I might not return much before nightfall, I started anew.

After we had crossed the creek again and had walked about a mile, we came on about a half-dozen pigs on the beach, most probably varying their diet with a few clams. When they saw us the little herd dashed across the sands and into the tangled jungle. Following them I found they had here a beaten path, which showed that this was one of their regular run-ways. I conjectured that this path would lead to the stream at some point, and so took advantage of it. In and out it went, well defined, through the thicket and the jungle; here through dense brakes of fern, there under great trees, until finally the stream was reached at a point higher up than I had ever before ascended. All about were great numbers of calabash trees full of gourds, literally thousands of them in all stages of growth, some fallen to the ground from over-ripeness. The inhabitants of this island need never want for such utensils as could be made of this vegetable product. What greatly surprised me was the size of the stream at this point. It had not seemingly diminished either in depth or width, though I had naturally expected it would be considerably less; for we were over three miles by its winding course from the mouth.

The path, without the aid of which I could not have penetrated the dense growth, led along the bank of the stream close to the water. About a quarter of a mile further on the course of the stream changed, coming around a bend from the west, straight from the cliffs. I pressed on and soon found myself in a deep, narrow gorge, the path still running alongside the stream on a narrow margin of rocky shore, the cliff towering straight up on either hand. On the top of the rocks, at the level of the central plateau, was a dense forest, the trees of which, growing close to the gorge at each side, interlaced in a mass of foliage above, at times shutting out the sky. I followed the stream along the path entirely through the central plateau, and came out on the other side in what I have before spoken of as the north valley.

I was now in a bowl-shaped depression, walled in on the east by the cliffs of the central plateau, through which I had just come by way of the stream-cut gorge; on the west by the western rise or ridge which formed the shore cliffs, and which circled around to the north; and on the south by the connecting ridge between the plateau and the cliffs. The stream wound away in lazy curves through the flat bottom, and its head-waters seemed as far away as ever. To the right hand the sunlit gleam of water caught my eye at a distance, and I passed through the bushes until I discovered a narrow cleft in the rocks to the northwest, through which came a glimpse of the distant sea. There was a park-like appearance to some portion of this enclosure that was delightful. Across the middle, east and west, ran a little knoll, which formed the water-shed. All the water which fed the stream evidently came from the drainage of the valley south of this knoll. What water drained from the north slope probably had to find its way to the sea through the distant cleft.

I followed the stream until the path at its edge faded away to nothing, and then turned off toward the centre of the valley through the open grassy glades which were interspersed among the beautiful groves and clumps of trees. Very soon I came upon decided evidence of the hand of man. An old orange grove was here, planted regularly in rows; the trees broad and spreading, and at least fifty years old, were loaded with the golden, russet-tinted globes. The fruit was sweet and delicious. One variety, a tree with gnarled branches and mossy trunk, bore literally thousands of the small, yellow mandarin oranges, with a skin loose and thin as paper. Here too were rows of red-berried coffee-trees, thorny limes, and low-growing lemons, with here and there a dark-leafed grape-fruit. The whole plantation was more or less choked with weeds and undergrowth, clearly indicating abandonment, perhaps for years.

Near by were the great banner-like leaves of the banana and plantain, in abundance. This was a most valuable find, and it removed from my mind all fear of lack of food. Man can live almost upon the plantain alone. And it has been said that this valuable fruit furnishes food to more millions than any other vegetable product, not even excepting rice. Pushing on through the luxuriant growth that cumbered the earth, I came out finally into a little clearing on the top of the rise and found before me several low buildings. The weeds that grew all about, choking the paths and overflowing in all directions, too plainly told the tale of long desertion and abandonment. There was a principal dwelling-house of a single story, built of adobes, with a wide veranda; also three smaller houses at a little distance, — servants' quarters probably; a large, low shed about which were scattered great heaps of old bagasse, or crushed sugar-cane, which indicated a sugar plantation; a tobacco-curing shed, in which still hung some shreds and fragments of withered tobacco; and other outhouses. There was an air of desolation about the place that was most depressing, as I stood waist-deep among the thrifty growth of weeds in the clear, hot sunshine, looking in astonishment at the scene.

I opened the front door and went into the house. All was vacancy and desolation, — dust, cobwebs, stains of water that had leaked in and pooled in spots upon the floor, dead flies, bugs, and spiders. There was a broken window-pane in one room, and through the small opening thus made had entered a great litter of dead leaves, which lay strewn about, indicating by their number the considerable time that must have elapsed while one by one they chanced to blow through the narrow opening. I was glad to get out again into the open air.

Here had been at one time a considerable plantation. Hundreds of acres had doubtless been under cultivation, and the busy sounds of life had been heard where now, save for the mournful complaint of a dove cooing from the orange grove for its mate, all was still.

That this plantation should have been unknown to me all this time seemed surprising to me at the moment. But in truth, had I not followed up the course of the creek, it is quite probable I never should have discovered it; for all about on every hand were rocky walls and dense foliage, both hiding it from view and rendering it difficult of access. There were really but two roads to this place from the outer world, one by the way I had just come, and the other by way of the sea through the distant cleft above spoken of.

Traces of a broad road led from the buildings toward this cleft, and I followed it down past the remains of sugar, corn, and tobacco fields, until I stood on the margin of a deep, rock-walled cove, open on one side to the valley, where was a rude landing-pier, and on the other by a narrow gate or passage to the sea. This was the harbor and port of the old plantation. The cove, though so small, would have floated a man-of-war, and was almost land-locked, the narrow entrance not being above thirty feet in width at the water level.

I remembered that when I made the circuit of the island on foot I waded across the mouth of this cove at low water. There must therefore be a bar, with barely water enough at low tide to get a boat over;

but at high tide there would probably be twelve or fifteen feet. That I did not see the wooden pier at that time was due to the fact that the cove took a bend to the left after entering from the sea. Had the rocks been less abrupt, I should doubtless have turned in at that time and endeavored to cross the island here instead of going a mile farther north, beyond the limits of the valley.

I wandered over the abandoned plantation in all directions for several hours, but found nothing of special interest except a flock of half-wild domestic chickens, descendants doubtless of some left by the former residents here. I gathered a dozen leaves of tobacco, thinking that Mr. Millward might like to have a cigar. After eating the frugal lunch I had brought, supplemented with some fruit, I sat down under an orange-tree and rolled me a cigar of some of the dried leaf, which I lighted with the burning-glass, and proceeded to enjoy a quiet smoke of the fragrant tobacco. While I sat thus slowly and placidly cogitating over the means of reaching the treasure, and varying that line of thought from time to time with speculations as to the former inhabitants of the island, suddenly the whole plan which had been floating unformed in my mind took concrete shape, apparently of its own accord and without effort. The riddle was read and the problem was solved.

The day had worn away, and the afternoon was half over when I concluded it was high time to be gone. So I got me a great banana-leaf, gathered a goodly lot of fruit, taking samples of all, including some of the coffee-berries, and tying the whole securely in a bundle with the banana-leaf and some bark strips, started for home, which I safely reached an hour before sunset.

As I came in sight of the house I saw standing poised on a rock near the creek the graceful figure of

Alice Millward, evidently on the lookout up the beach to see if the wanderers were coming. I waved my hand, and she at once jumped down and began to put the supper in readiness. And when I reached the house I found the table all spread beneath the porch, and the hot baked armadillo smoking on the board. I untied my great bundle and spread out before them the supply of oranges, lemons, plantains, bananas, etc., in a tempting heap.

As soon as Mr. Millward caught sight of the red berries, he cried, "Ah, delightful! you have found coffee! That was the chief thing your island lacked, friend Morgan. Now we can have our morning cup of coffee. But where did you find all this?"

"Come, father, let us have our supper, while it is hot," interrupted Alice Millward, "and the fruit will be a dessert for us. And I am sure while we are at table Mr. Morgan will tell us his adventures, and where he has been to-day."

This was too plainly desirable on all hands to be gainsaid, at least so far as the first part of the proposal was concerned.

Of course I had to go over the whole ground and describe the old, abandoned plantation as minutely and completely as I could, and to answer a hundred inquiries about it. The question was raised whether we had better not go there to live while we remained on the island, but it was decided that for the present we had better remain where we were, for several reasons; one reason was the trouble of removal, another the fact that we would there lose the refreshing sea breeze, and there were others quite sufficient to determine the matter in favor of staying. But at any rate we would as soon as possible sail around in the boat to the plantation cove and make a visit to the plantation. Speculation was indulged in as to who had lived there, and when and why the place had been abandoned. The explanation offered by Mr. Millward was quite satisfactory. He had frequently known of plantations being made on the outlying islands, and stated that they were always subsequently abandoned because of the difficulty of reaching a market for the products, the necessity for frequent voyages in the sloops and small vessels, and also the difficulty of keeping workmen and assistants long in such places, except as slaves.

After the supper was over I rolled a dry tobacco-leaf into a couple of ungainly cigars and handed one to the old man. The pleasure he expressed at this simple offering was quite extravagant.

"Indeed, young man, you have made here a wonderful find, — quite equal in every respect to the coffee. This is the true solace and comfort of the contemplative man. I thank you most sincerely."

But he would not light the cigar; he had other views of the proper use to make of it. Drawing from his coat pocket a venerable brown pipe, he proceeded to break up my cigar and fill the bowl with the fragments.

"Now," said he when he had finished, "if you will give me a light I will warm the heart of this old companion, and my own at the same time."

"Mr. Millward," said I, after we had the smoking fairly started, "I have found the way to the treasure in the sunken galleon."

"Ah, then you have hit upon a plan of making the air-pump. Well, I am in a mood just now to believe you can do it. Pray let us know about it."

"No, sir, I have not found any way to build an air-pump. But I have found, I think, that we shall not need one."

"But how can you get air to breathe under water unless it is pumped to you?" said Miss Alice.

"I do not expect to go under water," said I in reply. And continuing, "I am inclined to enjoy your perplexity a little, for perplexity is what I have been enduring myself until a very simple idea occurred to me this very afternoon. But it is not fair to expect you will understand without explanation in a moment what another could not understand for months. The simple fact is this: if I cannot go under water to the ship, why should I not bring the ship out of water to me? It is the old case, you see, of the mountain and Mahomet."

"Yes, I see it is," said the old man, — "with this difference, that you propose to have the mountain come to Mahomet.".

Thereupon I laid my whole plan before them, which was briefly this: to attach to the hulk, one at a time, sinking them under water, enough empty calabashes to raise it and float it gradually in to shore, where at low tide it would be above water. The mechanical principle was the common one belonging to every device which converts speed into power; as, for example, the lever, the screw, or the inclined plane. Little by little with slight exertion of power each calabash or gourd could be pulled down under water to the wreck, and would continue thereafter to lift as many pounds as were required to pull it down. When this lifting power was multiplied by enough of the calabashes, the wreck would surely be raised. It was, after all, only a modification of the method of raising hulks by sinking and attaching barges partly full of water and then pumping the water out and causing them to rise and lift the wreck. In that case the slow application of the power was accomplished by pumping. In the proposed method it consisted in pulling down the calabashes one at a time.

Mr. Millward likened the operation to the lifting of an entire building by the hod carrier who carried a few bricks at a load up the ladder.

"But how will you attach your numerous calabashes to the hull?" said the old man after a little thought. "It will take a great number."

"That I will explain to you in detail," said I, and thereupon set forth minutely the entire plan of operation. The explanation was satisfactory to his mind. He at once said to me that he thought the thing feasible, and was satisfied that it would probably succeed.

What those minute details were and how successfully they were carried out will appear when we come to the account of the attempt which was subsequently made.

"Now," said I, "we have a great quantity of rope to make, some hawsers, and a huge supply of small rope and cord. To do this will take a long time, and I have a notion that some sort of a spinning or twisting machine will be necessary. We must establish a regular rope-walk here in a small way."

This immediately led to a long discussion and a consideration of rope-making machinery in general, at the conclusion of which I thought I could see a way of making a sort of spinning-machine for twisting rope-yarn out of the cocoa husks, and also a reel for laying such strands up into rope. Having worked out the plan in my own mind I resolved to set about it at once. Mr. Millward had given his hearty assent to remain on the island long enough to make a full effort to recover the treasure, and I began now to look forward to a successful completion of my task.

The full moon that evening was shining over the calm sea out of a clear sky with a pure silvery radiance, and a cool, gentle breath of air, scarcely enough to ripple the surface of the sea, fanned our faces as we three sat looking out upon the water from under the little porch. It was a lovely night, almost too beautiful to put to such commonplace use as sleep. In a little while Mr. Millward asked me to push his couch into the house, as he thought he would retire. After that Alice Millward and I sat for an hour longer, enjoying the moonlight and talking low so as not to disturb him.

She told me much about the wandering life she and her father had led; of the many kind and thoughtful acts of the poor benighted laborers who formed his audiences; of her own efforts to learn Hindostanee that she might help him in his work; of the hardships and sorrows of these people, and of the strange characteristics of the various races, Hindoo, Chinese, and negro that made up the heterogenous mass to which her dear father had undertaken to teach the word of God.

"How do you like the idea, Miss Millward," said I, "of staying several months longer on the island?"

"I am delighted," answered she. "It is pleasant to see my father improving so rapidly; and the days pass quickly with the work we have to do. You know I like such housework, and have never had much chance to do it. Now here I am in sole charge of all the housekeeping arrangements, nobody to say I must not do this, or must do that. I feel quite as though I were empress, with none to dispute my sway. Ought I not to be contented?"

"I am very glad you are contented," said I, "and hope you may continue so. For I want to see you happy. Indeed, Miss Millward," I continued, with a slight tremor in my voice in spite of myself, " having done myself the honor to save you from the sea, I feel somehow responsible for your comfort and welfare, at least, I mean, while you remain on this island, and until you and your father reach civilization and your friends again. And even then I shall — I shall not like entirely to lose sight of you. It gives me pain to think that our ways may then perhaps lie far apart from each other."

Now there was a twang of maudlin sentimentality in this, which I recognized as I spoke the words, and this was magnified and intensified by the moonlight, and the trembling voice, so that I felt somehow as though I wanted to knock my head against something hard. I somehow felt too that she ought in all consistency to laugh at me. But she did not laugh. And though I could see her clear-cut beautiful profile in the moonlight, there was no sign of even a smile upon it. God bless me! how wonderfully pure and sweet she did look that night.

After a short silence I added, " I hope after we leave the island we shall not become wholly strangers, you and I and your father."

"Why, Mr. Morgan," said she, smiling now, and turning her candid eyes to me, " I thought we had just decided not to leave the island for some months. I am very sure that we, — my father and I and you can never become strangers. We must always be the best of friends whatever happens. It is not so easy to forget a good friend as you seem to imagine. And you have surely been one to us, — and especially to my poor father in his helplessness. But the dew is falling fast, and I must now go in. Good night, my friend, my good friend."

I sat long after that, alone in the moonlight, with the dew sparkling on each leaf in silvery lustre, thinking of my new found love, and hoping and despairing by turns, until the regular and peaceful breathing of the old man reminded me that I was uselessly dissipating precious hours that should be devoted to sleep.

CHAPTER XIV.

A REMARKABLE CURE.

AS the weather was now so fine, I thought it best to begin the gathering of calabashes, before going regularly to the work of rope-making. I should need an immense quantity of these gourds, and they must be as dry as possible and perfectly sound, or they would be unserviceable for my purpose. The collection and transportation of these gourds would have proved an immense task but for a happy thought which occurred to me; that was to make the stream do the major part of the labor. With this view I drove a row of stakes across the creek just above where the boats were moored. These stakes were placed close enough together to catch every gourd that floated down stream. After this precaution was taken I went with my axe to the calabash grove and began the work of gathering the gourds, throwing them into the water of the stream. Soon they were bobbing along down stream in a steady procession. I worked faithfully at this for more than half a day, and until I had just time to get home before supper. When I arrived I found that Alice Millward had been busy fishing out the floating gourds, and had a huge pile on the sand, and that the creek was still literally filled with them for several rods above the row of detaining stakes. In coming home I had followed down the stream, wading, with a pole to dislodge all that had caught on the way.

Wet and tired and hungry though I was, I went immediately to work throwing the gourds out on the bank where they might begin drying and hardening, and it was long after sunset before I finished this disagreeable labor. I was very glad to change my wet clothing and to sit down to the cheerful supper-table which the patient Alice had kept waiting for me.

"You must have worked very steadily, Mr. Morgan," said she; "there has been a constant stream of those great calabashes coming down all the afternoon."

"I see that you also were not idle," said I. "The great heap of gourds I found taken out must have kept you pretty busy."

"Oh, indeed, I was very busy, and kept the creek clear for quite a while," said she; "but then they began to arrive like a marching army, and soon overwhelmed me. I suppose you have enough of them collected now, have you not?"

"No, Miss Millward, perhaps there is half enough. I shall go again to-morrow."

"The sight of that immense number of calabashes makes me better able to realize the magnitude of the task we have undertaken," remarked the old gentleman, in a thoughtful tone.

"But that should not trouble us," I said; "we have plenty of time before us, and a little done every day makes a great deal. Now I roughly calculate that we must have a pile of gourds as large as the Spanish galleon, if you can imagine it lying on the beach; for the floating capacity of these round gourds in a heap would not represent, owing to the interstices between the individual gourds, more than half that of a single, great gourd of the size of the heap. Or to put it in another way, let us say we want a sufficient number of gourds to hold half the air that the galleon would hold if empty of water. Such a capacity would require, I imagine, a pile of gourds as great as the galleon. At any rate we will offer that for as good a guess as we are able now to make. I suppose we might estimate the cubical contents of the galleon, and so determine mathematically with reasonable accuracy just how many gourds would do the work of lifting it, — that is to say, of equalling its displacement or sufficiently approaching it. But I think we shall be near enough with our guess without that trouble.

The next day, starting earlier, I finished collecting the gourds by noon, and had them all out of the creek before two o'clock in the afternoon. As the wind was light and favorable, I proposed that we spend the remainder of the day in a voyage to the plantation, stay there all night, and return in the morning. This was heartily agreed to, and we speedily loaded the few things we were likely to need on board the "Alice," including an armchair and Mr. Millward's couch. When all was ready for the embarkation I carried him down and seated him, well braced, just aft of the centre-board.

We now hoisted sail and passed out over the bar. As we came into the neighborhood of the sunken galleon it was just three o'clock by Mr. Millward's watch, the sun was shining brightly, and the water was clear. If I could pick up the submerged buoy I could now with the water-glass show my companions the wreck. My sight poles on shore were down, and I could only guess at the locality. However, with Miss Millward standing on the fore deck keeping a bright lookout for the bunch of submerged gourds, I cruised about as near as I could guess to the neighborhood. In a few minutes she caught sight of them, and we were speedily made fast. We hauled up directly above the wreck and put the glass over the side; then all, including Mr. Millward, who managed to do so by our joint assistance, took a good look at the venerable hulk.

As the old man was looking I explained to him, "You see, Mr. Millward, the ship's forefoot sticks up a little clear of the sand."

"Yes, yes, that is true."

"And you will see that there is plenty of room there to drag the bight of a hawser well under the keel."

"Yes, I see."

"Now look at the stern, and you will notice that it overhangs very much, and that the rudder has broken away and become detached."

"Yes, quite true," said the old man; "and you could easily drag the bight of your second hawser under the projecting stern."

"Exactly," I replied; "and then we shall have the old relic swung securely from two points, and come up she must if only her old ribs and bones are strong enough to stand the strain. She must float or break in two."

"Mr. Morgan, we must and will succeed," said the old man, excitedly. "That craft is to all appearance sound and strong. I have heard that wood when under water completely does not decay as when exposed to the air. We shall find her still strong enough to be raised."

"I trust so and believe so," I replied.

When the fair Alice came to look at the wonders of the deep through the glass her delight was extravagant.

"Why," she cried, "I can see the old cannon all covered with sea-weed. And what a strange, old-fashioned ship! Two cabins built one on top of the other, and in front a sort of house. I can even see the doorway in the cabin, and the funny little windows, and a fish swimming in at one of them as though he lived there. Shells are growing all over the whole vessel like lichens on a rock. What a lovely, horrible sight!"

When we had spent an hour at this sight-seeing we cast off from the buoy and made sail for Plantation Cove, and very soon came abreast of it. From the sea, except for the break in the beach, the opening into the cove was scarcely distinguishable in the wall of the cliff, which here came out in a sort of cape or headland. Just in this headland was the cleft. I wore round and ran straight in for the mouth of the cove, and found water enough easily to cross the bar. We glided swiftly through the rocky gate with the momentum, and floated out on the deep, quiet waters of the cove, the breeze being entirely cut off by the cliff, except a faint, uncertain gust now and then, which found its way in as a draught will sometimes blow down a chimney. There was just enough motion to carry us alongside the pier, which now at low tide stood high above us, so high that it would be impossible to get Mr. Millward on shore by its aid. For this reason I pulled the boat along until her nose was against the rocky shore at the side of the pier and made her temporarily fast, while I carried Mr. Millward on shore, and landed his daughter. I then pulled pack to a place where a rude ladder led from the pier down to the water, and moored the boat securely, head and stern, with sufficient line so that she might ride safely at all tides, then I overhauled the sail we had brought along for a tent, carried it ashore and set it up, built a rousing fire, and gathered a quantity of fern for bedding. As soon as the fire was started Alice set about warming up a bean porridge for supper, that we might have it early enough to visit the plantation before dark.

We hurried through the supper, and then leaving Mr.

Millward comfortably seated in the armchair, I started with Alice for a little walk up to the rising ground to show her a view of the orange grove and plantation buildings which could be seen from this side. Along the old road, a great part of which was overgrown with weeds and straggling volunteer plants from the various crops that had formerly been cultivated here: Indian-corn, tall, tasselled sugar-cane, pink-blossomed tobacco, with great, velvety leaves and up-shooting stalk, an occasional dried cotton-plant with shreds of cotton still clinging to the brown bolls, yams run wild and growing in broad green bands of fleshy vine across the path in tropical luxuriance, — these and countless wild weeds and plants not only filled the fields but trenched upon the road.

Before we reached a point at which the groves and houses could well be seen Miss Millward had already gathered a great armful of samples to carry back to the tent that her father might see them. We went along up the road until we came to the remains of a gate, — two upright stones roughly resembling pillars, and having iron hinge-pieces let into one of them. The gate itself had been thrown down at one side. Here we were in full sight of all the buildings, and of the grove of fruit trees. I left her here a few moments while I waded through the weeds to gather a bunch of bananas, some of which were ripe and red. As I came back I saw her beckon to me to hasten; and I ran as fast as I could, until I reached her side.

"Listen," said she, "I thought just now I heard a cry."

We listened a moment, and then I heard distinctly, from the direction of the cove, her father's voice as though calling for help.

"It is father calling us," she cried, and immediately began running down the road.

I threw down my bunch of bananas and soon passed her, impeded as she was with her skirts and the weeds. I plunged through the last heavy growth of weeds and canes that separated me from a clear view of the tent, and was thunderstruck to behold a man coming toward us from that direction. At first I thought of the pearl-fishers, and feared that violence had perhaps already been done to the helpless Mr. Millward, whose voice we had just heard calling for assistance. My first impulse was to turn back and stop Miss Millward, whom I could hear struggling through the weeds behind me. But in a moment I was still more astonished to recognize in the approaching figure Mr. Millward himself! I do not believe I should have been more surprised to have seen a dead man rise and walk. I had never seen him, you will remember, otherwise than helpless, and my mind was completely habituated so to regard him. Now here he was, upright and walking with apparent firmness toward me. I was inexpressibly astonished, and for the moment quite speechless. I stood there with open mouth staring at him when Miss Millward came panting through the weeds to my side.

"Father! oh, father!" she cried, and without a moment's pause hurried on as fast as she could to meet him. Collecting my own wits I speedily followed her. When they met she fell upon the old man's breast and began to sob out, "Oh, what is the matter? Oh, why did you call?"

She had evidently forgotten, or failed to comprehend for the moment, that there was anything surprising in the fact that he was up and walking about. This oversight was doubtless due to the fact that, unlike myself, she had been long accustomed to see him walk, and the helpless condition was the one she was least accustomed to. However, without endeavoring to analyze our relative feelings of surprise, let us listen to the curious account given by Mr. Millward of his sudden recovery of the use of his lower limbs.

"After you had left me," he said, "I was sitting comfortably in the armchair looking at you until you disappeared among the vegetation. Presently I became aware that a little breeze had risen and was driving the smoke of the fire toward me. This was disagreeable, but as it could not be helped I quietly endured it, thinking it would not be for long, and that you would be back soon. But very soon thereafter I found the dry fern all around me on fire, and fearing I should roast to death I twice called as loudly as I could, hoping you would hear me in time. The flames, however, came very fast, my chair caught fire, my hands were slightly scorched, and I was at the same time smothering with the smoke. I sprang up and put out the fire with the blanket which you had wrapped around my limbs. Then finding I could walk, I started to meet you. That is all. God in his merciful providence has restored me."

That was all. But it was quite enough. We turned back and walked together to the tent. I could not get used to it. That this man whom I left helpless in his chair less than half an hour before, should now be actually standing firm on his feet, and walking about, as though nothing had been the matter with him, was entirely too much for my practical, matter-of-fact mind. Mr. Millward evidently noticed my bewildered air, and laughing said: "Rest easy, Mr. Morgan, I believe this recovery will be permanent. The excitement of the sudden danger must have roused my torpid nerves, and did suddenly for me what doubtless would have taken place a few weeks later in a slower way. Now let us thank God with all our hearts for this mercy."

The delight of the daughter, when she realized the pleasant truth was very touching indeed; she wept, embraced him, and patted him with her hands, cooing and sobbing and laughing all at once, while the old man in silence passed his hand gently from time to time over her beautiful hair.

From the scattered embers I rebuilt the fire, and after the sun went down, we all three sat in front of it talking over this strange occurrence. Intervals of silence would now and then fall upon us unbroken for several minutes. It was very hard indeed to realize the remarkable change. Perhaps the most curious thing was the effect produced upon Duke. The dog eyed Mr. Millward with an air of such ludicrous doubt, edging away from him, and then coming back wagging his tail to be patted, that we could not refrain from laughing heartily at his conduct. He resented our merriment with a sheepish, tail-between-legs air that only made us laugh the more.

Leaving the father and daughter to sleep in the tent, Duke and I went down to the boat. There, gently rocked by the incoming tide, I slumbered peacefully through the night until long after dawn, and was then awakened by the old man's hand laid gently on my shoulder. It was time for breakfast, which we made of oranges and plantains, the latter baked in the hot ashes. Mr. Millward had already been clear to the plantation buildings and returned with this spoil. He was still weak and feeble. That after his long inactivity his muscles should have strength enough for him to walk about at all, was, in truth, matter of surprise, even not considering the recent paralysis. The possession of so much physical vigor was doubtless due to the continued and regular rubbing and massage treatment he had received.

It was thought best, now that we were here with the boat, to collect and take back with us as much as we could conveniently carry of the produce of the groves and plantations. One thing Mr. Millward was specially desirous of getting was a good supply of coffee-berries, which we might cure in the usual manner by drying them in the shade, and thus finally get the kernels for use. Oranges would also keep well; and bananas and plantains would ripen even better in the bunch hung up at home than upon the tree. So, too, there was needed sweet-potatoes and yams, and a good supply of tobacco for curing. With shovel and hoe and improvised baskets made of huge plantain leaves we went to work, digging and gathering and carrying, — Miss Alice and I doing the chief part of the work, while Mr. Millward, feeling somewhat feeble and exhausted, was content to stroll about a little or to rest in the shade. Wandering about among the outhouses he came across a setting hen on a nest of fifteen eggs, and brought in hen, nest, and eggs all together, the devoted bird courageously allowing herself to be captured rather than leave the nest. This prize we stowed in the cuddy-hole of the boat, shutting her and her beloved nest in safety together.

I found an old, dilapidated fanning-mill, and a small grindstone mounted in a frame with a crank to turn it. Anything of this sort I thought might be useful to me in contriving my rope machinery; so I loaded it on the boat.

About the middle of the afternoon we got on board, and after sculling the boat out over the bar set sail for Home Creek, where we arrived safely about five o'clock. While supper was being made ready I built a safe coop for the old hen, with sticks driven into the ground, and put her with her nest into it, giving her corn and a gourd of water, and left her to hatch her brood if she chose. We were all very tired that night and went early to bed.

The next day Mr. Millward and I went to work to contrive some sort of device for spinning the cocoa-husk fibre into rope-yarn. The old fanning-mill came very handily into play in this job. The fan was geared to run at a high rate of speed, and by disconnecting the sieves and shakers and taking off the fan blades, this final piece of shafting could be made to revolve at a rattling gait by a comparatively slow motion of the crank, and with very little expenditure of force. We turned the old machine up on one end and mounted it on stilts to bring the final or fan shaft into convenient position. Then on the end of the fan shaft we mounted the spinning device, whittled out of hard wood and pieces of cane. This consisted primarily of a spool about a foot in length mounted in a framework so that its axis would be at right angles to the fan shaft. The revolution of the fan shaft would now cause the spool to revolve with an end-over-end movement; so that a piece of cord, if one end were tied or wound upon the spool, would be twisted. The next thing was to contrive some method for causing the spool to rotate automatically on its own axis at a slower rate, so as to wind up the cord as fast as it was twisted by the other motion of the spool at a high rate of speed.

This movement cost us an almost indescribable amount of the closest and hardest thought. To complete the machine up to this point took only two days. Then we stuck fast for a whole week debating the matter and trying contrivances which would not work, and which, when they came to trial it seemed as though we should have known would not work, so complete and humiliating was their failure. Finally we changed the whole structure by mounting the spool loosely on the end of the fan shaft itself with its axis coincident with the axis of the shaft, fitting the spool to run by friction on the shaft, while the frame which led the yarn to the spool was rigidly fixed on the same shaft. Now the rapid motion of the frame would do the twisting and the cord would wind only as fast as it was freely fed, the spool slipping at a commensurate rate on the shaft. This worked all right with a piece of cord already made; but whether it would make the yarn out of unformed fibre was a matter to be determined by trial. This trial we could not make until we had built a feeding-table on which to pile the mass of fibre, fitted with a tube of cane to guide the forming yarn to the twister-frame. When this was done the machine proved satisfactory and did the work it was designed to do rapidly and well. It required two to work it, — one to turn the crank and thus furnish the power, and the other to feed up and manipulate the fibre so that it would be smoothly and properly interwoven with the twisting end of the forming filament.

The construction of this rude machine took us ten days of hard study and work. But when it was done we had taken a long step in advance. When we learned it would work we celebrated the occasion by twisting a spoolful of yarn, about a hundred yards, — I turning the crank, with the sweat of honest toil dripping from me, while Mr. Millward fed in the fibre. This yarn, which was quite firmly spun, we doubled, and allowed it to twist together upon itself making a stout cord nearly fifty yards in length and of the size of signal halyard stuff. It was strong and firm, and as we judged would easily stand a strain of fifty pounds without breaking. That it was not absolutely smooth and even, was a matter of comparatively small consequence, the vital thing being strength and compactness.

To say that we were both delighted with the result of our labors, is only faintly to express the real condition of mind with which we hailed it.

Alice Millward had come down to see the trial of the machine, and was a witness of the making of the first piece of cord, and we all joined together in the rejoicing.

Now began a period of steady, hard work, manufacturing rope. We first rigged up the machine under the shed, so that we might have protection from the sun and the rain, and then set to work, regularly each day, excepting of course on the sabbath day, during which we always rested and held divine service at least once. We divided the working day as follows: from breakfast until nine o'clock we spent gathering husks enough for the whole day's work, bringing them to the shed and pounding up and separating sufficient of the fibre for a run of half an hour. Promptly at nine o'clock I took the crank and began a steady half-hour's grind; then to give my muscles a change we would go again at pounding and separating fibre for half an hour; then came another half-hour at the crank, and so on until the blessed hour of noon arrived, when we would take dinner and rest until one o'clock; then hard at it again, rain or shine, until five o'clock.

Mr. Millward could sit at his feeding work and was thus able to endure it; but it was doubtless very hard for him, though he never uttered a complaint and seemed to thrive on it. My work at the crank was very hard indeed, and at first when night came every bone and muscle in my whole body would ache with the strain. As the days went by, however, the work grew easier and easier day by day, until I felt it no longer as a strain upon me.

At five o'clock we set to work getting up the necessary fuel and doing the chores about the house, and such little things as Alice wanted attended to. Exactly at six o'clock Alice, who carried the watch, would come out and call us in for supper, to which two tired men were sure to do justice, especially to the hot coffee which we now had at each meal in plenty. After supper we generally sat on the porch talking over various matters of interest. Mr. Millward, who when a younger man had spent ten years as a missionary in India and South Africa, related many interesting reminiscences of his life in those strange countries: of desperate fights with savages in resisting forays; of hunts for game and encounters with wild beasts; of the rude forms of worship and superstitions of the African tribes, and the complex religion of the Hindoos. His memory was wonderfully accurate and stored with countless incidents, curious, strange, and interesting.

CHAPTER XV.

LOST AND FOUND.

IN about two weeks a brood of twelve chickens was hatched out, and the old hen fastened in the coop made no end of clucking and feather-ruffling in her anxiety that the fluffy, yellow-feathered little innocents should come to no harm. They ran in and out between the bars at pleasure, and very soon made friends with their mistress Alice, who could, or thought she could, distinctly recognize each of the little brothers and sisters, and distinguish one from another. In proof of this she named one after each of the twelve months of the year. By feeding them every day she soon got the whole brood so that it would come at call, and some of the chicks would frequently jump into her lap, or eat from her hand in a perfectly fearless manner. It was pleasant to hear her talk to her little pets and call them by name. The one she called April was a feeble little yellow chick, much put upon and driven about by the others, especially by the stout-legged, fluffy, brown ball named October, which seemed to be ever on the watch to snatch a bug or worm from the weakling.

"Now you bad, bad October," I one time overheard her say, "I shall certainly have to lock you up, if you do not let April's bugs alone. You selfish little creature, you drop a nice, fat worm of your own to snatch a bitter little bug away from poor April, and when you get it you don't like it. Serves you quite right, and April has got your worm and run away with it, too. Why, December, I do believe you are losing the beautiful stripes on your back. Come, June; come, September, and you too, August. There, there, — no fighting; brethren should dwell together in unity." Her father called the brood her Sunday-school class, and remarked with a smile, " Girls are all alike; they must have something to love and pet, and the more helpless it is the better they like it."

The work of rope-yarn-making went steadily on day by day, the pile of the product of our labor growing by slow accretion, until it was a great heap. This was such very tedious work that you may be sure I kept up a steady thinking all the while how to lessen and lighten it. I thought of two schemes before long that would very materially diminish the amount of rope-yarn required. The first of these schemes to take form in my mind related to a substitute for the two great hawsers which we had thought would be required, one to go under the bow and one under the stern of the sunken galleon. I said nothing about this idea until it was fully matured in my mind. Then one day as I finished a half-hour's grind, with the perspiration streaming from every pore and the breath about all gone from my body, I said : —

" Mr. Millward, what do you say to quitting for the day? It is now nearly noon. I feel as though I would like to go fishing."

He looked at me a moment, and then replied, " I don't wonder. I feel that way myself. If you are for a fishing excursion I am with you with all my heart. ' All work and no play makes Jack a dull boy.'"

Immediately after dinner we overhauled the fish lines — real ones with genuine hooks this time, which belonged to Mr. Millward's stores — and collecting a supply of whelks, clams, and shrimps for bait, were all ready for embarking by the time Alice came down to the boat. Just beyond the bar and the rollers we anchored the boat, and the sport very soon began by Mr. Millward pulling up a fine red-snapper, and continued until we had caught half a dozen fine fish. Then they ceased to bite for a long time, and the cause was made apparent by Miss Alice hauling up a three-foot spotted shark, which managed to break the line and get away. But though after that we sat patiently for an hour or two, there were no more fish to be had. The pirate was cruising about, and honest fish were not out in that neighborhood.

"Mr. Millward," said I after a spell of silence, uninterrupted by bites, " I think we are done making rope, or nearly so at last."

"Why, we are not half done, according to a liberal estimate," replied he, looking up in surprise. "We have barely enough rope for the gourds, to say nothing of the much greater quantity needed for the two four-inch hawsers."

"But," said I, "suppose we don't need the hawsers? I have an idea that it will be much easier to build a framework of beams strong enough to lift the hulk by, and thus dispense with the hawsers. At any rate even if it took almost the same amount of work — and it will not — I would favor a change of labor. The rope-making is getting very monotonous."

"I most certainly agree with you in that," he replied; "it does seem an endless task. But tell me how you propose to construct and attach your framework."

Thereupon I laid it out in diagram on the seat of the boat with the point of my knife, and explained it until both understood the plan. They were intensely interested. Alice was leaning over with her hand upon my shoulder looking and listening, and as I felt her breath fan my cheek I came to a dead stop. The old gentleman looked up from the rude diagram and said, "Well, go on, go on ; I understand it thus far, — what next?"

This seemed to bring the situation to Alice's mind, for she instinctively blushed, and gently drew away. My heart beat with a thump that I could almost hear ; but the old man did not seem to notice my confusion nor the innocent action of the girl. He was bent intently on understanding the proposed plan which promised to shorten our dreary yarn-making task, and had no eyes or ears for anything else.

Recovering myself I went on with the explanation of the diagram. I showed how we might make two triangular frames of heavy beams or spars firmly joined, how these two frames might be connected together at the apex of each by a long beam or spar in such manner as to be distant from each other something less than the length of the galleon ; how the connection between the long beam and the two triangles should be a flexible or jointed one, so that, as the whole structure, suitably weighted with stones, was lowered to the galleon the triangles could be held away, and then allowed to swing in toward the galleon and come under her head and stern, thus cradling the hulk in a support at each end which would become more secure when a strain was subsequently put upon the frame. The calabashes for lifting could be attached to the horizontal connecting beam and thus a proper distribution of the strain ensured without trouble. After careful consideration Mr. Millward said this scheme would do. We then discussed the amount of work required for the building, conveying and placing of such a framework, as compared with the work which would be required to make the two large hawsers ; and after mature deliberation decided in favor of the framework, as far the best and quickest method.

The fishing was over for the time. No more bites, and no prospect of any. So we pulled up anchor and went in to dress the fish and make preparation for a grand chowder, to be compounded of yams, fish, red pepper, and a clove of wild garlic. When this was in the kettle and the kettle over the fire (we all three took a hand in its preparation) Mr. Millward and I began to overhaul the rope-yarn, to make an estimate of how much, if any, more would be needed, in view of the recent change of plan. It was at this time that I conceived the second scheme. It occurred to me that a good deal of rope might be spared if we could enclose each calabash, or bunch of calabashes, in a wicker cage made of willow branches. I suggested this, and we went at once to the willows and cut some slender wands, and made such a cage as I had in mind, out of fine wands and tied with bark. This cage securely enclosed four calabashes; as the wires of a lantern-guard enclose the globe, and at the same time afforded a ready means for attaching the rope without wasting any of its length in loops and bends about the calabashes. This scheme would save at least one fourth to one third of the amount of rope needed.

We estimated that four of the large calabashes would lift in the water as much as the strength of the rope employed would permit, or at least would be as much as we cared to attempt to pull down at once into the water. The trees that furnished the wands were plentiful along the lower part of the creek, and there would be no lack of osiers. I have spoken of these trees as being "willows;" but, in truth, I believe they were some species of water-loving oleander. They were, however, quite like willow in appearance and growth, and furnished abundance of long, slender branches, pliable and strong, with a bark that easily came off and was itself quite strong enough to tie the joints with. I believe this tree is a better one for basket-makers' use than the common osier willow, though I do not know if it is ever used for that purpose.

It was with heartfelt satisfaction that we could now believe that enough rope was made, and that the daily monotonous grind which had been going on for weeks was at last over. Nor was the basket-work in caging the gourds likely to be of a trying character, as it was light, easy work, in which we could all engage at any time, rain or shine, and enliven with talk.

The very day after this Mr. Millward and I began to cut the osiers. We tied them in bundles of a hundred or more, and put them into the water to keep from drying out until used. When we had quite a large stock on hand we began each evening after supper to make the cages, enclosing four of the gourds, now quite dry and hard, in each cage.

In the mean time, as regular work for each day, we began the construction of the framework. For this we needed seven great spars, which had to be cut on the upland from a species of pine which grew there, trimmed to the required shape on the ground, and from thence got down to the sea.

We selected the trees as near the creek as possible, and by means of levers rolled them into the water, which was barely deep enough to float such great sticks. The labor was a great deal for two men to accomplish, one being old and feeble. It took us every working day for three weeks to get these timbers down to the mouth of the creek. But it was finally done, and then commenced the framing together of the two triangles and their attachment to the beam. This we did with ties of strong inch and a half rope in several turns. At last, the complete structure lay floating in the creek ready to be towed out to the galleon.

While we were at work getting out the timbers on the upland it happened nearly every day that Alice Millward would either go with us in the morning or come out at noon bringing a lunch to us of hot baked yams and bacon, and so go home with us at night; or when I had wet work in the creek, following down a launched timber, she would return with her father in advance. We always went to this work quite early in the morning and returned home at least four hours before sunset, as the cage-making work demanded some of our time. On rainy days we did not go out at all, but kept busy with the basket-work.

One day it happened that at noon when we expected Alice with the lunch, she did not come promptly as usual, and after waiting nearly an hour over time, we both became quite anxious to know why she did not arrive. I told Mr. Millward to wait where he was, to receive her if she came, while I went back to the house with Duke to see if she was there. Hurrying along, the dog and I arrived in a little over half an hour at the house, going by the shortest cut and as rapidly as possible, running indeed part of the way where the nature of the ground permitted. As I had greatly feared, she was not there. Nothing indicated any disturbance; everything was as we had left it in the morning, and I concluded at once that she had started to come to us with the lunch, and had either lost her way in the dense growth, or had received some hurt on the road. The obvious thing to do under such circumstances was to follow up the regular path which we customarily took, and which in my haste to reach the house I had not pursued on my return, and to look for traces of her on the way.

When I came to a little glade where the candleberries grew plentifully I noted a place where I thought it possible for her to have mistaken the path. Two conspicuous bushes, separated from each other by a distance of perhaps five rods and covered with vivid scarlet blossoms in great masses, were on the opposite side of the glade. The way ran to the right hand side of the right hand bush. Now if she had taken a course to the right hand of the left hand bush, she would be travelling quite thirty degrees away from the true direction. This was brought to my mind by the circumstance that several times Miss Millward had come with these red blossoms in her hand, or decorated with them in hat or dress, probably gathered each time from the bush by the side of the route. I went over at once to the left hand bush, and found that a branch had been freshly broken off. It was probable, therefore, that here was the place of divergence from the true route. Without paying much attention at the moment, Miss Millward had doubtless been misled by this false guide, and in passing had broken off a branch of the flowers as usual.

That this surmise was correct was evidenced a few paces further along by fresh leaves and twigs of the bush which she had thrown down after securing the coveted blossoms from the branch; and finally by the branch itself partly denuded of its blossoms. But beyond this I could find no trace. Perhaps a skilled woodsman or tracker could have easily followed the trail that no doubt existed, plainly enough marked for those who could read it; but unfortunately I knew not how to read the subtle indications that are said to be so plain to those versed in that sort of writing. I then tried to start the dog on the trail by leading him to a point where I knew by inference it existed. But either he did not choose to take up the scent, was unable to do so, or did not understand what I desired of him. At any rate he made no effort to follow the trail.

I then endeavored to reason out the probable course the girl had taken, by trying to conceive myself misled in the same manner. Suppose I had diverged thirty degrees unconsciously to the left of the route, when should I discover the error and what would be my course when I did discover it? By this method of imaginative analysis I was able to follow with reasonable certainty her probable course through the forest for about forty rods, which brought me to a dense jungle all interwoven with thorny bamboo and utterly impassable. There was nothing at all like this on the true route, and at this point, if not before, and most probably at this exact place Alice Millward must have become conscious that she had lost her way. Now the thing for me to determine was, what did she next do? Most probably, finding herself lost, she at once sought to retrace her steps until she could arrive at some familiar place from which to take a fresh departure. If she had gone back to the glade she would have found the blossoming bushes and probably from thence have been able to get a correct start. It was fair to infer, therefore, that she must have missed the glade, passing it either on the right hand or the left. But if she had passed it on the right hand the angle of such a course would have speedily brought her out into the open ground from which the sea and the beach, and possibly the house and shed were visible, and she would have had no difficulty in getting home. Therefore the inference was justifiable that in endeavoring to retrace her steps, the girl had veered to the left hand; this would lead her to the heavy timber that lines the creek in that direction.

As soon as I had reached this conclusion, I started immediately to tell her father of the situation. I soon reached him and found him very anxiously waiting my coming. I told him briefly where I thought she was now probably wandering, and my reasons for the conjecture. It considerably eased his mind to be able to think she was merely lost.

It was decided that he should return to the house at once and await me there, or after getting there come back up the creek to meet us, if I should find her.

Without delay I started for the thick woods where I hoped to find the girl. As soon as I was well into the heavy timber I began to shout at intervals every few minutes, and then listen for a reply; but none came, and I wandered in and about the forest in this manner for several hours, shouting until I was so hoarse that I could scarcely be heard ten rods away. Finally, when it was almost dark, I found her far up the creek, and almost to the cleft or chasm through which I had passed on the day I discovered the plantation. She was on the bank of the creek and coming down toward me through the tangled undergrowth. I tried to call, but was so hoarse from the long continued shouting that I was not heard, and so she did not see me until we were quite near each other.

"Oh, Mr. Morgan," she cried, with a voice full of tears, "I am so glad to find you!" Instinctively I put my arm around her and took her hand in mine.

"Let us hurry on," she resumed, "and find poor dear father, he must have been so anxious about me."

I told her he was waiting near the creek, or at the house for us and we would soon be there, as it was not over an hour's walk.

She was softly crying to herself, and apparently much shaken. She clung to my hand as though fearful of losing her guide. We walked on in the rapidly gathering dusk, and she became gradually more quiet and assured, so that she soon began to talk freely of her adventure. It seemed that she had only just found the creek, and though, as she said, it seemed to run in the wrong direction entirely, she had reasoned that if followed down it would finally bring her home. She had just about determined to go into the water and wade down the stream itself if the tangled growth became too thick on the banks, as it seemed quite likely would happen soon, and as, indeed, was the case a little way on. I fancied the distress of mind and body that this would have caused in the darkness now fast coming on, and my heart grew soft and tender. I told her then of the way I came to find the route she had most probably taken, the incident of the red blossoms, and all the course of reasoning by which I was led in the search.

She then took out of her dress the bunch of blossoms, and said, "'Then it is to these flowers I owe this meeting?"

"Yes," said I, "to the gathering of those red blossoms. Don't you think I have earned them as a reward?"

Without a word she handed me the bunch, glowing red as the sunset tints which yet marked the sky.

Somehow I felt, as we stumbled along the darkening way, her hand clasped in mine as it rested on my arm, that our hearts had come nearer together than I had ever dared before to hope might be the case, and my own heart was filled with a wild, new-born hope. She seemed to be mine as I lifted her over the fallen logs, and helped her past the rocks and obstacles. It very quickly grew quite dark, and it was no easy matter under such circumstances to keep the right course, so that we could not talk even if either of us had felt a desire to do so. In silence we struggled along, until finally we came out into the open. The sea with its wonderful self-light was plainly visible before us, and the ceaseless murmur of the surf as it came to our ears was a most welcome sound. A bright fire built by her father to guide us shone like a beacon before us, reddening the palm-trees near the house. Soon we could see him standing near it on the watch. And in a few minutes she was clasped in his arms.

CHAPTER XVI.

A BAD PORT.

WHEN the lifting-frame was complete, there was no reason why it should not at once be floated out and secured in place at the sunken hulk as soon as possible, and as the weather was very fine at that particular time, and the water clear, we concluded to do it immediately. We took both boats, Mr. Millward and Alice in his boat, and I alone in the "Mohawk." With a line from the floating frame to each boat we towed it along so easily and rapidly that in a couple of hours we were over the wreck. We anchored the two boats one at the bow and one at the stern of the galleon, and pulling the floating frame between the two, fastened it safely by a line at each end to the boat anchors. The next task was to get some heavy rocks with which to sink it, and attach them to the frame in such manner that when the latter was down in position to engage the wreck bow and stern, the rocks could be released to permit the frame to rise by its own power of flotation. It would then, we thought, be secure against displacement, as there was evidently very little, if any, movement of the water at the depth the galleon lay. Leaving the frame attached to the anchor-lines we went to the north cape with the boats, and loaded on twelve stones of considerable weight, which we carried out and secured to the frame by slip-knots in such manner that by a pull from above on a rope each might be released.

When the stones were attached we found that ten of them were just enough to sink the frame slowly. By means of a couple of ropes, one at each end of the frame, paid out from the two boats by Mr. Millward and me, we guided the contrivance in its descent until it landed exactly in place. Alice Millward with the water-glass watched the frame, and indicated to us how to manipulate the ropes. Thus she would call out, "Slowly, Mr. Morgan, a little more forward; a little more aft, father; now you are going right," until it was in proper position. We then pulled the ropes attached to the stones, releasing the slip-knots two at a time to keep the balance properly, and when relieved of this weight the frame floated up, enclosing and grasping the wreck at each end. This part of the work was therefore successfully and easily completed.

The frame was in position, and it now only remained to attach the calabashes, one cage of them at a time, and we hoped the galleon would be lifted. In preparation for this work, — which we would not be ready to undertake for some time, or until all the calabashes were caged and fitted with attaching ropes, — we had, before sinking the frame-work, passed over the spar that connected the two triangles the bight of an endless rope, for use as a down-haul with which the calabash cages might be pulled down. This endless down-haul line we proposed to hitch to a buoy when we left, so that it might be supported within reach until wanted.

Being very anxious to test the working of my plan for pulling down and attaching the calabashes, I had brought along a single cage of them for the purpose of trying the experiment of pulling it down and attaching it to the longitudinal spar. This scheme was a very simple one, and I sincerely hoped it would prove successful, as it had given me considerable study in its contrivance, and was, I thought, the best and easiest way to accomplish the result. The following description will make it clear. To the cage holding the calabashes was attached a rope four feet long. On the free end of this attaching rope was a hook made of a stout forked branch. Secured to the endless down-haul rope was a similar hook. By catching these hooks together, the cage could be pulled down until the two hooks passed under the spar and came up on the other side. Now by crossing the down-haul rope the hook on the attaching rope, I thought, could be made to hook over that part of its own rope which was on the other side of the spar. Then by reversing the pull on the down-haul its hook would be released and the calabash cage be left attached to the spar by the stout rope passing around the spar and hooked to itself.

The experiment, to our great delight, was entirely successful and satisfactory; and when we had fixed the down-haul rope securely to a buoy we set sail and returned feeling highly encouraged at the outlook for our labors.

As this business of pulling down and affixing the calabashes was likely to be a long and tedious job, to be successfully prosecuted only in good weather, we determined to begin it as soon as we could get a sufficient number of cages ready for a start; and thus we could work in suitable weather at the wreck attaching the cages, and in unsuitable weather at home in preparing them for attachment. It would be only at the very last that we need watch for the wreck to rise, and prepare for towing her in to shore. Until enough calabashes to float her had been sent down, such as were attached would of course be simply anchored to the wreck.

It was oppressively warm that evening after we had returned home, and we all brought our chairs down to the shed to better enjoy the slight breeze which breathed in from the sea. We sat thus, watching the breakers roll in through the dim light, and crash on the sand with a long, running sound that passed from left to right along the beach, slow but regular as heart-beats in their constant reiteration. Mr. Millward was seated at a little distance from Alice and me enjoying his pipe, the fire in the bowl of which shone at intervals with a red glow, as though in rhythmic sympathy with the sound of the surf. The stars were bright and sprinkled all over the clear, dark sky, which was lit now and then by the long, fiery thread of a meteor ruled rapidly across the azure dome, and lingering as an impression on the retina long enough so that by turning the eye away the line of fire was transported to another quarter, — fading out, however, too fast for us to locate it distinctly.

It was a peaceful, quiet summer night, and we sat silent, enjoying together the restfulness of it. I looked at the dim outlines of Alice as she sat by my side leaning her cheek upon one hand, and my heart was filled with conscious depths of love and tenderness; then past her at the shadowy figure of the old man and the intermittent glow of his pipe. A great peace seemed to possess my soul, a wonderful content of spirit, and I said to myself, " This is the peace of pure content and happiness." Often since have I recalled that night, and felt that man, born to trouble and sorrow on this earth, — beautiful though it be, — can hope for no greater bliss than such hours afford him. Happy hours come not at call, nor often, nor long remain. Satisfied ambition brings them not, nor gratified pride, nor gathered wealth; but they come only when there is united this trinity of conditions: rest from labor done, the healthy body, the presence of those we love. When these three things are united, the peaceful, happy hour will come. And when this sweet angel of peace shall hover over you, drive it not away, my friend, by taking troubled thought of the morrow, nor by grieving over the past, nor regretting opportunities missed. Enjoy it in contented silence while you may, and with little thought of past or future.

An unusually brilliant meteor shot in a long diagonal line from the zenith nearly to the horizon, and there burst in a ball of fire like a rocket. Alice laid her hand on my arm as though to call my attention, but without a word. The touch was light; the little hand remained but a moment on my arm, and was then as gently withdrawn. But, light and momentary, it thrilled me through and through; the angel of peace took instant flight, and thought came back with a rush. The restless fear that we might be parted; that she could never love me; the instinctive wish to know with certainty her heart; a thousand contending emotions stirred me. With all my will I strove to calm myself and still the wild beating of my heart. What strange power was this which the girl had acquired over me, that a mere touch of her hand sufficed to banish quiet, fill my brain with teeming fancies and my breast with longing and unrest? The quiet stars still shone as before, the surf still fell in measured cadence, the gentle, rustling breeze still fanned my cheek with its soft, cool breath; but peace and quiet and rest had departed. My soul was fevered, and anxiety preyed once more upon my heart.

The night-blooming cereus had unfolded its waxen, white flowers, and the warm air was laden with its strange, sweet perfume mingling with the fragrance of the dew-moistened foliage. Now there stole up out of the verge of the sea the thin, pale crescent of the young moon, a mere rounded line of silver tilted back as though reclining in its new feebleness, and giving but little more light than the brilliant lamp of Venus that hung, a point of corruscating splendor, near it.

Again, as the silver horn emerged from the dim horizon line, I felt the soft touch of her hand upon my arm, and in low tones she said, " Is it not beautiful?"

For answer I took the hand in mine. Cool and soft it felt to my fevered grasp. She withdrew it not, but, passive, let it lie for a few minutes. Some say that souls while still embodied do and can communicate with each other in some occult and mysterious way. If that be true, then surely my soul must then and there have greeted Alice Millward's.

Mr. Millward, who had once or twice nodded over his pipe, now rose and knocking out the ashes reminded us that it was time to go to bed; and he and Alice retired to the house. As I had no fancy to be shut up in-doors on such a night, I brought my hammock down to the shed and swung it there where the sound of the sea would lull me to sleep, while the breeze fanned by with its cool breath.

The next morning we went diligently to work caging the calabashes in sets of four, rigging each cage with its short attaching rope and hook. The hooks I cut with axe and knife from the bushes of the nearest jungle. The work was congenial and light. Under the shed we arranged some tussocks of dried grass so that we could be seated low down; and thus ranged in a sociable triangle we worked, chatted, laughed, and joked; the old gentleman revived his experiences of former years; and altogether it was a very pleasant time. Whenever the weather was favorable we would load the completed cages of calabashes on board Mr. Millward's boat, and all three of us would sail to the galleon and sink and attach them one at a time, in the manner already indicated.

Little by little the great pile of calabashes near the shed diminished until it was nearly gone. We had attached literally thousands of the gourds to the framework which grasped the wreck, until now when we looked through the water-glass the hull was no longer visible, by reason of the mass of caged gourds sunk far under water, each one of course pulling upwards to the full extent of its buoyancy. Still we kept on. I began to think that I should have to make another trip to the calabash trees. But it was not to be so.

One morning we arrived at the galleon with a huge load in both boats which we had got ready during the two preceding days. We had not pulled half of them down when I felt the hauling-line slacken in my hand. Now I had fully expected this very thing sometime to take place; but when it did occur I thought for the moment that the line had frayed and parted, and did not realize that the hull was rising. Then as suddenly I understood, and shouted to Mr. Millward to cast off his boat from the buoy, as the wreck was rising, and suiting the action to the word did the same for my boat. We had no sooner cast loose than slowly the gourds lifted their heads in a confused mass to the surface, rattling and knocking together in the swell. The water all about became dark with ooze and sand and fragments of weed stirred up from the ocean's bed. I felt sure that the old hull was floating beneath in the frame, because, though I could not see it on account of the condition of the water, I knew that had the framework let go, its beams would have floated up and would now be in view among the floating gourds.

At the sight Mr. Millward jumped upon the gunwale of his little schooner and waving his hat began a cheer, in which we all joined. The old hulk floated at last! Its long rest was broken and a new voyage begun.

By a piece of sheer good-luck it so happened that the tide was coming in and nearly at the flood, the swell was setting to the land, and moreover the little breeze there was came from the right quarter to drift the wreck in to the point of rocks. Everything was favorable to success in beaching the galleon there.

In the greatest imaginable excitement we hastened to get the hauling-line on board the schooner, and securing both boats to it made all sail and endeavored thus to help the old hulk along by towing. It was sluggish business. The boats would rise and fall with the swell and lean down to the breeze, then come up, the sails empty, and then down again, and so on. But we moved, and in the right direction, though slowly, very slowly at first, and then a little faster as the rattling mass of gourds and the heavy load beneath it got fairly under way.

I never saw Mr. Millward so wrought up with excitement as at this time. And indeed we were all in something of the same condition. For here was the result of long labor culminating before our eyes. Small wonder, then, that there should be much hilarity. The galleon was afloat, and our ship was coming in! Halfway to the beach Mr. Millward, in a sweet and powerful voice, rolled out that good old hymn, "We are going home," and back from the rocks came the echo of the last word, "to-morrow." We all joined heartily in the chorus, with the best of good-will.

In about an hour, and as near as could be at high tide the Spanish galleon grounded between two rocks on a sandy bottom just at the north cape of the island, and we beached my boat near by in a sheltered place to the southwest of the cape. The other boat we sailed down to the creek, got something to eat, put the axe and some other things on board, and came back to the cape, where we anchored to await the falling of the tide.

As we sat in the boat lifted by the swell, and watched

each wave wash through between the rocks where lay the galleon, I began to realize that Mr. Millward's spirited song about "going home to-morrow" was not very likely to come true for a good many to-morrows. There was a regular tide-way through this passage, and I began to doubt whether the sea had not played us a sad trick in bringing the galleon to such a port.

That the situation of affairs may be better understood, it will be necessary to describe precisely the lay of the land. The two rocks were separated from each other by a narrow passage about thirty feet in width at the end where the galleon entered, and narrowed to perhaps ten feet at the other end in a length of a hundred and fifty feet. Through this passage the swell washed with great force. Indeed, the galleon and its supporting mass of gourds had been carried in on the heave of the swell and the hull dropped there with a crash on the bottom. The frame-work and cages had been at once torn loose, and the spars and gourds lay jammed in the narrow exit beyond, the water churned to foam by the obstruction they offered, dashing continually against them and tearing them one by one loose from one another until the sea all beyond was littered with the fragments.

Even as we watched, this débris little by little washed out and away. The hull of the galleon, it is true, lying on the bottom and well under water where at high tide it was full five and twenty feet in depth, would suffer no such damage probably in the present state of the weather. But on the other hand the fall of-the tide would most likely not be great enough to leave her above water, and there was no telling what might happen if a gale of wind should come along, especially with a low tide. Indeed I speedily made up my mind that there was not only going to be great danger of the wreck breaking up and getting away from us entirely by washing piecemeal out through the exit into the sea, but also, if this dire misfortune should be long delayed, that we should not be able to get at the cargo for the racing of the water, even when at its lowest. I must confess that when this fully dawned on me I felt greatly discouraged.

At last after a weary wait the tide reached its lowest, and as I feared, we found that we dared not go into the race-way with the boat. Each swell swept through it with a great rush, breaking into foam in the narrower part, so that a boat would have been dashed to pieces unless fortunate enough to swim fairly out through the exit, and would then be extremely liable to be overwhelmed. We drew up to the rock which lay adjoining the beach and landed, so that we might look down on the galleon from above. There she lay with the deck just awash at the water's surface, except when a green sea came whelming through, and then she was buried to the depth of several feet. The old hulk was a most venerable and curious sight; shells of various kinds grown fast all over her ancient deck and sides; long streamers of sea-weed floating from her like hair; coral branches, sand, ooze, mud, — a thousand reminiscences of her long sleep on the bottom were now plainly observable in the light of day.

We all three stood looking down upon this curious sight in silence, which was finally broken by Mr. Millward, saying, —

"I am afraid we are as far away from the treasure that lies in that old ship as we were before we raised her."

I did not feel like talking about it, and therefore said nothing, but stood with hands in pockets looking at this exhibition of what I regarded as the perversity of inanimate matter. That the bewitched old galleon should have run her nose exactly into this place of all others, when there were miles of fair sloping beach on which she might have stranded, seemed like a deadly stab in the back by a treacherous adverse fate. It was enough to make a man swear, if that would have done any good. And possibly it might have eased my feelings temporarily if I had possessed talent enough in that direction to have done full justice to the subject.

This would have been a good time to give up the whole project, — to wash my hands of all Spanish galleons in general and this perverse one in particular. But I must say that no such thought entered my mind. I was disgusted, and very much disappointed, and not a little angry; but as for giving up, that was simply impossible. The situation stunned me, and there seemed no way out of it; but I could not entertain the thought that the recovery of the treasure was impossible.

Alice Millward came up and drew me away by the arm. "Do not look so downcast," said she. "Surely we need not grieve over this failure. If we cannot get the treasure we are no worse off than we were yesterday."

"But you do not know," said I, fiercely, "what it means to me. I have been working to save my birthplace."

"Never mind, never mind, Mr. Morgan," replied she, gently, "let us go home to the house now and think it all over there, where the hateful thing will be out of sight."

"We can do no more here and we might as well be starting," added the old man. Between them they led me to the boat, the old man saying various things about not putting your trust in things of this earth; that riches are not enduring; and other like remarks, all of which fell on my ear without at all penetrating to my understanding. To tell the truth, I was utterly dazed and unable to give the thing any sort of consecutive thought.

We made the run quickly to Home Creek, and all went early to bed, a most disheartened lot of mortals. Contrary to my expectation, I soon fell asleep and slept soundly all night long.

CHAPTER XVII.

THE WAVES IN HARNESS.

WHEN a carefully concocted plan carried out industriously and faithfully results in a total failure to achieve the end sought, the consequences are disastrous in more ways than one. There is first the loss of all the labor, which is important; and secondly, and far more important, there is also inevitably a loss of confidence in one's own power to achieve success.

I went to my hammock under the shed that night humiliated to the last degree, with a sense of utter contempt for my own judgment, — in short, in a sneering mood, criticising the folly I had displayed in not foreseeing events and making due provision for them. In a rank spirit of self-criticism and self-condemnation I reviewed what I had done, and what I had left undone, and deliberately pronounced myself a stupid ass for all my pains. Nevertheless, as before stated I went very quickly to sleep, and slept the traditional sleep of the just until after dawn.

When I awakened, the new risen sun hung bathed in fleecy clouds of primrose just above a sea all golden and flashing with his level beams; the dew gemmed each blade and leaf; the cool morning air trembled gently among the glistening foliage; the birds sang in noisy chorus far and near; everything was fresh and rested and hopeful and fair and encouraging.

I felt braced and full of confidence and hope; all the worry and trouble of the night had rolled away and gone. Never say die! There is no such thing as fail.

The only question now is, what shall we do next? How shall we protect the wreck where it lies, and overcome the obstacles that have risen in our path? I went whistling a jolly tune down to the bathing-place in the creek, took a cool plunge in the clear water, and returned light-hearted, confident, and happy, to rouse my companions, that they also might feel the inspiring effect of the beautiful morning. I wanted somebody to talk with, to discuss the hundred half-formed projects with which my brain already teemed. I wanted to get to work again on some new line, and felt that no moment should be lost. I went to the door and called them; then built a fire and put the kettle on for coffee.

When Alice Millward came down to the fire, radiant in the beauty of health and freshness, her cheek flushed, her beautiful eyes sparkling, and a rebellious tendril of silken hair trembling over her brow in the breath of the morning, I so looked my admiration that she instinctively blushed. I turned away, busying myself with the fire. Somehow I could not help whistling snatches of the merry air that had been running in my head all the morning.

She caught my eye presently and said in a tone of full conviction, " Mr. Morgan, you have found some way of getting that treasure. I know you have by your manner this morning."

"You are mistaken, Miss Millward. I only wish you were not. The fact is I have only just found that it is possible to begin again calmly to think and plan. But that discovery is quite enough to cheer one. It is a good deal to have recovered from the stunning disappointment of yesterday, and to have regained composure and confidence; for that is equivalent to regaining one's faculties. Don't you think so?"

"Yes, I suppose so," she answered, with a little air

of thoughtfulness, " but I really do not know; for to speak the truth I do not think I felt the disappointment so severely as either you or father. Of course I was sorry, but then you see I was not so deeply interested, perhaps, as you two were."

Mr. Millward now came up, and after the usual morning greeting said, "I imagine it will now be in order to begin to think of getting back to civilization. Our labors here seem to have come to naught."

"No," said I with some heat, "I shall not leave until I find it utterly impossible to explore that sunken hull. I could not rest comfortably elsewhere so long as a bit of hope was left. Of course," I added, after a moment's pause, "I cannot ask you to remain. But I do hope you will consent to stay a few days longer. We ought to protect the wreck from destruction in some way before the next gale. And I think it can be done."

"But how?" said he.

"Ah, that is the question, that is the problem," I replied. "If we could build a breakwater across the mouth of the chasm in some manner the hull would lie safely where it is. We could then leave, and come back with divers to get the treasure at a later time."

"To stand the shock of the waves which will dash through that place in a gale of wind from the right quarter, your breakwater will require to be a powerful structure. And the building of it would be an engineering feat of no small magnitude, I take it." And the old man shook his head slowly, as though to say he did not believe it possible.

Even as he was talking, however, the half-formed plan which had been floating hazily through my mind took definite shape. The chasm, the rocks, the swell and waves racing through were all so pictured in my mind that there was no need to go again and look at the place, because it was then before me in imagination as vividly as though I actually beheld it. The remedy for the danger was clear and plain to my mind. I went up to my two companions and taking a hand of each, said as earnestly as I felt: "We can do it. I see how it can be done. It is, I now believe, a piece of rare good luck that the old galleon drifted into that place. For consider; if she had struck upon the open beach she would inevitably have gone to pieces in the breakers, and who knows whether what of her cargo we want would have washed up to dry land. I tell you now, and believe me it is true, fortune has favored us."

"But the breakwater," said the old man, impatiently, "how can we construct such a thing?"

"Very well," said I, with a smile and an air of mystery, "you shall know; but as the coffee boils, let us have breakfast, and we will discuss it over our coffee."

"I am quite agreed to that," replied he, "but fear it will need to be helped out by all the aid the good coffee can give it, my boy. However, I am open to conviction. You have done wonders in getting the wreck where she is, and I hope you may be right in your belief that the berth is a lucky one."

When we were fairly seated, the corn bread broken, and the steaming hot coffee poured out by the hand of Alice, the old man nodded at me as much as to say, "Now fire away."

Alice voiced the same request in words, saying: "Now give us your great plan, Mr. Morgan. I am sure it will be a success. How will you construct the breakwater?"

"My dear Miss Alice, I expect to induce the sea to do that work for me in the most part. I shall harness the wild waves of ocean to my dirt cart, and make them labor to protect the old hull they would delight to destroy." And I calmly filled my mouth with corn bread, while Mr. Millward looked at me as though he feared I had become demented by the recent disappointment. There was silence for a moment or two. Then, looking furtively at me, he said: —

"But I do not understand how you expect to harness your steeds, even if such unruly creatures were willing to work for us."

"Still, you will confess it is very simple," I said, oracularly. "We have only to offer these waves work they always delight in doing, and you may be sure they will work day and night, high tide and low tide, to get it done, and when it is accomplished they will sigh and moan and crash and roar for more. That is the ceaseless, persistent disposition they have, and the harder the wind and the bigger the waves the quicker will the work be done. My plan is simply this: to get the waves to work throwing up sand to fill that chasm and bury the wreck if necessary in sand. If it is buried we can easily dig it out. But we need not wait for the entire chasm to be filled. It will be enough if the mouth and exit passage are filled. Look out at yonder beach and see the unruly breakers at their daily task of throwing up tons and tons of sand, and as constantly dragging it back again that they may have more of their delightful occupation. You have only to throw down a rock, or a branch, or some obstacle to retain the sand and hold it from being dragged back, and it will presently be buried beneath the heap which it has retained."

"I see what you mean," said Mr. Millward, setting down his cup of coffee, which he had held in his hand, "but I do not yet understand how you propose to prevent the constant scour that is going on in that race-way. You must first stop that scouring action, and then I agree that the place in time will fill with sand."

Then I proceeded in detail to explain how by cutting down trees and throwing them into the mouth of the chasm I hoped first to get the tops buried in the sand, and then by adding brush and branches to create finally a bar of sand at this point, which could be constantly added to by more tree tops and branches and the sand cast up, until it was as high as the waves could reach. Near by grew mangrove trees in a little lagoon. These would answer our purpose as well as any; they could be felled into the water and floated to place.

All excitement and full of hope, now that a feasible plan had presented itself, we discussed the matter in all its bearings, until Mr. Millward, rising, declared we must waste no more time, but go to work while the weather held good. There was, indeed, no time to lose, as a northeast gale meant destruction to the old hulk, if it should occur before the guard could be built.

At once we loaded into the boat blankets and a sail for shelter, and provisions for several days, including five great calabashes of water, intending to camp at the point so as to be near our work while the present danger should continue. By nine o'clock we were out of the creek and under way, and soon reached the place where we intended to land. We moored the boat in safety under shelter of the rocks to the west of the point, where she would be safe except in case of a severe storm; then we put up the sail that we had brought for a tent, and landed such things as were wanted there, putting Alice as usual in control as housekeeper.

The long spar which we had used to connect the two triangles of our lifting-frame, we found beached to the west of the rocks, and torn lose from the triangles, which had washed away and disappeared. It was Mr. Millward's suggestion that we could utilize this piece of timber to good advantage by cutting it to the right length, and wedging it across the mouth of the chasm at about the height of low water, for the butts of the trees forming the abattis to rest upon. To get this spar into the water and tow it around to the mouth of the chasm was the first job we undertook. For this purpose we used my boat, the "Mohawk," as being the lightest to row. By dinner time (about one o'clock) we had the spar sawed off and dropped down between the rocks, where it wedged itself, as the wall was slanting at each side. To secure it more firmly in place we resorted to the expedient of tying a great stone on the end of a line and dropping it down on the spar several times at each end, standing for this purpose on the rocks above. We kept up this pile-driving operation until the spar began to splinter slightly. It now lay across the mouth of the chasm at about a foot above low water, so firmly wedged in place that no wave could displace it, unless it should be powerful enough to break the great, tough beam in twain, which was not very likely.

After dinner we took my boat into the small lagoon on the west coast near the north point, and began the other branch of our work by cutting down a couple of trees which stood near deep water, and grew in the water itself on branching roots uprising in a complicated maze. These trees, one at a time and by dint of hard work, we towed out into the sea and brought round to the mouth of the chasm. Here we manœuvred until we got the butt end pointed at the spar, and then let go at the right moment so that the swell as it entered the chasm swept the tree bodily into the exact place we wanted it to go, the butt lying on the wedged-in spar, and the top presented to the waves. To weight the top down and make it sink we threw into the branches several heavy rocks. When in place the tree lay at an angle of about forty-five degrees with the horizon, the butt resting on the spar, and the branches on the bottom.

I had some fear that the shock of the tree striking against the spar might dislodge the latter; but it had no effect of that kind, the spar being much too tightly wedged. Moreover the chasm, as I have already stated, narrowed gradually from the mouth inward as well as from the top downward. So the blows of the waves only served still further to tighten the spar in place. We managed to get the two trees in place and weighted with rocks before we were called to supper at sunset. We had made a fair start, and accomplished a good day's work. The supper, spread on the ground and eaten by firelight, was a merry meal, though we were very tired and glad to get to sleep. We needed a strong rope that had been left at Home Creek, and I concluded to walk there along the beach after supper, and sleeping at home to return at early dawn with the rope before breakfast. So I bade my companions goodnight and started down the beach. The way was easy, and I reached the house in little over an hour and turned in immediately to secure a much needed rest.

When I returned with the rope in the morning, as I came near the tent and while it was still hidden from view by the intervening foliage, I heard the voices of father and daughter joined in a hymn, — the clear, rich soprano of the girl, flute-like and full, mingling in harmony with the noble baritone of the old man, whose voice was still unbroken by age. I paused a moment to listen to the wonderful song of praise, in which were mingled the deep booming bass of the surf, the myriad voices of the birds trilling an accompaniment, and the interwoven notes of the hymn, rising and falling together in sweet accord, — and my own heart was lifted up to the great Creator to whom such praise, I thought, might prove quite as acceptable as though sung by a full-voiced choir beneath cathedral arches to the accompaniment of the majestic chords of an organ.

When the strains of the hymn had ceased I came up, and the hearty greeting which I received was very pleasant. Indeed, the friendly sense of comradeship had become very strong among us all; and I have no doubt they were as glad to see me after this short absence as I truly was to see them.

After breakfast Mr. Millward and I began again at an early hour the work of filling, towing, placing, and weighting the trees. This day we placed five in position. The next day we brought and placed five more, by which time the entire mouth of the chasm was so full of the trunks, branches, and twigs that we could get no more in place. The fourth day of our labors we spent in casting loose rocks in among the branches. The fifth day we passed in watching this *chevaux de frise* and noting the effect of the waves, as they came frothing through the mass of twigs and branches. The structure — if such it may be called — held firmly and broke the swell completely.

We could do no more. The remainder of the work must be accomplished by the waves themselves in their own time and way. For this we must wait their pleasure. There was still quite a strong current through the chasm, and I wished very much that this could be lessened, as its tendency was of course to carry through a large portion of the sand which might otherwise be retained. When I spoke of this to Mr. Millward he immediately proposed that we should partly fill the narrow exit passage with rocks and limbs to check this current, and on the sixth day we began this job. Instead of floating whole trees, which we could not have managed to get into place without the aid of an ingoing swell, we cut and carried limbs and branches, which, together with rocks, were thrown down from above, until the end of the exit passage was a frothing mass of water struggling through the tangle. This very much lessened the current, and we were well satisfied with the work. That evening we sailed the two boats back to Home Creek and moored them in their former haven. The next day, which was the Sabbath, we spent in rest at home, leaving the waves now to do their work, and confident that no harm could come to the hulk if the fair weather would continue for a few days longer.

In the morning, while we were seated beneath the shed, Mr. Millward read selections from the Psalms, in his deep, sonorous voice and impressive manner. We joined afterward in prayer and hymn, and when this simple service was over I started with Alice for a walk on the beach to the south, while Mr. Millward composed himself for a comfortable smoke in the shade. The walking on the sand just above the reach of the waves, and yet where it was wet by an occasional toppling roller that came spuming up the slope farther than its fellows, was excellent, for the wetted sand was hard and firm, and cool to the feet. Everywhere lay fragments of sea-weed, shells, and the curious forms of sea life cast up by the waves. We amused ourselves by collecting specimens of the many-tinted weeds, mosses, and fragile structures, whether vegetable or animal I know not, nor could any save a naturalist draw the dividing line. Alice explained how these delicate forms could be spread out and dried, by first floating them in water until they were untangled, and then lifting them out by a plate of glass and drying them on paper.

"I look forward now," said she, "to the time when we shall be sailing away from our island home, and I would like to carry with me something by which to remember this beautiful beach."

"Are you getting tired of the life, Miss Millward?"

"Ah, no," she quickly answered, "not tired of it; far from that. It seems now quite like a home to me. You must remember that it is many years since father and I have remained so long in one place as we have been here. I have grown quite to love this beautiful island. And the work and the life is a real pleasure to me. But yet I fear that father is pining to be back to his work, or to civilization, though he has not yet said so in my hearing. It is hard, you know, for an old man to change his habits."

"I suppose you would find it pleasanter if you had some one of your own sex as a companion," said I.

"Perhaps so," thoughtfully, "but I have never had any girl friends, you know, in all my life; for we have been here in this region, among the islands, since I was quite a child, and have gone about from place to place so much that I have had no chance to meet such friends as I might feel like making my companions. The people are mostly of quite another religion from ours, — those who are white I mean, — and though I have many friends among the colored people, the Hindoos and others, the friendship has not made me any comrades. Father has often said that he feared it was his duty to send me north among people of my own kind, that I might learn better what life in this world really means. But I think I do know, for it must be much the same everywhere; and I should not like to leave father here alone."

The thought of the wandering life which this motherless girl had led, among poor, half-heathen people, touched me, and I had it on my tongue to contrast such an existence with the very different sort of surroundings she might have had elsewhere. But why should I do this? Even if she could understand it, which was doubtful, no good could come of creating in her mind longing and discontent; though I honestly believe discontent never could have found entrance to such a candid and happy mind, no matter what might be held up for her imagination to consider.

The sun soon beat down with fiery rays, and I cut for her a leaf of fan palm to form a sort of parasol. The picture she made in her light dress, against the blue sea all filled with glowing brightness, the shade of the graceful leaf falling upon her, will live long in my memory. It seemed to me that her pure soul shone out from the beautiful eyes that now and again met mine. Rare combination of something that seemed straight from heaven with what was sweetly human and of our earth; the clear, pure spirit, and the beautiful woman glowing with health and filled with life and color and made for human love — was there ever before, whispered my tortured heart, such an incomparable being? Dare I speak to her of what fills my mind and soul? No; most certainly not.

Now in point of fact I was making love to this girl with all my might, and did not know it. I wooed her all unconsciously, and had not dared to woo her at all. The divine passion, I have since been told, needs no word or sign; and this girl, divinely pure and yet sweetly human, inexperienced as she was, must have felt that I adored her. If she had never heard of the love of man for woman — and most likely she had never given it a thought — still she must have known my devotion to her quite as well as though the burning words that ever kept throbbing up from my heart for utterance had passed my lips. But I could not know. And so I alternated between the medium plane of faint hope and the cold depths of despair. I conclude, as I now look back, that I was not doing so badly as I then thought.

We sat down on a rock together to watch the little hermit crabs, each with a stolen shell that it had converted into a house, now peering out, now drawing itself in, now dragging its house along the sand in search of food or a better location, — funny little creatures, that seem to link the spider family to the crabs. Her hand was on my arm; we sat close together; the curved, flat edges of the spent waves nearly reached our feet as they stole up the sand; the solemn sound of the sea was in our ears, and the enchanting song of a first love filled my heart.

And then we wandered slowly on along the beach, now and then compelled by a higher flow to step aside; we examined the lovely shells that lay in numbers and great variety bleaching on the margin of the dry sand, or wetted by the rising water; the little skipping sand borers; now and again a gaping clam or hideous sea slug; dry shells of the great horse-shoe crabs; bladder-weed and ocean tangle; and all the wonderful débris that the sea casts up. Then turning in toward the land we came among the tall, graceful stems of the cocoa-palm, their feathery heads trembling and rustling in the gently stirring air. Here we found in a low shrub the little nest of one of those diminutive wagtail wrens, and while the anxious mother fluttered near, feigning a wound or inability to fly in order to draw us away from her precious little ones, we looked at the four tiny, gaping-mouthed children clad in down and naked helplessness, until the distress of the comical little matron induced us to move away from the nest in pity.

We found too the purple passion-flower and gaudy

cactus blossoms bursting out in showy splendor from thorn-armed, fleshy leaves, bright-feathered parrots and parroquets, a little humming-bird that bore a flashing jewel in his breast and made a misty halo round about him with his rapid wing, beating the air so fast that it seemed to the eye a faint sphere of cloud.

And so we wandered on side by side, talking of what we saw. I parted the thorny bushes for her path, lifted her over the rocks and logs, and hand in hand we crossed the grassy open where I had gathered seeds, now ripe again, and thus came finally home, as the sun stood in the zenith.

We found the old man sleeping peacefully in my hammock under the shed, with Bible in hand lying open on his breast. Duke lay on the ground below him, furtively opening an eye now and then, though without stirring when we came up. On the fire, now burned nearly out, slowly steamed and simmered the dinner stew, whose appetizing odors floating to us apprised us of the fact that we were very hungry, just as the cool shade told us we were very warm, and the inviting arm-chairs suggested that we were really tired.

CHAPTER XVIII.

EMBAYED.

WHEN I arose shortly after dawn the next morning, it was with no small degree of satisfaction that I found the sun brightly shining, and every indication present of a continuance of the fair weather and gentle breezes which had now held continuously for ten days. Very anxious to know the condition of the breakwater, Mr. Millward and I, shortly after a hearty breakfast of fish freshly caught, started for a walk up the beach to the resting-place of the galleon. We found no apparent change in the condition of the larger breakwater, — the one across the mouth of the chasm, — but strangely enough the smaller one, across the exit passage, had so far silted up with sand as to form an almost complete obstruction to the flow of a current through the chasm at low water. Indeed, the sand had almost buried the branches we had cast in, and was risen so far as to be plainly visible just below the surface of the water. This was an altogether unexpected result, and it now looked very much as though the silting and filling was to take place from the exit backward to the mouth, instead of from the mouth as we had calculated. However, it mattered not to us how the capricious waves chose to do their work, if only it were done.

We had brought the axe along, and without delay we began to cut and pile into the exit passage more limbs and branches and rocks, until the place was full to a level somewhat above high-tide mark. To facilitate further the formation of this bank, we cast many branches into the waters of the chasm just back of the newly formed sand-bar, that it might be caused if possible to rise high enough to prevent any through current and consequent scouring action even at high tide.

We tried hard to ascertain whether the sand had begun to accumulate at the breakwater across the mouth; but were unable to do so because of the lack of transparency of the water, which held in suspension a large percentage of sand and foreign matter stirred up by the swell. We both expressed our confidence that as soon as the current through the chasm was stopped, the sand would begin to silt in and fill up the main breakwater.

It was two hours after noon when we returned to the house again. After dinner we all three turned to the work of digging sweet potatoes in my old garden, and storing them under the shed. All the crops were doing finely and we found some green Indian corn just ripe enough to boil. In the cool of the evening we sat under the shed to watch for the new moon to rise, discussing the theory and probable action of sand deposit by waves.

Mr. Millward's theory — and I believe it to be the correct one — was that the sand was held in suspension only while the water was in very considerable motion; and that it fell to the bottom almost instantly when the motion of the water ceased. He likened it to stirring sugar, not yet dissolved, in a glass of water. As soon as the stirring stopped the sugar fell to the bottom. "Thus, for example," he explained, "when a wave comes up on the beach in front of us, it is more or less charged with sand; the sand is deposited just when the wave has spent its force and paused before the return flow. But, of course, the sand so deposited on the naked beach would be picked up again and carried back, to be again brought up, and so on in ceaseless round." And the reason, he insisted, why the sand gathered at the last breakwater in the chasm instead of at the first one, was simply because at that place the current and consequent motion were least.

Each morning I walked up the beach to the chasm, sometimes alone and sometimes accompanied by Mr. Millward. In two days the breakwater at the exit was completely covered with sand, which rose above the level of high tide, and the sand had already begun to silt into the chasm back of the exit. On the third day we found a great shark embayed in the chasm and dashing around the old hull every little while, as though in a flurry of excitement. Each time a wave would break in he would endeavor to swim out, following the retreating water, — for now there was no longer a current through, — but the trees and limbs prevented him. Mr. Millward said he seemed like an evil spirit set to guard the galleon and its treasure; and indeed it would have been a dangerous thing for any one to attempt exploration of the wreck while this man-eating sentinel patrolled the narrow water where she lay.

The sight of this voracious fish reminded me very forcibly of the great danger which would have attended any attempt to reach the hull by diving when the galleon lay out in the sea. Had I brought my diving-apparatus safely to the island, as I originally intended to do, it is quite possible, and even probable, that I should have found a grave among the gastric fluids of some such shark. Strangely enough, in all the many times I had looked at the wreck through the water-glass while it lay out in the sea, I had never seen a single shark, though other fish had been visible in considerable numbers and variety. But doubtless, as is the treacherous nature of this tiger of the sea, he was lying there concealed and instinctively watching the boat in expectation of prey. It made me shudder involuntarily to think of the possible encounter that I might have had. As the shark imprisoned in the chasm was no present inconvenience to us, we allowed him to remain undisturbed where he was.

As we stood on the rock which adjoined the shore, watching the frothing of the surges through the breakwater at the mouth of the chasm, I pointed out to Mr. Millward that every few minutes, at intervals of about every third wave, the water rushing back met the incoming wave exactly at the breakwater and the resulting interference produced there a temporary quiet in the waters.

"Now," said I, in reference to this fact, "if your theory is right we ought to be getting a discharge of sand at the breakwater every time there is such a meeting of the waters there."

"Of course," said he, "there is no doubt of it; and we shall soon be having a bar at this point. Whether this bar will rise high enough to stop the water materially from coming in before the whole chasm has silted full of sand is something we cannot determine except by waiting to find out by actual test."

"Nor does it greatly matter," I added, "for in either event the galleon would be safely housed."

The weather held fair for a week longer, and at the end of that time it had become quite evident that a bank of sand was steadily forming at the mouth of the chasm. It was already nearly up to the surface at low water, so that the inrush of water was very small compared with what it had been. We had gone up to the chasm in the morning as usual, and then again in the evening of the same day, as the weather was very threatening and the heat intense, and a glassy calm was on the sea, which, almost devoid even of a swell, spread out in a flat, metallic-looking plain with scarcely a wrinkle. A storm was surely brewing, and we might expect it that night or the following day at latest. But as there was nothing to do, except to wait its arrival and abide the result, I only went to the chasm to satisfy my curiosity. When I arrived, an hour or two before sunset, and examined the place carefully, I thought the galleon would probably be safe, unless the surge became so heavy as to sweep the breakwater out on its return flow. Mr. Millward was of the same opinion.

About midnight that night I was wakened by a tremendous crash of thunder. The sky was black with heavy clouds, lit up at short intervals by the lightning, and it had already begun to rain. Owing to the heat, I had been sleeping in my hammock at the shed. I immediately got up, partly dressed myself, and carried my hammock to the house, where I found my companions both wakened by the thunder. I called Duke in and secured the door, expecting a heavy rain, which speedily came down with a rush and steady roar upon the thatched roof. The wind followed from the old quarter, the northeast, and soon became almost a gale, beating and driving the rain against the walls in angry gusts.

Mr. Millward and I, talking through the darkness, speculated on the probable result to the galleon; but being unable, of course, to reach any satisfactory conclusion, we dropped finally to sleep, thus forgetting our worry and anxiety.

In the morning, after a cold breakfast, without coffee, — for the fire was out, everything in the way of fuel was wet, and there was no sun visible, — I started for the chasm. Breasting the stiff gale, which was accompanied by spits and dashes of rain, I made my way along the beach, full of apprehension as I saw the huge rollers come crashing in, and the heavy swell that had been raised by the gale. When I came to the north cape, and the rocks forming the chasm were in sight, the scene was indeed one of grandeur, and my worst fears seemed to have good grounds. The tremendous swell running in against the rocks broke with a thunderous noise; the spray flew high in the air, and was blown apparently clear over the rocks.

I had hurried along thus far as rapidly as I could travel against the strong wind; but now I hesitated, dreading to go far enough to see what had happened to the galleon. However, no good could come of waiting, so I plunged ahead and soon came to the rock which joined the shore, and ascended it that I might have a fair view of the chasm. I found that the chasm no longer existed as we had known it. Instead of an open race-way through which the current rushed, or into which the rollers broke, there was now a peaceful little pool, in the midst of which the galleon was dimly visible, sunk some feet below the surface. The water in this pool was not very clear; for every few minutes a mighty shower of spray flung on high fell like rain upon its surface, and the rocks all about were drenched, and covered with little rivulets. Even the spot where I stood was not exempt, but I took the wetting with cheerful fortitude under the circumstances. Both breakwaters were completely covered with sand. The one at the mouth was almost like a sand-hill, and reached nearly to the stem of the galleon, but was so drenched by the falling spray that I did not care to go upon it. The one at the rear, or exit, was far enough away so that the spray did not fall upon it to any great extent, and I therefore climbed down upon it to see how firm it was. I was very certain no one seeing this bank of sand would have imagined how it had been made. There was no indication whatever that the hand of man had had anything to do with its construction. It looked quite as though the sand had lain there for ages. The waves had done their work most thoroughly, and the aged hulk now rested in a quiet, land-locked harbor, as safe and secure from the sea as though it were in a dry dock.

Wet through by rain and spray combined, but elated and in the highest of spirits at the condition of our work, I hastened back as fast as my feet would carry me, helped on by the wind now at my back, to convey the joyful intelligence to my companions. Duke, who had accompanied me, seemed to read my satisfaction in my face and actions, for he bounded along frisking and barking as though the whole thing were a grand frolic. When I came to the creek he had already run on ahead to the house, so that Mr. Millward and Alice were apprised of my return, and were at the door looking for me as I came up to the house.

"What news do you bring?" asked the old man, anxiously.

"The best of good news," cried I, "the very best of good news! The galleon is safely and snugly at rest in a basin where a tornado could not reach it."

"Well, that is good!" said the old man, fervently.

"Excellent!" echoed the daughter, and added, solicitously, "but you are very wet, Mr. Morgan, and you must change your garments at once. It will never do to have the courier who brings such good tidings take harm by his journey."

After I had gone into my little sleeping-place and put

on dry clothing, we sat down, and I had to describe minutely what I had seen. We then went into general committee to discuss ways and means for getting at the cargo of the sunken hull. Mr. Millward was for setting sail at the first favorable wind for Martinique to get divers and return with them. But I could not bring myself to agree to leaving the galleon to chance for so long a time as that might require. We had already successfully overcome so many difficulties that those remaining seemed trifling in comparison; though I am free to confess that just how we were to get at the contents of the hull was not at all clear to my mind at that time.

We had discussed the situation a long time, and as I had nothing to offer but mere resistance and unwillingness to leave, I felt that the old gentleman was gradually getting the better of the discussion, and had fairly driven me to the last ditch, when Alice came to my assistance with a suggestion that supplied a new stock of ammunition to my retreating forces.

The dear girl's suggestion was in these words, " Why don't you pump the water out of the basin and leave the galleon dry?"

Why, indeed? What was to hinder? It would be difficult to make an air-pump, but not at all difficult to contrive some sort of water-raising device.

"Thanks, fair Alice, for the idea. It rehabilitates me," thought I; and meeting her eyes I added aloud, "You have hit upon the very idea, Miss Alice. We can get the water out of that basin with far less trouble than a voyage to Martinique and return would cost."

The old man was silent.

Turning to him I said, "Your daughter deserves our warmest thanks, Mr. Millward, for this suggestion. Now we have only to contrive some water-lifting device, and we can set to work on the final task. What do you say?"

"I say that if it is feasible I will stay of course."

We discussed all the water-raising contrivances we had ever heard of, from the primitive Egyptian shadoof — a bucket on a balanced pole — to the rotary steam-pump. But steam-pumps were not to be had, and it was aggravating to think about them. However, I went conscientiously through the entire list, and was listened to most patiently. It chanced that among other devices there was one I had heard of as being used in India by the natives to raise water for irrigation. It consisted of a wheel to which were suspended a number of gourds. Mr. Millward at once remembered seeing these very machines in use, and told how he had witnessed the breech-clouted coolies toiling with them on the banks of the rivers. He immediately agreed that we could easily build such a machine, and that it would accomplish the work.

"'The amount of water raised in a day from the river with one of these rude machines and poured into the irrigating canal by the efforts of a single native workman is truly astonishing," said he. After thinking a moment he added, "But you overlook one thing, Mr. Morgan. These machines are only adapted to lifting water from a river or other source of supply which remains at or near a constant level. Now, here the water to be lifted will be getting constantly lower, and as it falls the wheel also must be lowered and would soon be so low that it would no longer bring the gourds high enough to discharge their contents above the breakwater. You see that, do you not?"

In truth, I had not seen it at all. But when the difficulty was thus suggested it was plain enough that such a wheel would never do for what we wanted. I did not answer this most pertinent suggestion, for the very good reason that it could not be controverted. The wheel idea was quite out of the question.

After a little while he resumed by saying, "But I have also seen a modification of the same sort of machine, in which the gourds were attached to an endless rope instead of to the wheel itself. This device is used by the same people where the water is to be raised to a greater height than can conveniently be done with the wheel. I think we might possibly make such a modification work successfully."

"Can you recall how this modification was constructed?" said I, anxiously.

"Perhaps I can recall enough to enable you to get the idea," he replied, throwing back his head and closing his eyes in the effort to remember. "Yes," said he, after a little reflection, "I think I can. I remember the general features very well indeed. However, the most vivid recollection I have, connected with these machines, is the hideous, creaking screech of their ungreased axles as they were turned hour after hour all through the hot summer nights, the natives 'spelling' one another at the work. How well I remember the dry, hot nights when I lay listening to these sounds from far and near. You could easily tell when the laboring coolie was tired by the gradual slowing of his machine and the lengthening of the interval between screeches. Then a fresh man mounted the treadmill and the screeches quickened; and so these monotonous alternations continued through the still night."

After a few reminiscences of his old life in India the old man proceeded to give a description of the machine as nearly as he could recall it. It consisted of a drum, or skeleton wheel, about six feet in diameter, mounted on a platform over the water; each end of the drum overhung the platform and carried an endless rope, to which open-mouthed gourds were tied at regular intervals. The drum was revolved by stepping on its bars as in a treadmill. The gourds were carried down into the water empty and brought up full by the endless rope. Troughs at each side received the water as the gourds tipped to return. In short, it was a sort of chain-pump, or modification of that well-known device. From his description, aided by my own imagination and a full knowledge of the result sought, I was able to reconstruct in my mind this machine, or at least to see how one could be built that I conceived would answer the purpose. We agreed that we would start at this work as soon as the weather was pleasant enough to be out of doors with reasonable comfort.

It was very tedious to be without any fire or means of obtaining one during the rain. The house was getting damp; we missed our hot coffee; cold victuals were not pleasant, and our supply of cooked food was about gone, so that if the rain continued we should speedily be reduced to raw bacon and cocoanuts. As the leaden sky gave no immediate promise of sunshine, Mr. Millward and I concluded to try our hand at producing fire by friction. For this purpose we attached a piece of hard wood to the final shaft of the old fanning-mill, and setting it in rapid motion held a piece of soft wood against it as it revolved. I turned the crank while he held the wood. It presently began to char and smoke, but no fire came, though I ground away until the sweat poured off my body. We were about to give it up as a bad job, when Mr. Millward hit upon the idea of rasping off a quantity of fine wood-dust by grinding a piece of wood on the end of the iron shaft itself. When he had collected some of this and sprinkled it into the hot, smoking cavity of the softwood stick the motion soon caused the light material to catch fire, and we were speedily rewarded with a glowing coal from which we were able to start the fire, which you may be certain was not permitted to go out again. I very quickly had a hot fire in the oven, one near the shed out of doors, and a third in the fireplace of the house. With fire, life became speedily more endurable.

The comforting and cheering influence of an open fire, the sight of the blaze or the glowing coals, is a mysterious thing, and is not to be explained by the mere personal comfort due to the warmth, for a close stove or a steam coil will give that as well and perhaps better and more equably. There is an instinctive something deep down in the heart of man that responds to the open fire, and makes it act like a tonic on the disposition. This feeling is common apparently to all mankind. Everybody alike, old or young, rich or poor, is cheered by the glow and blaze of the fireside, the crackle of the burning, the sight of the flames on the hearth. Men who have been brought up from childhood to live in houses heated by the modern steam, hot-water, or hot-air apparatus, or have lived in the tropics where fires for warmth are rarely if ever needed, no sooner approach the blazing hearth than they feel its cheering influence. I have thought sometimes that the explanation might be found in heredity, — in a deep-seated habit of the human mind descending from parent to child through countless ages and generations. Far back of history, in the dim twilight of primitive life, we may imagine our ancestors living in such wildness as can scarcely be found on earth to-day even among the lowest savages; and we can picture the primitive hunter returning exhausted from the chase to seek his rest and comfort by the open fireside. By the fireside he rests, by the fireside he eats, here he meets his family, here in his nakedness he is warm, here are all his joys and loves and comforts. Every pleasure and every comfort are directly associated with the sight of the glowing embers and the bright, leaping blaze. And this has been going on through thousands and thousands of years. When Nature so impresses their habits upon her creatures that the dog, ages after it has become domesticated, will yet run round and round before lying down on a carpet, because its wild ancestors did so in order to flatten the tall grass in which they slept, is it too much to believe that man should have kept the habit of associating comfort with the sight of an open fireside?

Whatever may be the true explanation, the fact was that the glowing fire in the chimney cheered our hearts, and made us merry, as we sat laughing and talking and joking, and listening to the old man's tales that night; and this pure delight was not in any wise lessened by the moaning of the wind and the intermittent dash of the rain upon the walls and roof. We three and Duke, in a sociable semi-circle lighted only by the flickering rays of the fire, enjoyed the shelter, the homelike sense of comfort, and the quiet of perfect content that night, and it seemed to all, I doubt not, as it did to me, a pity that the hour of bedtime should come around to break up so pleasant a party.

CHAPTER XIX.

THE PEARL-FISHERS.

FOR two days longer the rain continued, and then with a gentle southerly breeze the sky cleared and the sun came out again, lighting up once more the land and sea and releasing us from the confinement indoors, which had begun to grow irksome. Of course the first thing to be done was for all three of us to be ferried over the creek and to walk up the beach to the galleon. The two sand-banks were now dry and the water in the basin was quite clear and transparent, so that the hull was plainly visible, the raised poop and forecastle being only about three or four feet under the surface. All her masts and spars had fallen and disappeared long ago. A cluster of corals seemed to indicate where the foremast once had stood. A curious thing was the appearance of a single pane of glass which was visible in the side of the cabin. This pane had changed its transparent quality to a milky condition of pearly irridescence, and shone under water like a gem as it caught and reflected the light from above.

This vessel never could have been noted for speed, I thought, as the hull appeared to be a regular tub, with high bows and stern, a great breadth of beam, and a low mid-deck or waist where lay the green remains of what had once been four brass carronades. When sailing close-hauled she probably went to leeward faster than she drew ahead. Doubtless such was the ancient fashion of ships, and it accounts for the fact that the old voyagers were sometime wind-bound, until the green moss and weeds grew plentiful on their hulls, and the water and provisions gave out, and the dreadful scurvy came to sweep away half the crew. I could picture this lumping old craft as she might have looked when the old admiral commanded her beneath the broad flag of Spain, — her crowded decks, her tall masts, the gorgeous array of bright-colored garments worn by the dusky grandees who were on board, the images of the saints, the crucifix at the wheel, the shaven priest, and all the pomp and ceremony that attended her clumsy progress to strange ports.

I knew the history of her last voyage well. I knew how she had twice rounded Cape Horn and stanchly buffeted the storms of two oceans; of the troops she had landed, the treasure she had taken up, and the final scene when with sails set and colors flying she sank beneath the waves. Long ago every soul who then lived had gone to the other world; the admiral, his officers and his crew, the king and queen and all their court were now returned to dust. Yet here lay the fabric of teak and oak, still strong and stanch and enduring, and the store of gold that I hoped to get. Were the shades of these departed ones aware that a heretic was planning and contriving to get the long sunken treasure, so much of which had been once designed for the coffers of the holy mother Church?

We made a careful survey of the basin, and selected the lesser bank of sand, that forming the breakwater at the narrow end of the chasm, as a suitable site for the pumping-apparatus. Mr. Millward pointed out to me the fact that the water stood higher in the basin than the then level of the sea, — a proof, he insisted, that the water did not percolate to any considerable extent through the firmly packed sand. This was a highly important fact to us. Had it been otherwise we never could have hoped to pump the basin dry, or below the sea level.

With a line we took some measurements which we expected to need, and then set out on our return to the house.

As a matter of convenience we decided to build the water-raising machine complete and set it up and test it at the creek near the house, where we could be near such domestic comforts as we possessed; after which we could load it on the boat and convey it to the chasm. And this work we set about at once. As I have already indicated what this machine was to be I need not here again detail minutely its construction. The wheel we made chiefly of stout bamboo, the water-troughs of hollowed logs; the bearings, in deference to Mr. Millward's recollection of the uncouth screeching of the machine's Indian predecessors, we supplied liberally with grease. In ten days the thing was complete and set up at the creek for trial, — troughs, platform, and all. I had arranged that the water might flow from the troughs into a ditch leading to our garden to irrigate the growing crops.

When all was ready I mounted the wheel, and like a horse in a treadmill (perhaps a better simile would be like a hod-carrier climbing an endless ladder) began to turn it. Up came the full gourds, splashing the water at quick intervals alternately into the two troughs, whence it flowed down to the ditch in tinkling rills, steadily and continuously, as long as I chose to keep up the ladder-climbing action. It was going to prove rather hard work, I fancied; but nevertheless it was a perfect success, as I was continually lifting more than half my own weight in water with as little exertion as could have been required to accomplished that result. Then Mr. Millward tried his footing on the machine; and finally we had to help up Alice to try it in turn. Altogether it was unanimously pronounced a grand success, and we only waited for a fair wind that we might take it down and embark it for the chasm. Unfortunately for our patience, the wind veered around into the northeast again, and was quite too heavy to allow us to make the voyage with safety, as the rollers came tumbling in over the bar at the mouth of the creek at such rate that there would be great danger of swamping the boat in any endeavor we might make to get outside.

I was so impatient at this delay that I had half a mind to take the machine apart and attempt to carry it piecemeal overland. But it was useless to repine over the inevitable. It was not probable that I should gain an hour of time by undertaking to lug the machine overland, and I should simply have a great labor for naught. There was therefore nothing to do but to possess our souls with patience and await the issue.

Aside from the wind, which blew half a gale, the weather was pleasant, and the sun shone warm and bright. As we had nothing better to do, it was agreed that we should make an overland excursion to the old plantation for the purpose of getting some fresh fruit. One morning early, after a good breakfast, we ferried over the creek and started with light hearts and in holiday spirits up the beach, the wind blowing stiffly and the breakers crashing in beside us. I assisted Alice Millward with my arm, for the breeze was strong enough to make walking against it difficult for a woman. With bowed heads we beat slowly along until we reached the hog path, and were glad to turn into it and get under shelter of the vegetation, which broke the wind and made progress comfortable. Neither of my companions had ever been over this road before, and I explained what might be expected from moment to moment as we advanced. When we came to the cleft in the rocks where the stream came through, Alice and her father were delighted with the romantic and picturesque beauty of the place; the bold, precipitous rocks, the stream, the overarching trees growing far above, the dense beds of fern, tall and feathery, were all duly admired.

When we emerged into the north valley, we found a great herd of pigs that scattered and ran wildly at our approach. I managed to lasso a little porker, just old enough to roast, which we proposed to have for dinner. The orange grove was as before plentifully laden with oranges in all stages of growth, many of them quite ripe, a delicious refreshment. We soon reached the house, and building a fire in the broad fireplace of the kitchen, spitted the porker in front of it, and leaving him to twirl slowly before the fire on a twisting cord, we wandered over the old garden and plantation, Alice and I often hand in hand. I felt sure that she was pleased at my undisguised attention to her comfort, and that it gave her pleasure to be with me; and this in turn gave me unspeakable delight.

We were among the bananas and plantains seeking some of the latter to bake as an accompaniment for our dinner of roast pig, when I heard what sounded like the distant report of a gun. The sound was so faint and distant that I could not be entirely sure of my impressions, until I had asked Alice, —

"Did you hear that?"

"Yes," she replied, "it sounded as though somebody had fired a pistol far away over yonder on the high land."

We listened intently several minutes for a repetition of

the sound, but as we heard nothing the impression soon passed away; for our conversation, however uninteresting it would seem if written down, was, I assure you, of most absorbing interest, at least to me, though we talked of nothing in particular, and like children laughed at everything out of mere high spirits. We went now with our plantains to the house, where Mr. Millward was gone to look after the roast. He came out to meet us, smiling at our evident enjoyment as he heard the merry ringing laughter of his daughter, over some nonsense or other I had been putting into words. As we all three stood in the shadow of the great veranda, upon its brick pavement, between the joints of which the rank vegetation was sprouting, I heard again, and this time borne on the wind quite distinctly, two shots in quick succession. There was no mistaking the sound this time. I saw instantly in the faces of both my companions that each had heard the unusual sound. Mr. Millward cried quickly: "A gun! who can be firing a gun on the island?"

"What can this mean?" thought I. And again we listened, but there was no repetition of the report.

"Somebody besides ourselves is on the island," said Mr. Millward.

We stood now looking at each other in silence for several minutes. My mind reverted at once to the pearl-fishers. They had doubtless returned, and the shots we had heard indicated that they were pig-hunting. The same thought had occurred to Mr. Millward, and he immediately expressed his fear that the pearl-fishers had come back. Indeed, it did not need any great power of divination to determine this, because the chances were as a hundred to one against any other visitors. All the picnic and holiday hilarity of our excursion was over. We were full of anxiety and care at once. The probability was that we had neighbors, of a most undesirable character, — lawless adventurers who would have small respect and consideration for us if we stood in their way, or even if they thought so. If they discovered that we had surprised their secret it was impossible to say what they might do. I had often thought of the contingency which now apparently presented itself, and had cogitated much and to no purpose as to what I should do when it arose. And now the thing so long feared as a possibility was actually upon us. Unexpectedly at the last it came like a skeleton to mar our happy feast. We hurried through our dinner in anxious mood and immediately started back home, laden with the fruit we had collected.

When we reached home everything was as we had left it. There had been, so far as we could tell, no visitor in our absence. We arrived about three o'clock in the afternoon. I was restive with the uncertainty and anxiety that the sound of those three gunshots had occasioned. I felt that I must know speedily the exact truth. Our own personal safety, to say nothing of the treasure ship, was possibly involved, and I determined to go at once to Farm Cove, where they would probably be encamped, and reconnoitre the enemy secretly. Of course there would be danger of encountering the pig-hunter, or party of pig-hunters on the way, but I must endeavor by caution to avoid this. When I announced my intention both Mr. Millward and Alice opposed my going; but I was able very soon to convince them that it was necessary.

About four o'clock I started alone, not permitting the dog to accompany me. I took the small axe from Mr. Millward's boat, my lasso, some food, and a small gourd of water slung as a canteen over my shoulder. I told them I might not return until the next day; but that if I did not get back before the next night they might conclude I had been captured; and in that event it would be wise for them to embark in their boat and make the best of their way to Martinique. But Mr. Millward proposed a better plan, which was that if I did not return by the next night, he and Alice, provided the weather was such as to permit it, would take both boats out of the creek and anchor just beyond the breakers, and wait there another day. This was such an excellent idea that I at once agreed to it.

Bidding them farewell I plunged into the forest and made my way cautiously to the central elevated plateau, climbing the rocks by the path which I had first ascended. Here the open nature of the growth made the utmost caution indispensable, for I might at any moment now come upon the visitors, if they were still out pig-hunting. It was necessary that I should see them before they saw me. This made my progress very slow. Looking carefully about in every direction, and listening for every sound, I advanced a hundred yards or so and repeated the observation, concealing myself as thoroughly as the nature of the ground permitted. On the connecting ridge between the central plateau and the shore cliffs I came upon convincing evidence of the presence of visitors on the island. Here a pig had been killed and disembowelled. The viscera still fresh lay upon the ground, and a broad mark where the carcass had been dragged along led away toward the shore cliffs in the direction of Farm Cove. I had now little doubt that I should find the visitors at that place. It was fully an hour before sunset, and I thought it best to conceal myself and wait until dark before advancing further. I secreted myself therefore amid a thick clump of ferns, and patiently waited for the friendly shelter of the night.

As I sat thus buried in the ferns among the moss-grown rocks, looking out through a break in the forest toward the southern sky, where lay a battlemented mass of sun-dyed cloud, heavy and fantastic in outline, there passed through my mind thoughts of the life and curious adventures of that Henry Morgan, my ancestor's brother, who two hundred years ago had roamed these seas and besieged the Spanish strongholds. Fancy pictured in the tinted clouds the fortified city of Porto Bello, the seaport of Panama on the Atlantic side of the isthmus, which the intrepid Morgan attacked with four hundred and sixty of his men, having resolved to reduce this strongly fortified place as a preliminary to the capture of the rich city of Panama itself. There was in my mind the vision of the gray walls, the gorgeous banners, the smoke and roar of guns, the white-faced priest and pale nuns looking from the convent walls, the scaling-ladders, the grim, determined Anglo-Saxon sailors, mingled with the equally determined Dutch and the black-bearded Frenchmen, constituting Morgan's little band. I could see in fancy the flashing, blood-stained blades, and hear the hoarse battle-cry. I could even fancy my ancestral uncle himself, broad-shouldered and commanding in appearance as he needs must have been, standing, fire-balls in hand, on the scaling-ladder, grimy with powder, and with his face set toward the doomed city. There must have been something more than mere brute force in this great leather-clad ancestral uncle of mine with his flashing eyes and sturdy figure; for did he not control absolutely at one time all this region; conquer the all-conquering Spaniard; quell mutinies among his reckless followers with ease; lead them without food across the fever-stricken isthmus, travelling amid inconceivable obstacles ever onward until they were actually reduced to eating their leathern doublets; then with this starved crew did he not besiege and capture the rich city of Panama? When a mutiny rose and some of his desperate followers threatened to desert him for a piratical cruise in one of the captured ships, Morgan, like Hernando Cortez, but with his own hand, chopped down the masts and rigging. Ah, there must have been a spirit in this man greater than a mere piratical thirst for blood. Then too, did not his sovereign, Charles II., bestow upon him subsequently the order of knighthood, make him Sir Henry Morgan, and place him as governor over the island of Jamaica? He died without descendants of his own, the honors bestowed upon him in the later days of his career are no longer remembered, and in the region he once dominated his name is used to frighten children with. He is now remembered only as a buccaneer, a name almost synonymous with "pirate;" a dauntless, reckless, blood-thirsty, unconquerable embodiment of energy and will, brooking no power near him save his own, — truly a leader of men, but exercising his leadership to no good purpose. Though he once controlled the Spanish main, we fail to see it recorded that he ever did good to any man.

Here was I now, two hundred years later, perhaps the sole surviving representative of his family, his sole heir, seeking to recover a treasure that he conquered, a treasure which I had already brought up from the depths of the sea, and which only waited to be possessed. I felt the old spirit of the dead Morgans fire my heart at the thought of the possible intervention of a crew of lawless pearl-fishers to snatch the prize from my grasp. The treasure was mine, doubly mine, — first by conquest of one to whom I was heir; and secondly by right of discovery and recovery from the sea. "No! by the Eternal, they shall not have it!" I cried, half aloud. "By the bones of my all-conquering ancestor, they shall never have an ounce of it, not so much as a glimpse of it!"

When it grew dark I resumed my progress toward Farm Cove, stealing along as cautiously as I could over the somewhat broken way. Every few steps I would pause and listen. It was dark as a pocket, and the cloudy sky was scarcely discernible. But still, by keeping the wind on my right cheek it was not difficult to preserve the proper direction, and I knew that however dark the night, the sea would be visible when I reached the cliffs, just as the sky was faintly distinguishable now through the black foliage above me.

It took me fully an hour to cover the comparatively short distance that remained, and it was not done without several falls on the way; but fortunately I made no great noise, though an occasional dry branch would break under foot with a sharp crack, which in the stillness sounded alarmingly loud to my tense senses. In due course, groping along, I came to the cliffs and could see the faint glimmer of the water through the foliage. Then as I parted some branches I caught sight of the red reflection of a fire on the leaves below, then the bright blaze of the fire itself, and a canvas tent which was lighted by it. Increased caution was now demanded. It would not do to step on a dry branch now, so at each step I felt cautiously with my foot that nothing might intervene between it and the ground. Fortunately I came out upon the path which led down the rocks into the little vale that lay, as I have previously described, like a bowl, open on one side to the sea and nearly surrounded by the cliffs. Down this path I stole cautiously, and was half-way down before the intervening foliage would permit a fair view of the encampment.

And now I was almost near enough to hear the conversation that was going on among the people assembled there. Indeed, I could hear the hum of voices, but was unable to distinguish words. In the light of the bright fire I could see four men seated on the ground playing cards on a folded blanket. They were evidently gambling. One of the four was a yellow-skinned Chinaman, who sat facing me. Opposite him and with his back toward me was a great, burly negro, while the other two players were dark-skinned, black-haired native Indians or Caribbeans. The game was an animated one, and the players were completely absorbed in it. Near by the fire, seated on a fagot of wood, was a third Indian, his head bent forward and resting on his hands as he looked steadily into the fire. From where I was located I could not see into the tent, which consisted of a square of canvas thrown over a pole and stretched shed-fashion to the ground, with the opening toward the fire. But I could plainly see on the canvas the shadow of a person seated within the tent. On a limb near by hung distended the dressed carcass of a hog. I could just make out that some sort of a craft was moored at the mouth of the little stream.

I watched this scene for several minutes scarce daring to breathe. The three Indians, each carrying a long knife in his belt, were, I conjectured, the divers of the party; the Chinaman was doubtless the cook; and as for the negro, I could not determine approximately his place.

Suddenly the players fell to quarrelling, and one of the Indians, with an angry cry, sprang up and drew his knife. Instantly the whole party was on foot, and I fully expected from their excited manner and attitude to see blood shed. Just at this juncture the person in the tent — a man — came quickly out, with a drawn revolver in his hand, and sprang into the mêlée, cursing and shouting in a loud, deep voice of command for them to desist. He was a broad, compactly built fellow, of forty years or thereabouts, evidently possessed of great muscular strength; for he was able with his unoccupied hand to seize by the shoulder the Indian who had drawn the knife, and with one effort send him reeling backward almost to the ground.

"Caramba!" cried he, in guttural Spanish. "Dogs, stop this fighting, do you hear? If I find you at it again there shall be no more card-playing. Go to bed, or keep quiet, you quarrelsome scoundrels."

The fight was over. All seemed alike to fear him, and when I saw his countenance in the firelight I could not wonder. It was a dark, powerful, and passionate face, framed in by a short black beard. Dark enough for a Spaniard, there was yet something in the countenance that made me think he was not of the Latin race; more likely a dark Englishman or an American. Perhaps his dress and general appearance contributed to this conclusion. He was the only white man in the party, and that he was master, or chief, did not admit of a doubt.

Now that I had seen this cut-throat-looking gang and their chief, my apprehension as to what they might attempt if they found us on the island and in possession of their pearl-fishing secret was by no means allayed. As to what would happen if they by any chance should discover the galleon, I felt only too certain.

Crouched down among the dark leafage by the side of the path I remained, a prey to many thoughts, for a quarter of an hour longer, and then stole cautiously back up the path to the high ground above, and began my return home through the darkness. When I had put a considerable distance between me and the party I had left, I began to breath more freely. In the murky darkness I more than once missed the way, and finally came out at a place where, though I could plainly hear the murmur of the waters of the creek below me, it was impossible to descend.

However, by travelling first in one direction and then in the other, I at last came upon the little gulley which I had before descended, and getting down was able to proceed with greater speed along the more familiar route. It was midnight when I at last reached the house and roused Mr. Millward and Alice to relate to them what I had seen.

As we were safe for that night at least, I proposed that we should go to bed again and get our rest, and discuss our situation in the morning.

CHAPTER XX.

THE CAPTAIN OF THE GANG.

THOUGH considerably exhausted by my toilsome tramp and the excitement of the reconnoissance, I got very little sleep after I retired to my hammock that night. Not until near dawn did unconsciousness come; and as is usually the case under such circumstances, though my mind during these hours of sleeplessness dwelt continually on the danger that threatened not only our plans but ourselves as well, nothing came of the thought except added apprehension. There is scarcely ever any good result from what may be best termed "worry." The mind, like the body, refuses to act when deprived of its usual rest. One may indeed fancy he is thinking most deeply, during the still hours of the night when he should be sleeping, but in truth such thought is rarely genuine; it is only puerile worry, totally lacking in virility and potency to solve real difficulties. The fatigued brain like a coward magnifies all obstacles, and at the same time overlooks their solution, and ignores the hopes that rise to illumine the fresh intelligence of the rested thinker.

The consequence was I did not waken in the morning until called to breakfast by Alice Millward well on toward eight o'clock.

The gale had sunk to a gentle breeze from the same quarter. The bright blue sky was flecked here and there with high clouds, soft and fleecy white, their shadows a mellow, purple gray. It was a fresh, bright, beautiful morning, such as breathes hope and confidence in the apprehensive mind. I immediately began to discount the probabilities of impending disaster that had oppressed me, and our talk at the breakfast table was all in a hopeful strain. What right had we to suppose the pearl-fishing gang would discover us? It was not probable they would stay long, — a month or two at farthest, — and there was no telling how long they had already been here. They would be busy at their work on the other side of the island, with nothing to cause them to wander about except the pig-hunting, when they wanted fresh pork. If they should chance to descend from the central cliffs, they could not see our habitation or boats, unless they should happen to come around the island to the beach above or below us.

It behooved us therefore to lie close for the present, and the chances seemed to favor our escaping notice. By carefully guarding against raising a smoke during the day with our fires, we should greatly diminish the chances of being discovered, and at night we would keep no fire. We could lower the masts of the boats, and by mooring them a little farther up they would be partly hidden by the willows. So, too, as to the galleon; unless one actually climbed upon the rocks and looked down into the basin, there was nothing in the external appearance of the place from sea or shore to denote its existence. The vines I had planted now grew most luxuriantly over the shed and the house, so that a casual observer from a distance might well fail to distinguish human habitations. There was, however, the naked palm tree with its cross-piece which I had rigged long ago as a distress signal, standing most conspicuously. This must come down at once; it would be plainly visible at a great distance up and down the beach, and from the sea. A few blows of the axe would soon remedy that. Thus we discussed the situation; and although bad enough in all conscience to cause us much mental disturbance, it did not seem without hope.

After arranging our belongings so that they would attract as little attention as possible, we sat quietly down to await events. We read aloud by turns from Charles Dickens's beautiful story "Our Mutual Friend;" Mr. Millward revived his early experiences; we improvised a checker-board and finally a set of chess-men, and Mr. Millward and I pondered long over intricate situations arising from Evans gambit. Nevertheless the time hung heavy on our hands, owing to the shadow of anxiety that was over us. Mention was seldom made of the pearl-fishers, but they were always more or less in mind. Thus passed three days, during which we heard nothing from the other party on the island.

On the morning of the fourth day, two hours before dawn, I departed for a second reconnoissance, intending to conceal myself in some place where I could remain during a portion of the daylight for the purpose of getting a better knowledge of our neighbors and their doings. By starlight I readily made my way to the cliffs about Farm Cove, and there, just as the dawn was breaking, concealed myself in a bed of fern growing among the rocks. From the lay of the land I judged there would be no difficulty in seeing the camp from where I was hidden, and such proved to be the case. By the aid of a glass belonging to Mr. Millward I could bring the camp up to an apparent distance not exceeding two rods.

The whole party was asleep, so far as I could judge, when I first observed them. About an hour after sunrise the Chinaman rose up from his blanket, and after yawning and stretching himself in sleepy fashion proceeded to build a fire and cook a breakfast for the party. This was soon done, and then he went from one to the other of the sleepers and roused them. The breakfast for the white man was carried into the tent.

After the eating was over the whole party, except the Chinaman, went down to the boat, which was a good-sized sloop, of twice the tonnage of either of ours, and embarked, pulling out of the creek by a warp laid out to a buoy for that purpose. They had a good-sized dingy, or better, a yawl, in tow. When they reached the buoy, which was at a distance of forty rods or thereabouts from shore, they made fast to it, and the three Indians with the negro got into the yawl and pulled away a hundred yards or so to the south, the white man remaining on board the sloop, where I could see him sitting near the tiller smoking a cigar.

When the party in the yawl reached the distance mentioned, the negro being at the oars, they came to a standstill, and I could see the Indians strip for diving. The operation was wholly new to me and interesting. They took turns one after another. The fellow whose turn it was to dive got over the side and took hold of a line, to the end of which a great stone was tied, and which was provided with two loops, in which he inserted his feet. When he was all ready one of the other Indians allowed the rope to pay out rapidly, and down sank the diver carrying a sort of bag hung around his neck. After the Indian had been down what seemed to me an extraordinary length of time for a man to stay under water, he came up without the bag and clung to the side of the boat seemingly in a state of utter exhaustion. The two Indians in the boat then helped him on board and he immediately lay down, while his companions hauled up the stone again and brought inboard the bag, from which they emptied perhaps a bushel of great flat oysters. Then another took his turn, and so on in rotation, until a considerable heap of the great bivalves, each of which was four or five inches in diameter, was collected. These they carried to the sloop and began again, shifting their position a little each time under the direction of the man on the sloop, who sat watching and smoking the whole time.

I had heard remarkable stories of the length of time pearl-divers could remain under water, some accounts putting it as high as ten minutes, and I was sorry I had no timepiece with me to find out how long the men before me actually stayed down. As a substitute for a more accurate method, I timed them several times by counting my own pulse-beats. Allowing seventy-five beats to the minute, which I believe was about right, the longest time I could make out was a little over two minutes. The shortness of the time was a surprise to me, for judging from my untimed observations the apparent duration was frequently between five and ten minutes. I think the exaggerated accounts we receive are due to the natural tendency of an observer who does not actually measure the time to think it longer than it really is.

The oyster-gathering thus conducted in my view was a slow business, as the divers did not go down oftener than once in fifteen or twenty minutes, and were seemingly in no hurry to go down at all, though willing enough to come up. This was the frequent occasion of rough and stern command from the man in the sloop, who kept up a more or less constant talk across the water with his subordinates. When a diver would come up too soon or with a light find, a string of imprecations in Spanish would greet him; so, too, when one hesitated too long before he plunged in.

When I had watched this performance for an hour

or two I began to think of getting back home. The Chinaman had finished his work and was seated at the foot of a tree knitting a white cotton sock, his fingers plying the bright steel needles as fast as ever I saw a grandmother do it. He sat precisely facing my place of concealment, and every now and then would look up and around, his needles still going with automatic regularity. This was very annoying. I did not dare to move so long as he sat there; for if he should chance to look up while I was scaling the rock just back of me — a height of perhaps ten feet — to reach the summit of the cliff, discovery was almost certain. I was obliged, therefore, to remain where I was.

In order to improve the time I examined the interior of the tent with the telescope. The only thing I saw of interest there was a double-barrelled breech-loading shot-gun slung to the ridgepole, with a belt of cartridges. You may be sure I coveted the possession of this weapon and its ammunition, and had there been any way to get it, should not under the circumstances have hesitated to appropriate it to my own use and the defence of my friends. But even if I had succeeded in getting it without being seen by the knitting Chinaman its loss would at once be discovered and the presence of others on the island immediately suspected. I now turned my glass on the Chinaman and soon saw him close his eyes while still knitting away. He looked up now no longer, but his fingers kept on plying the needles. His head gradually sunk upon his breast. The man was evidently knitting in his sleep! A moment later his hands fell into his lap, and after a few more of the automatic movements became still. I lost no further time in climbing back to the summit and getting out of sight in the forest, from whence I made my way home safely.

We continued to lie close at home after this, as before. In order that no smoke should rise by day we now made a practice of cooking at night-time in the fireplace so that the fire would not be visible. We did not venture out on the beach at any time during daylight where we might be seen from a distance. This life continued thus for a week, and I had about made up my mind to take another trip to Farm Cove to see if the pearl-fishers were still there. This, however, became unnecessary, for just as I had reached that conclusion we were informed of the fact that the visitors were still present by the sound of several shots from the centre of the island.

To occupy some of the time that hung so heavy on our hands, Mr. Millward and I took down the pumping-machine and loaded it on the big boat, to be in readiness to carry to the basin when we should feel it safe to do so. We went out fishing after dark in the smaller boat several times to eke out our supply of provisions by a stock of fresh fish. One night I was fortunate enough to turn a fine turtle, which gave us a good supply of meat and a plenty of eggs. The latter made a fairly good omelet, but had a slightly unpleasant oily taste.

Thus passed another week of enforced idleness. I cannot deny that the society of Alice Millward proved an ample compensation to me for this delay in our plans. We were almost constantly together, and there grew up between us, I was certain, a perfect feeling of comradeship, even if it went no further on her part. A thousand times during this period of intimate association my great love for this sweet girl, who grew sweeter and dearer as I came to know her better, impelled me to speak to her of my regard. But I did not do so. It seemed to me then that by so doing I might risk the delight of her companionship. As our present relations stood we were happy in each other's friendship. Her beautiful eyes looked into mine so frankly and cordially, her hand lay often so confidingly in my own, her smile was so friendly and sweet, that I dared not risk the utterance of words which, if they found no response in her own heart, would make mine so desolate. You may perhaps quote to me the old adage that "faint heart never won fair lady." But please remember my situation. You would not ask a shipwrecked mariner to give up the plank on which he floats; no more could you ask me to risk the only joy I knew. If there lurked discomfort in the uncertainty, certainty might develop more than discomfort — utter despair. I trust that I am not a coward in all things; yet in this thing my heart beat faint at the possibility of disappointment.

It seemed to me that her father more than half guessed the state of my heart. But he never said a word to indicate it to me, and I only judged so from his manner at times; for example, from the fond way in which he would look at his daughter, or stroke her hair, — little things which suggested to my mind the idea that he thought of the time when another might claim her from him. My turbulent heart would beat then at the bare possibility that I might be that happy man. It must be a great sorrow for a loving parent, who tenderly cherished a daughter through helpless infancy and childhood, till she blossoms into womanhood, to see her wooed and won away by a stranger — a sorrow that is not less poignant because untainted by any selfish desire to hinder the loved one from leaving the home nest, and acquiring new loves and affections which shall inevitably displace to a great degree the old ones. It is small consolation to the heart bereft that it is the course of nature. That does not bring back the lost one. The parent would not have it different, and yet the grief is there. Akin to this is the fond regret of the mother who sees with mingled pride and sorrow her babe grow out of its sweet helplessness. Day by day the little one must seem to become less and less a part of herself. Her old love may take on a new form, but it is not so dear a form.

One beautiful morning as we sat in the shed eating a late breakfast and engaged in a lively conversation concerning the successful manner in which we had evaded the notice of our neighbors at Farm Cove, wondering if they were still there, and if so how long they would remain, we were all surprised to see Duke come running into the shed as fast as he could go, and plunge under the table with his tail between his legs and a cowed air about him that was quite strange to the dog. The action was remarkable, for Duke was a well-bred dog, and this conduct was not only peculiar but also in very bad form. I got up immediately and looked up and down the beach. There, not ten rods away and coming straight toward the shed, was the chief of the pearl-fishing gang. Positively for a second or two I felt paralyzed. Mr. Millward and Alice were almost immediately beside me; and as soon as I could control myself I said to them in a low tone, "It is the leader."

The man advanced with a perfectly assured self-possession, and when near took off his broad panama hat, bowed with great dignity and no lack of courtly grace, saying in Spanish, "The day is better for beholding you."

"Good morning, sir," said Mr. Millward.

"Ah, very good; you speak English," said the stranger in our own tongue and with no trace of foreign pronunciation or accent. "I am glad. It is my own language. You will pardon me for intruding upon you. But I only followed my dog which has been lost for some time, and which I have just found. He ran into your premises, as you noticed just now."

"Then your name must be H. Senlis," said I to him with as much politeness of demeanor as I could command.

"True, my friend," replied he, suavely; "no doubt you may read it on the dog's collar. H. Senlis is my name, and Duke is my dog. The rascal mutinied and ran away from me, but that makes him no less my property."

His property was at that moment cowering under the table, looking very much as an escaped convict might at the appearance of his keeper.

"Of course, Mr. Senlis," said I, "if the dog is yours, as it seems he is, we lay no claim to him. He came to us as a stray animal. You have a right to your property, though we should be sorry to lose him. If you had not claimed him it was our intention to carry him away from the island soon at our departure."

"Poor Duke!" said Alice; "we shall not like to part with him."

Off came the panama again with a most profound bow, and he said, "Do not distress yourself, lady. It is not my intention or desire to take the dog from you. It became necessary for me to punish him for insubordination. He ran away. He is still in a mutinous mind, and I have no use for him unless it be to punish him again, and that is hardly worth the while, as I fear he is incorrigible. Permit me then to surrender to you" — another profound bow — "all my right and remaining title in the animal."

The man's effusive, overdone politeness, the bold, undisguised stare which he gave to Alice, all tended to confuse the girl so that she answered nothing to this speech.

Her father noticing this broke in by saying, "We were just at breakfast when you came up. Will you partake of our fare?"

"Surely I will, and with much pleasure," answered the stranger; and thereupon as we gave way he entered the shed, and when I had procured him a seat we all four sat down at the table. As he came in Duke rapidly departed from under the table.

The stranger's appetite appeared to be excellent, judging from the quantity of baked pork and beans and hot corn bread he disposed of, and the gourd of steaming hot coffee he drank.

"How do you happen to be here?" said he at length to Mr. Millward.

"We are castaways," answered the old man, and added, "When I landed here a few months ago I was helpless, unable to move a limb, in short, paralyzed. But I am recovering, and may say, indeed, that I am now almost myself again."

"Then you have been here several months," said the stranger, his eyes fixed on Mr. Millward.

"Yes."

"Why do you remain here, now that you are well? Or is it that you cannot get away?"

"Can you assist us to get away?" said Mr. Millward, and I was somewhat amused at the delicate diplomacy of this reply.

"Well," said the stranger, "it may be possible. I will see what can be done. Our boat is rather small and heavily laden. But I will see. I will see, and let you know."

At this point I broke in, saying, "When did you land?"

"We came yesterday," said he, coolly; "a party of us are here pig-hunting."

"There is a great plenty of pigs to be had," said I, accepting the lie without remark. "When do you intend leaving?"

"We shall not remain long, — two or three days, or perhaps a week," said he; and after a pause he added, "but I will let you know in time."

He inquired our names, and where we wanted to go; praised the breakfast unstintedly; bent furtive glances of coarse admiration on Alice from time to time; and conducted himself all through with the utmost assurance.

When we rose from the table and went out on the beach, he drew some long, plantation Cuban cigars from his pocket, offered us each one, which we did not refuse, and we began to smoke together.

Presently he spied on the beach one of the cages of gourds such as we had used in raising the galleon, — an extra one, not used. He walked up to this object and contemplated it for several moments, turning it over with his foot.

Finally he said, "Mr. Millward, I am a good deal puzzled over this thing. I suppose it was cast up here by the sea. Can you tell me what it is for?"

"I cannot, Mr. Senlis."

"Well, it is very surprising indeed. In our sloop in the open sea a hundred miles west of here we came across thousands of these things floating in the water — literally thousands of them, all just like this one, four gourds in a willow cage, with a wooden hook at the end of a line. If it is some sort of fishing-apparatus I don't understand how it could be used. And where did they all come from?"

Though this made me feel decidedly uncomfortable, I could hardly forbear laughing, as the thought of the sea full of gourds, and the puzzle which they would present to a chance navigator, came thus forcibly to mind.

He looked at the thing a moment longer, gave it a vicious kick as though to punish it for daring to puzzle him, and then turned away.

Mr. Millward then took him to our flourishing garden, and said the visitors would be welcome to a supply of fresh vegetables if they desired it. A huge bunch of plantains caught the captain's eye, as it hung in the porch of the house, and he said, " Do you find plantains on the island ? "

" Yes," answered Mr. Millward, " and bananas as well. If you like we can supply your party with both."

" If we expected to remain long it would be an object. But we shall be going so soon now that it is scarcely worth the trouble."

We then returned to the house at the visitor's suggestion, and he with the most formal courtesy, as though parting with a hostess, took Alice Millward's hand and thanked her for his breakfast and said adieu to her and us.

"You will hear from me in a day or two, a week at most. In the mean time I hope you will not disturb the pigs. Perhaps it would be better if you should keep away from the higher part of the island entirely, as it might drive our game into the lowlands where it would be more difficult to find."

After a pause, as though considering something, he added : " Personally, I should be pleased to have you visit our camp, which is on the other side of the island. But I will not now ask you to do so, for the reason that it will be difficult for me to induce my companions to submit to the inconvenience that would result from our making room for three additional persons in our boat.

Perhaps on the whole it would be best that they should not know you are here at present, and until I have had opportunity to prepare them for your reception. I will let you know in time. And now farewell until I see you again."

With this he stalked off over the savanna to the southwest, without again looking back. The cool, self-possessed manner in which the man had lied was astonishing. And we were utterly unable to determine his purpose, beyond the fact that evidently he wanted to conceal the nature of his business on the island.

CHAPTER XXI.

SELF-BETRAYED.

THE consternation and bewilderment caused to our little party by the pearl-fishing captain's visit may be better imagined than described.

The captain's burly figure had hardly disappeared when Duke came back wagging his tail. Alas! poor dog, he little knew the trouble he had caused his friends. He came up and laid his head down on Alice's knee to be patted, and made much of her as was his wont.

Of course we discussed the recent event in all its bearings. The only definite result of the long talk, however, was the general conclusion, which can perhaps be best stated in Mr. Millward's words, as follows:

"We are discovered," he said, "just as we were congratulating ourselves that we would not be. The man does not know, however, that we are aware of the pearl-fishery. He believes, on the contrary, that we are not aware of it. If we are not apprised of his secret he can have no object in doing us harm. He tells us the first convenient lie that occurs to him to gain time to think matters over. However bad he may be in fact, it is not to be expected that he will go to the length of wantonly murdering three people for no purpose; and I feel, therefore, that we are safe as long as he does not fear that we have discovered his secret. That he intends to offer us a passage on his sloop I do not believe at all. That would be to betray his business here at once; for even if the general character and appearance of the men and apparatus did not suggest it, when we reached port it would inevitably come out. I am inclined to believe he told the truth when he said that the party did not intend to remain long on the island. Now, if we can keep matters as they are at present, the gang will doubtless remove all evidence of their occupation, and then quietly leave the island, and leave us to get away as best we may."

This all seemed reasonable and probable. Our cue, therefore, was plainly not to discover the pearl-fishery secret, but to remain quietly at home and await events, without attempting to invade our neighbor's privacy.

That this was a wise conclusion was made evident that very day in the afternoon, as follows: —

In plain sight of the house and on the skirts of the savanna, or open grass-land, there grew a huge silk cotton-tree, with buttressed trunk and spreading branches. I chanced to be looking that way and noticed a flock of parrots fly to the tree and then, instead of lighting on its branches as they seemed to have intended, break up into a confused body as though something therein alarmed them, and scatter in all directions. My first impression was to go up to the tree, which was perhaps an eighth of a mile distant, to investigate. Then the idea occurred to me that the flurry among the birds might have been caused by the captain or some of his gang lurking there to spy upon us. To satisfy my mind on this point, I went to the house and got Mr. Millward's glass, and putting it through a crevice which I cut in the wall for that purpose, examined the neighborhood of the distant tree very carefully. Presently I saw, perched high in the branches, and partly concealed by the foliage, so as to be quite invisible to the naked eye, my old acquaintance the Chinaman. There he was comfortably ensconced among the limbs, knitting away at his white sock, just as I had before seen him. Undoubtedly he was on watch to spy out our doings.

"Watch on, my celestial friend," thought I; "we shall endeavor to conduct ourselves to the eminent satisfaction of your black-whiskered patron."

I reported the discovery of the spy to my companions, and we had a quiet laugh to ourselves over the matter. The only thing we did in consequence of the discovery was to tie up poor Duke in the shed for fear that he might find the Chinaman and occasion him some uneasiness of mind. For, in truth, the fact that the captain had set his Chinaman to watch us was a thing that comforted me amazingly. I reasoned it out in this fashion: So long as the captain knew we stayed safely at home, so long would he feel that his secret was safe; and so long as he felt his secret safe, so long would he lack motive to molest us. The spy was a guarantee that he would know that we were not spying about ourselves.

Four days passed thus. Each day I cautiously examined the tree with the glass, and each time found either the Chinaman or the negro mounted on guard. Whether they kept up the espionage at night as well as by day I had no means for determining satisfactorily. From the actions of the dog at times I imagined, however, that they did so.

On the morning of the fifth day of this watch, at about eight o'clock, we received a second visit from Captain Senlis. He brought the carcass of a young pig just killed, and inquired, after a little general conversation, where the plantains were to be found. I endeavored to tell him as plainly as I could where the old plantation was located and how he might get there, and finally volunteered to guide him to the hog-path and put him in the right course to reach the north valley. He remained with us half an hour, and then expressed a desire to be guided as I had suggested. Now this required that we should cross the creek, and as I had no notion of letting him see our boats, we waded over the stream breast-deep, and walked on up the beach. When we got to the hog-path I pointed it out to him, and explained that he only needed to follow it until he reached the gorge, and to pass on through the latter into the valley; that he would then have no difficulty in finding the fruit trees; but that in order to get out of the valley he would be obliged to return through the gorge, as the surrounding cliffs were very precipitous. He asked me then suspiciously if I had ever attempted to scale the cliffs surrounding this valley. I truthfully answered that I never had, and indeed, never had occasion to do so.

He asked me minutely about the topography of the valley, and I described it to him as well as I could, — the surrounding wall of cliff, the little harbor, the buildings, fields, orange groves, etc. He was particularly interested apparently in the harbor, and I thought I could readily understand why, though of course I did not hint that I knew he was thinking of it as a secure place of concealment in the prosecution of his future diving operations. At length he started into the path, and I followed for a little way continuing the conversation. When we were well into the forest I said I need go no farther, and we parted, he going on and I returning on the path.

When I came out on the beach it occurred to me that this was an excellent opportunity to walk up to the basin and take a look at the galleon, to see how she came on. There was nobody in sight, and I was already half-way there. I had bitter cause subsequently to regret this foolish performance, as you will presently see.

When I reached the place I climbed upon the rocks and looked down into the basin. There was the galleon peacefully resting in the clear, calm pool, visible from end to end through the transparent water. I stood thus contemplating this object, so interesting to me, for perhaps a quarter of an hour, and then came down upon the beach and started home. I walked quietly along, in no special hurry to be back, entirely without suspicion of any misfortune, and thinking of the time when our troublesome neighbors would be gone, when suddenly I saw in the damp sand tracks which I at once recognized as having been made by the feet of the Chinaman. There was no mistaking these footprints. They could only have been made by the peculiar shoe worn by that people. The prints indicated that he had come diagonally out on to the beach to the edge of the water and then run in again toward the forest.

I took this all in at a glance and read its meaning instantly. The almond-eyed spy had followed me up the beach, and here was where he had run out to get sight of me as I turned in toward the rocks. No doubt he had seen me looking into the basin. I did not pause in my walk, for he might even now be watching me; but I edged in slowly toward the jungle and got out of sight. Then I looked back up the beach, but could see nothing. Would the Chinaman go up and look into the basin, or would he content himself with simply following me to see that I did not go toward Farm Cove? I determined to find out. There was nothing in sight. I could not go through the jungle, so I came boldly out and ran up the beach close to the bushes as fast as I could until I had gone about twenty rods. By going out to the water I could now see the rocks of the basin. So I lay down flat on the sand and rolled out nearly to the water's edge. If the Chinaman was there watching he might wonder; but no matter, I would take that chance. When far enough out I looked toward the rocks, and saw the spy there at the basin looking in just as I had done. It was enough. His back was turned. I sprang to my feet and ran back under cover. Our secret was out now with a vengeance, and all through my own stupidity. The situation was a desperate one. The treasure seemed in a fair way to be irretrievably lost. Without arms Mr. Millward and I could not cope with the pearl-fishing gang, and it was too much to expect that on this remote island, far from the power of the law, they would respect our prior right to the cargo of the old vessel which we had brought up from the deep. They would do what they pleased, and would doubtless speedily please to go diving in the basin; and we would be powerless to prevent it.

With head bent down I slowly made my way home. There was a gloomy party there that day. Of course no one blamed me for the misfortune but myself. That was, however, no consolation. I was so fully convinced that the truculent Senlis and his gang would seize on the treasure of the galleon, that I already counted it almost as good as lost. Still I did not entirely despair, and did not intend to give up all effort until the treasure was actually gone. But what could we do? Mr. Millward thought we could do absolutely nothing.

"Don't grieve over spilt milk, my boy," said he, kindly, in an effort to soothe my terrible disappointment. "There are far greater sorrows in this world than the mere loss of money."

Alice, too, was full of sympathy, and put her hand on

my shoulder without a word. But I could read well enough in her face what she would say.

No one could suggest any plan of action except that now it might perhaps be quite as well for us to embark and leave the island and the dangerous neighborhood of the captain and his crew. But I was not willing to do this until I knew with definiteness what were his intentions. We finally concluded that as soon as it was dark we would get the boats ready and go out to sea, where we could watch proceedings in safety.

About four o'clock in the afternoon the captain came sauntering down the beach. I knew quite well that he had seen the galleon, or at least the inference that the Chinaman had reported it to him was almost certain. But though he crossed the creek and came to the shed where we were all seated and talked with us a while, he said not a word concerning the subject that was uppermost in all our minds. Could it be possible the Chinaman had not told him? No; I could dismiss that idea from my mind; it was too improbable. He knew of the wreck, and moreover he knew that I knew of it. His present demeanor was simply the outcome of his naturally secretive disposition. But there was one thing he did not know, and I did not intend to let him know it. And that was the fact that we were aware he knew of the galleon. So I said nothing that would lead him to suspect that I had been watching his spy; nor did the others.

The man's deceitful nature, which I well comprehended by this time, coupled with the offensive air of gallantry which he exhibited toward Alice Millward, together with the fact that I felt sure he intended to overhaul the galleon and seize upon the fruits of our tremendous labor, made me feel as though I should like to have it out with him there and then. And the effort I was obliged to make to control my feelings did not add to my comfort while he stayed. I was very glad, as we all were, when he left.

Just before sunset I strolled into the grove of cocoanuts about half a mile from the house, on no special errand but just idly thinking over the condition into which our affairs had drifted. I was so absorbed in my own thoughts that for the time I had forgotten our determination to stay close at home. As I was standing near a tall palm, with my hands in my pockets, I was rudely awakened from my revery by the whistle of a bullet close to my head, and the report of a pistol following immediately after. I got behind the tree in short order and watched to see if I could discover the author of this wanton attack. That it was the captain or some of his gang I had no doubt; most probably it was the captain, for so far as I knew he was the only one who carried firearms.

I waited where I was for half an hour, until the dusk had come, and then went home. I did not tell of this adventure just then, as it was not necessary to make my friends feel uneasy. They had heard the shot, but attached no special importance to it. This deliberate attempt to murder me made me feel strongly the danger of our remaining longer on shore. I had no right on any account to subject Alice and her father for a moment more to the tender mercies of such a gang of cutthroats. Let the galleon and its treasure go if necessary, we must put to sea at once. The full moon would rise by nine o'clock, and as we wanted to be off shore before that time, we had to hurry our preparation. The boats were fortunately both provided with a supply of fresh water in gourds, which would keep sweet, and it did not take us long to put our provisions on board, together with such things as we thought we might need for a voyage. The masts were down in both boats, having been lowered for the purpose of concealment. We were obliged, therefore, to have recourse to our oars, rowing the large boat and towing mine after it. We had forgotten Duke, but he came swimming after us just as we were about to leave the creek, and I helped him on board. As I did so my hand came in contact with his collar. I stopped the boat and took this collar off, for the reason that it bore the name of Senlis, and dropped it overboard into the sea. I smile when I think of the childish performance; but it seemed to me then that I could not bear to have anything near me pertaining to the truculent knave. And I have no doubt that Duke also felt delighted, and with much more reason. My companions both noticed the act, but said nothing.

Just as we got beyond the rollers I made out in the darkness the figure of a man running down to the beach. I knew he could see us better than we could see him.

"Pull, Mr. Millward!" I cried; "they are after us. Get down in the bottom of the boat, Alice, quick! they may shoot."

The words were hardly out of my mouth when three pistol-shots were fired in rapid succession, and the balls whistled close by us. From the flash I thought I could make out the captain as the murderous assailant.

He did not fire again and we were soon out of range, and casting anchor began the work of setting up the masts and rigging. The light of the moon, which soon rose, showed nobody on the beach. It was almost light enough to read coarse print, and this facilitated our work greatly. As soon as the boats were in sailing trim we stood off to the north with a gentle breeze coming from the south. By midnight we were off the north cape, and here we cast anchor in plain sight of the rocks surrounding the galleon basin and in such a position that we could see the pearl-divers' boat long before it could come within gunshot, if it should put to sea and attempt to round the cape.

I now told my companions of the narrow escape I had had at the cocoanut grove, which, owing to more recent events, was no surprise to them.

We arranged to keep a watch as follows: I would take the first watch until two o'clock; then Alice would watch until four, and Mr. Millward until six, and then I would take another turn while they slept in the morning. Alice insisted on taking her share of this duty.

Mr. Millward rolled himself up in the bottom of the boat and in five minutes was sound asleep. Alice and I sat in the stern sheets together. She insisted she was not sleepy, and wanted to change the order of the watches agreed upon, and to take the first watch herself. This I would not let her do, as I had determined if she went to sleep not to waken her. I could not persuade her to lie down. We sat silently thus for half an hour, when I saw that she had fallen asleep. I gently drew her toward me that she might rest with some comfort, and held her thus unconscious in my arms, the moonlight falling softly upon her sweet, pale face. I felt that here was a treasure to console me for the loss of the galleon.

The long, heaving swell rocked us gently, and the soft plash of the water against the boat sung a lullaby. More than once I found my heavy eyelids about to close. Then I would rouse myself up, for fear of disturbing the dear burden that rested upon me, and look about. Nothing came in sight. I could see the rocks where lay the galleon; the long line of breakers down the beach; the sea stretching clear to the horizon on all sides except where the island obstructed the view; the shore and foliage lit up by the silvery light of the moon; but no sign of our interesting neighbors. The hours passed on until three o'clock and after. One after another the constellations moved down to the western sky line, and still Alice slept peacefully on.

At last she moved uneasily and seemed about to awaken. I wanted very much to let her head gently down upon the seat, that she might not know how she had been sleeping, but my attempt to do this wakened her fully; and she at once realized the whole situation.

I said then, speaking low that her father might not be wakened, "Alice, never mind, you have been sleeping."

She looked up at me in a startled way and blushed until the flush was visible in the moonlight.

Again I said, gently, "Never mind about it, you have been sound asleep. Pray don't distress yourself."

Then how it came about I do not exactly know, and perhaps should not care to analyze it here at any rate. In her sweet confusion, while lying thus in my arms, I put my lips to hers, and pressed her to my heart.

The uncertainty was gone, never to return. My dear Alice was mine, mine alone. I had rescued a treasure, indeed, from the sea. Ah! do you know what it means, this finding out your true love? If you do, then no need for me to write it down; if you do not, then mere lifeless words cannot paint to you the pure delight, the flood of hope and fond emotion.

Of course we had much to talk about, as lovers do, and we sat talking low until the gray dawn stole into the eastern sky heralding the sun. I learned a good deal in that time. Perhaps the most instructive lesson was when Alice drew forth my old stained visiting card, and showed it to me.

Just before sunrise the old man woke up from his sound sleep, and came aft to where I was sitting with my arm around his daughter.

I lost no time in telling him what had passed between us.

"Is it so, Alice?" said he, putting his hand on her head tenderly and turning her face up toward his.

"Yes, father."

"Well" — after a long pause, and sighing — "I suppose it is only natural." Then turning to me he laid his other hand on my shoulder, and said: "My boy, you may be thankful to have such a wife. She will prove to you what her dear mother was to me. I thought I could see this coming, but it is hard to lose my little girl."

He then sat down beside us, and after a little silence said: "Now, my children, we are all here together. You have made up your minds to love each other. It will please me that you should love each other well; the more the better. And I want you to take me into the partnership. I am an old man, and I cannot lose my daughter. She is all I have on earth. Make a place for me, my son, in your heart, as I have already made a place for you. And you, Alice, love him with all your heart, and do not feel that I am an outsider, or my presence a hindrance to you. Often have I tried to console other parents by saying they gain a son when they lose a daughter. Now I am an called upon to console myself. I may do it by loving you both."

I was much affected by the old man's earnest manner and the deep feeling that trembled in his voice. I took his hand in mine and pressed it fervently. Alice threw her arms about his neck and passionately declared no one could take his place in her heart.

The sun rose upon this scene, and his level beams shone upon us with a flood of golden light. A bright new day had dawned for me in more senses than one.

CHAPTER XXII.

THE CAPTAIN'S FATE.

ABOUT ten o'clock in the morning we had the first news of our neighbors. Captain Senlis, the negro, and the three Indians at that hour came walking up the beach from the direction of our house. The negro had a coil of rope over his shoulder, and one of the Indians carried a water jug. It was plainly an expedition to view the galleon. When they came in sight the negro pointed out our boats, and they all paused a moment to look at us, as we swung at anchor just beyond range from the nearest point of the shore.

We were curious to know what would be their method of procedure with reference to the galleon. In view of the vast amount of incrustation of shells and coral, it would be no very easy task even for the pearl-divers to get at the contents of the old ship by diving and breaking into the hull. That such was their design I conjectured from the fact that the captain carried an axe, and one of the Indians an iron bar. When they had reached the rocks I took Mr. Millward's glass, and climbed the mast of the sloop to the cross-trees, where I could have a footing, and from which I could just see over the edge of the breakwater, and get a glimpse of the surface of the water in the basin, for about half its extent.

When they came to the rocks all five stood looking down into the basin for some time, the Indians pointing now and then, and the captain and the negro holding conversation together. Then they all came down into the breakwater. One of the Indians began to prepare himself for a dive, greasing his body with oil from a bottle and plugging up his nose and ears, in the slow, methodical way that I had before observed, and with the same apparent reluctance. When he was ready he sat down on the sand with such an air of indifference and disinclination to proceed that I could not help smiling. Then the captain began to gesticulate and talk in a way that made it plain, though of course at that distance I could not hear a word, that he was cursing the poor Indian at a stormy rate. There seemed to be some sort of hitch or difficulty in affairs. The two other Indians came up to the captain and began to talk to him. From the distant pantomime I fancied they were endeavoring to convince him that the rock at the shore side would be a better place to work from than the low breakwater. But this the captain would not see. He presently went up to the seated Indian and pushed him on the shoulder; but the man only looked stolidly. The captain then threw off his coat, kicked off his shoes, and plunged into the basin. He evidently intended to swim to the wreck, and stand on the higher portions of it. It required only a few strokes for a powerful swimmer such as he would doubtless be.

But the unfortunate man never reached the galleon. After he had plunged in he was hidden from my view by the breakwater. My glass was levelled carefully on the scene, and the whole of it was in the field. I expected almost instantly to see his burly figure rising from the three or four feet of water that covered the poop of the galleon, but he did not appear. Not only did he fail to appear, but there arose immediately the greatest excitement among the others. The Indians began to throw up their arms and shout and to cast stones into the basin. The negro covered his face with his hand as though to shut out some fearful sight.

The meaning of all this did not penetrate to my mind at once. I could not understand the disappearance of the captain. But the conduct of the Indians, in their shouting and stone-throwing, led me presently to conjecture the real state of the case. It was the imprisoned shark. I now recollected that he lay in the basin like a sentinel guarding the galleon. The captain had been attacked by the fish, and probably killed. The conduct of his followers would soon determine this. Mr. Millward called up to me to know what the evident excitement meant. In a moment more I caught a glimpse of what seemed a blood stain on the surface of the pool, though of course I could not be sure; for while the glass brought the view up to an apparent distance of not over ten rods, still there was a certain glimmer due to the refraction of the light which made such a thing as a discoloration of the water an extremely difficult thing to see. But putting all together, — the disappearance of the captain, the fact that the shark was there, and finally the conduct of the remaining members of the party, — I felt morally certain that he had met his fate in a horrible death from the treacherous fish. If such was the case (and there seemed to be no escape from the conclusion) I felt sure there would be no further attempts made by the party to get at the wreck until they could get rid of the shark. I told my companions what I had seen and my conclusions drawn therefrom, and they agreed with the latter.

I came down on deck, as we could watch the doings of the party on the rocks quite as well from there, though we could not see into the basin.

The three Indians and the negro were now gathered together in a group on the rock, evidently engaged in a consultation. Presently the negro started off down the beach toward Home Creek, and the Indians remained at the rock. We immediately concluded that he had gone to their camp to get a shark hook, or the gun, or some means of destroying the man-eater. I at once made up my mind that we did not want our sentinel destroyed, and that the only way to prevent it was to reach the camp ahead of the negro, and get possession of the shotgun and ammunition. There would be no one at Farm Cove now except possibly the Chinaman, who would be left there as a guard to the property. I recollected his propensity for knitting and sleeping, and thought it possible to catch him napping if I could arrive there before the negro. He would require over two hours to go, and would most likely sail back in the pearl-fishers' sloop, and would then be in a position, with the gun, to make the neighborhood too warm for us. I determined to be beforehand with him if possible. I could do this by sailing down to Farm Cove in my boat, along the west coast, which would not take longer than an hour. The Chinaman, if he should be keeping a bright lookout, which was not very likely, would not be expecting anybody from the sea. The chances of success in the enterprise seemed more than even.

I explained the plan to Alice and her father, and the necessity that existed for speed and promptness in its execution. After much hesitation, particularly on Alice's part, they finally agreed that the move was a proper and advisable one. I immediately cast loose the "Mohawk" and made sail, leaving the Millwards and their boat at anchor. As I parted from them I told Mr. Millward to keep a bright lookout, and if he should see the pearl-fishers' sloop coming before my boat, to weigh anchor and stand to the north, and then make his way as best he could to Martinique, and assured him that I would follow in my own boat if I came to no harm. The wind was light, and had shifted so that I had it fairly on the port beam, and made satisfactory speed on the way. I would have at least a half-hour to spare before the negro could make the distance by land, the route he was taking, and probably an hour, unless he made more haste than I believed he felt occasion to do.

When I came nearly opposite the cove I bore up close-hauled and headed fairly for the sloop, which lay moored at the mouth of the little stream, and came boldly in. If the Chinaman should be at the tent the intervening foliage would prevent him from seeing me, and if he was on board the sloop, which was not likely, I would soon see him. When I drew up alongside the sloop, keeping the sails full to prevent their flapping in the slight breeze, I found it deserted, and immediately made fast leaving my sails hoisted ready for a rapid retreat if it should be required. Now the greatest caution became necessary. If the Chinaman was at the camp I must see him before he saw me. Moreover, I conceived that there was no time to spare even if I had a full hour before me.

From my previous visits and observations the lay of the land was perfectly familiar to me. The best way to reach the tent would be to follow up the creek, where I would be screened from view by the oleanders that grew on its banks. This would necessitate swimming for a few rods just at the mouth, and I felt a little nervous at the recollection of the recent shark episode, but rightly concluded that the sharks could not be very plentiful hereabouts, or the diving could not have been carried on. Without delay I slipped gently over the side into the water and swam in until my feet found bottom. It grew rapidly shallow now until the water was soon only ankle-deep in the little narrow rivulet. Cautiously advancing I soon came to a point where the tent was visible. The gun and ammunition hung in their old place, but no Chinaman could be seen. The stream took a bend here, and by following it completely round I could gain a spot within a couple of rods of the tent. This I safely reached and looked around again for the Chinaman, but he was not to be seen. I then waited, watched, and listened for fully five minutes, but could get no trace or sign of him. The gun was so near that I then made up my mind to a bold dash for it. If I could get hold of the gun I did not care for the Chinaman. With this intent I started on a run straight for the tent before me.

I had not taken three steps before my foot came down exactly upon the celestial lying flat on his back asleep in the grass. I must have knocked the wind out of him completely, as my foot backed up by my whole weight struck him fairly in the pit of the stomach. He squirmed and struggled up to a sitting posture, but did not cry out nor make any effort to stop me. Indeed, I believe the fellow could not have cried out to save his life after the foul blow he had received in the diaphragm.

I turned to look at him as I ran on, but did not pause until I had the weapon in my hands, a cartridge in both barrels, and the belt of ammunition buckled around my waist. I was now master of the situation, as I supposed. I looked around the tent to see if there were any other firearms, but could see none. My back was momentarily turned towards the prostrate foe, when a curious whistling sound caught my ear, and instinctively I wheeled quickly around just in time to escape a knife which he had thrown at my back with all the dexterity of a juggler. Instantly I covered him with the gun, and there never was a Chinaman nearer death, who lived to tell it, than this yellow scoundrel at that moment. My finger was on the trigger, when he threw himself face down flat on the grass with his arms stretched toward me, the palms together. It was not worth while nor did I want to kill him, I reflected in a moment, and moreover I did not care to fire the gun, for there was no telling how near the negro might be. So, keeping an eye upon him as long as I could see him lying there, I hurried down to the boats. Just as I reached the place where they were moored I caught a glimpse of the light-blue blouse of the Chinaman as he ran swiftly up the path toward the top of the cliffs.

As I have before stated, the pearl-fishers had laid a warp from the shore to a buoy anchored well out, which they used to haul the sloop in and out by. I hastily cast off the shore end of this warp, which was fast to a tree, and taking it on board the pearl-fishers' sloop hauled that vessel, my own, and the pearl-fishers' yawl, all three, out to the buoy. I then made shift to haul up the anchor by aid of a winch on the pearl-fishers' craft, and left it hanging at the bow, cutting loose the buoy. We now began to drift, and I took a line to my own boat preparatory to towing the entire flotilla. All this had occupied some time, and just as I was fairly under way I saw the Chinaman and the negro run down to the mouth of the creek. The black fairly danced with anger, and shouted out curses loud and deep after me, to all of which I made no reply, but getting the sails on my boat trimmed, jogged slowly along with my heavy tow safe behind. I felt now for the first time since our disagreeable neighbors had come on the island that the game was once more in our hands.

About one o'clock the boat of the Millwards hove in sight, and knowing he would have his glass bearing on me I stood up in the stern sheets that he might plainly see all was right. By three o'clock we were once more together, and all three boats at anchor, in plain sight of the Indians on the rock, who exhibited the utmost excitement when they saw me towing up their sloop. In a little while afterward the negro and the Chinaman came up to the beach and joined the rest of their party.

Having no fear now of firearms, we had brought all the boats to anchor much nearer the shore, so that we were now in easy hailing distance of the shore party. After a talk with his companions the negro came out alone to the nearest point on the rocks and called to us in "darky" English. When I had answered his hail, he said "Wharfor you done tek our boat, boss? How you reckon we kin git off dis hyar island with no boat?"

"Do you want to leave the island?" said I.

"Yes boss, de captain's dead, eat up by shark. We don't want to stay hyar no longer. Fore de Lawd, I speak true."

"Tell the rest to come where you are," said I.

When they had all gathered there and stood in a row, I asked them in Spanish if they wanted to go, and they all began to speak at once. Then I motioned for silence, and bade them each to speak in turn, the right-hand man first, who happened to be the Chinaman. He wanted to go, and one after another they said the same.

"If I let you have the boat will you sail straight away, and leave here for good and all?"

To this they all assented except the negro, who said they wanted to go to the cove to get the things left there. There could be no objection to that, if they did not stay longer than was necessary to embark the property, and I so told them. Moreover, they would need a supply of water. If they set about it at once they could do all this and be away by midnight, as there would be a moon to light them on the way.

Having settled this to our mutual satisfaction, I cut loose the yawl that it might drift in, and directed them to come on and get their vessel.

The alacrity with which the whole party tumbled into the yawl was sufficient evidence of the desperate straits they had fancied themselves to be in, at the prospect of being marooned on the island. Before they got under way, I told the negro that if they chose to do so they might delay departure until the next day, which would give them more time to make proper preparation for their voyage; but that they must be under way before the next night. He agreed to this and said, —

"Boss, we got nothen agin you. You've treated us square, and we's mighty glad to get away."

The Chinaman grinned at me as they bore away, as though he felt grateful for not being shot, and had forgiven the blow below the belt. The Indians sat stolidly silent, but I felt surer of them than of either of the others.

As soon as they had sailed we brought the boats to the shore, in the sheltered nook I have before mentioned, and unloaded the pumping-apparatus before nightfall, to be ready to set it up in the morning.

That night we slept on board the boat, but kept a watch all night. I turned in immediately after sundown and slept until one o'clock. Then Mr. Millward wakened me and I kept watch until five o'clock, after which Alice watched for the two hours we both continued to sleep. There were no signs of the other party during the night. And I may state here, to avoid repetition, that they put off in their boat about three o'clock in the afternoon of that day, and before sunset were out of sight in the western board.

It took us all that day to set up the pumping-machine and get it into working order, in addition to the slight task of setting up a sail on the sand for a tent in which to sleep.

We had suffered so many set-backs now in regard to the galleon that we all felt like crowding the work to our utmost, for fear something new might turn up. I could not help feeling that the pearl-fishing gang, as soon as they could reach port and procure firearms, might take it into their heads to return for the spoils that they must expect would be found in the wreck. We could not hope, therefore, to feel entirely secure for longer than ten days.

When the pearl-fishers sailed we observed them with the glass and noted that the whole party was on board; therefore we should not need to keep a watch for the present. That night, tired out, I slept soundly, but was troubled with dreams about the galleon. For example, I dreamed that we had emptied her hold completely and found nothing in it but a sealed jar, which upon opening we found to contain a dirty visiting-card, on which was written, "I raised this galleon in 1830 and took out all her contents. This is for the benefit of the next man who tries it. Please let her sink again."

This, absurd as it was, when added to the real uncertainty and natural anxiety I felt contributed not a little to my discomfort. I could not help anticipating a possible disappointment. But then reason told me plainly that the probabilities were all the other way. Still, there was the ever recurring thought, "What if there should prove to be no treasure?"

The next day Mr. Millward and I began the pumping business in earnest. Of course I was able to keep much longer at it than he, and his share amounted to little more than to spell me occasionally for a short time. Since that leg-aching and back-breaking experience, kept up for four days, I never can see a horse in a treadmill without a gush of sympathy. On the fourth day the water was so low that the shark was almost aground, and I put two loads of buckshot into the living grave of Captain Senlis, whereupon it succumbed, and left the galleon unguarded.

By night of this fourth day the basin was pumped out sufficiently, and the galleon lay almost completely exposed, the water inside of her still leaking out slowly. Completely exhausted we went to bed early and left her to drain as she might. Human nature could endure no more. I was so exhausted that I went supperless to bed, and consequently woke early in the morning hungry as a hunter. While the others still slept I raked the embers together, built up the fire and put the coffee on to boil. I then roused my companions, and we were soon at breakfast discussing the probabilities of finding anything in the old hulk. At last the day had come around for which we had toiled and waited so long.

CHAPTER XXIII.

TREASURE TROVE.

It would be impossible to convey to another an adequate idea of the feelings I experienced when I clambered for the first time upon the deck of the old galleon. Alice and her father stood on the rocks as I advanced along the shell-incrusted structure, axe in hand, to the raised cabin or poop. I struck the cemented door with the axe several blows, until it broke and fell in with a crash. Then there came up a damp sea-smell from a dark, cavernous interior, into which here and there penetrated a narrow beam of light from small crevices and openings above. I was about to break in the window containing the iridescent pane of milky glass, when Alice called to me to spare it, if possible, for its exceeding beauty. So I dashed my axe through all the other incrusted openings, and let in a flood of light and fresh air to the long sunken apartment. Mr. Millward cautioned me to beware of foul air and gases; but the caution was needless, the air was pure and sweet and impregnated only with an odor such as a receding tide leaves behind. Testing it cautiously at first, I soon felt that it was safe, and entered the cabin, the floor of which was flush with the deck on which I stood.

On either hand were berths, the doors of some of which were closed, and some fallen open. Within the berths I found the usual bunks, and looked with dread for ghastly memorials of those who once occupied them. But if there had been skeletons there at one time, the bones were long since dissolved and gone; not a trace was left. All about were remains of sea organisms of various kinds, animal and vegetable, which had lived and flourished here in the dark deep under the sea. I could note here and there heaps indicating the decayed or covered remains of the furniture. A glass decanter and several goblets stood encrusted and cemented to what had once been a table. It was a strange sight, never to be forgotten.

With the axe I went about and stove in one after another all the doors, except one which resisted my efforts. This door was made stronger than the others, and was banded and barred with iron much rusted, and in places so oxidized as to be mere streaks and stains of rust. I inferred that here was the strong-room of the ship, and doubtless within its precincts would be found whatever of treasure the galleon contained. I reserved the opening of this apartment, which was located at the port side of the rudder, until my companions should be present to share with me the pleasure or disappointment that might result from a disclosure of its contents. Having done this much I returned on deck and announced the result of my investigations, and that I wanted all to be present at the opening of the treasure chamber.

The old man waded to the vessel as I had done, and I took Alice in my arms and carried her, helping her up to a footing on the deck. Duke, not to be left behind, came plunging in and swam to the side, following his mistress, and I helped him also on board. Then we all entered the cabin, and I began at the door with the axe. At the second blow the blade went through near the bottom of the door, and out gushed a stream of water which poured down the slanting cabin-floor, draining away into one of the berths. I enlarged this opening until the confined water flowed more freely, and then we waited until it had drained out and ceased to flow. I wished very much for the crowbar that I had seen in the hands of our departed neighbors, but it had gone with them, and so I was fain to continue the work with the axe. Little by little the barrier was completely demolished and the chamber lay open before us.

There upon the floor was a great heap of something half filling the room. With the axe I struck into it, and there shone out the yellow lustre of gold. Mingled with a black, oxidized mass of silver, all glued together, were great bars or bricks of the pure, indestructible, untarnishable, precious metal, unchanged by all the time it had lain sunken beneath the waters. It shone with the same dull yellow that it had given back to the light so long ago. Iron might rust, the bolts and bars might dissolve and fall away; the inferior silver might blacken, soften, and change; but the noble gold was proof against time, and against the insidious tooth of the bromides, the chlorides, and iodides, and all the other salts that the sea held in solution in its mighty waters. A simultaneous cry of delight from all went up at the sight. I clasped my darling close in my arms and kissed her sweet lips.

"See," cried I, "the gold! That means a home for us, my queen! It means the redemption of the hills and valleys, the woodland and fields where I was born, and where you shall rule, sweetheart!"

"It means very much to us, my son," said the old man; "it is at once your fortune and my daughter's dowry. Think of the good that can be done in the world by a proper use of this treasure which will be entrusted to your care and stewardship."

Duke came up and sniffed suspiciously at the pile, and turned away as though disgusted at the whole business, and the exceeding bad taste of his friends.

While I had been chopping at the door the dog was in the greatest state of excitement, expecting no doubt that some sort of game would be unearthed. But as it proved, nothing came forth, not even a chipmunk, and not even the stale scent of one. We all happened to be looking at this display of canine wisdom, which was so significant and so complete a commentary on the artificial character of the value pertaining to what we had found, that the effect was irresistible. We all burst into merry laughter, peal on peal, till the cabin of the old craft rang with such a burst of hilarity, echoing through its cavernous recesses, as it had not heard for centuries if ever before.

Now that the gold was found I was in a state of feverish anxiety to get it out of the galleon. It seemed as though misfortune hung over us in the cloudless sky. I could not hasten fast enough. The minutes seemed hours. A great dread was upon me. I could not have slept while the treasure remained where it lay. To my excited brain and wrought-up imagination it seemed that the very ghosts of those who once owned the gold would come to claim it. Though it would be days before the pearl-fishers could get back, I could not avoid casting anxious glances toward the western horizon. Mr. Millward appeared to partake in some degree of this same anxious condition of mind. I am certain no two men ever worked more freely up to the extent of their physical abilities than we did that day. We loosened up and carried to Mr. Millward's boat the whole of the precious metal, more than a ton in weight including the gold and silver together, and stowed it on a layer of canvas where it might serve as ballast, clearing out the ballast that was already there, and covered it over with the sail cloth of the tent, and over that a layer of sand to conceal it all.

That night we slept on board the boat, and we began to feel the anxious care of the charge that wealth brings. I got little sleep, and was restless, and up and down all night. In the morning we began and continued until late in the afternoon a systematic examination of the entire interior of the galleon, searching for more treasure, but we found nothing, and brought nothing more away from the wreck except the pane of glass, and the decanter and goblets which I, for souvenirs, removed at Alice's request.

There was nothing more to keep us on the island; the weather was fair and settled, the wind was favorable, and we might have started that night, but Mr. Millward thought it would be wise to provision the boat better and renew our water. Moreover, Alice expressed a wish to visit once more our house that we might bid farewell to scenes which we might never revisit. We therefore sailed for Home Creek in the sloop, leaving my boat behind me as we should have no further occasion for it. We reached the creek an hour before sunset, and moored the boat in her old snug place. Nothing at the house had been disturbed. By the level rays of the sun as he was about to sink behind the central plateau of the island I lit a fire, and soon we had one started in the oven as well. Then began the roasting, baking, and boiling, of pork and beans, bread, yams, potatoes, coffee, and whatever we had in store. It was midnight before we completed our task and went to bed.

Alice and her father slept at the house, and I made my bed in the boat, the gun by my side, and Duke curled up at my head.

The last day on the island dawned clear and bright; the blue sky unflecked by a single cloud hung high above; the favorable wind that we had sighed for in vain at times was gently rustling through the foliage and swaying the graceful palms; the myriad voices of Nature sounded all about in the song of bird and hum of insect and boom of surf. When I rose to greet the day I saw Alice standing on the porch in the full sunlight, looking out at the sea all glistening as it was with light from a million facets. Presently Mr. Millward came out, his white head bare and his commanding figure erect and unbowed by years. They stood together thus when I came up and joined the group.

There was little to do before we left. Our breakfast, for which we did not light a fire, was soon over. Then we loaded on our provisions, emptied and re-filled our water-gourds for the voyage, stored them, and were ready to go. I dug up my pearls from their place of concealment. Alice went into the house and brought out my nautilus-shell from the mantel. We would leave all else as it was for the benefit possibly of some shipwrecked successor, and carry away only what we needed for our use upon the voyage.

Then together we three, followed by the faithful Duke, made a round of visits to the various familiar places,— the salt-pan, incrusted now with white salt; the shed, beneath whose shade we had toiled so hard and passed so many pleasant hours; the house, the oven, the garden, now luxuriant in its rich abundance of growth; the cocoanut grove, — and to all bade a silent farewell. At the last, with tears in her sweet eyes, Alice begged that I would walk with her down the beach and sit upon the rock by the seaside as we had done once before in a time that now seemed so long ago. When we reached the rock she put her arms about my neck and said, "It was here I first knew I loved you, dear. I could not go away without coming here with you to say good-by to the dear old island."

Ah! fair Key Seven, good-by, good-by. How much

of happiness do I owe your friendly shores. Shine forth a gem of the sea. Smile ever in my remembrance as on that fair morning when, clad in all your loveliness, my bride and I bade farewell to your palms and sands and groves and streams, and listened for the last time to the chorus of your birds. Farewell, farewell. May we hope some day to come and visit these scenes again, and open once more the gates of this earthly paradise before we pass through the valley that leads us to the final home.

It was ten o'clock in the morning when we embarked and set sail from Key Seven bound for Martinique, a fair wind wafting us over the sea, the tinkling water at the bow and the broad wake behind speaking well for the good speed we made. By two o'clock the island hung a trembling, hazy, blue cloud in the west. We looked at it with regret filled with sweet remembrance, as it sunk lower and lower and finally, fading away out of sight, was gone from our view.

The run to Martinique was wholly uneventful, though it took us four days to reach port, owing to the light winds. Throughout the voyage Mr. Millward and I took turns at the helm, steering by the compass. Not a single sail was sighted, and we drew into the old pier just four hours before the steamer bound for New York made the port and tied up to the same pier.

Mr. Millward went at once to the captain of the newly arrived vessel and related enough of our story to apprise him of the nature of our cargo, and the desire we had to get to New York with it as soon as possible. The captain, a New Bedford man, came back with Mr. Millward to the boat, and we then arranged for our passage and the safe carriage of our treasure. The latter was stowed in canvas bags and sealed and weighed under our supervision, and carried on board the steamer. Then my heart grew lighter as the care of the treasure was lifted from my mind. We secured ample insurance from the local underwriter, made arrangements that the sloop should be sold and the proceeds sent to some of Mr. Millward's old parishioners in Jamaica, and then, just as the sun was setting, embarked for New York and home.

My story is done, for all our trials and labors and troubles were then over. Now we may ring the curtain down. But before it descends I may invite you to look at the last tableau.

It is a summer's day. The dust lies thick on the shady road. The katydid rasps its musical wing in the tall elms which shade an old farmhouse. On the porch, enjoying the faint breath of the evening air that comes gently over the fields of yellow grain, and through the orchard where the home-returning cows have stopped a moment, is a group consisting of a white-haired old man, who smokes his pipe in quiet comfort, a young man, and a beautiful young woman, at whose feet lies a noble Gordon setter. It is the party whose story you have followed. This farmhouse and these broad acres have been redeemed with long sunken Spanish gold. It is a loving and a happy party, whose hearts beat kindly for each other and for all.

The old man speaks: —

"My children, to-day is the anniversary of our departure from Key Seven. Let us thank God for all the good gifts that have come to us from THE SPANISH GALLEON."

THE END.

THE BRIDGE OF THE GODS.
A ROMANCE OF INDIAN OREGON.
By F. H. BALCH.
12mo, 280 pages. Price, $1.25.

THIS is a masterly and original delineation of Indian life. It is a strong story, charged with the elemental forces of the human heart. The author portrays with unusual power the intense, stern piety of the ministers of colonial New England, and the strange mingling of dignity, superstition, ferocity, and stoicism that characterized the early Indian warriors.

There is no need of romancing, and Mr. Balch's scenic descriptions are for all practical purposes real descriptions. The legends he relates of the great bridge which once spanned the Columbia, for which there is some substantial history, adds to the mystical charms of the story. His Indian characters are as real as if photographed from life. No writer has presented a finer character than the great chief of the Willamettes, Multnomah; Snoqualmie the Cayuse; or Tohomish the Seer. The night visit of Multnomah to the tomb of his dead wife upon that lonely island in the Willamette is a picture that will forever live in the reader's memory. . . . To those who have traversed the ground, and know something of Indian character and the wild, free life of pioneer days, the story will be charming — *Inter-Ocean, Chicago.*

It is a truthful and realistic picture of the powerful Indian tribes that inhabited the Oregon country two centuries ago. . . . It is a book that will be of value as a historical authority; and as a story of interest and charm, there are few novels that can rival it. — *Traveller, Boston.*

There is much and deep insight in this book. The characters stand in clear outline, and are original. The movement of the story is quick and varied, like the running water of the great river. — *The Pacific, San Francisco.*

Its field is new for fiction; it is obviously the work of one who has bestowed a great deal of study on the subjects he would illustrate. It is very interesting reading, fluently written. — *Times, Chicago.*

Sold by all booksellers, or mailed, on receipt of price, by

A. C. McCLURG & CO., PUBLISHERS,
COR. WABASH AVE. AND MADISON ST., CHICAGO.

THE BEVERLEYS.
A Story of Calcutta.

BY MARY ABBOTT,
Author of "Alexia," etc.

12mo, 264 pages. Price, $1.25.

The uncommonly favorable reception of Mrs. Abbott's brilliant novelette, "Alexia," by the public bespeaks in advance a lively interest in her new novel, "The Beverleys." It is a more extended and ambitious work than the former, but has the same grace of style and liveliness of treatment, together with a much more considerable plot and more subtle delineations of character and life. The action of the story takes place in India, and reveals on the part of the authoress the most intimate knowledge of the official life of the large and aristocratic English colony in Calcutta. The local coloring is strong and unusual.

A more joyous story cannot be imagined. . . . A harum-scarum good-nature; a frank pursuit of cakes and ale; a heedless, happy-go-lucky spirit, are admirable components in a novel, however trying they may be found in the walks of daily life. Such are the pleasures of "The Beverleys." To read it is recreation, indeed. — *Public Ledger, Philadelphia.*

The author writes throughout with good taste, and with a quick eye for the picturesque. — *Herald, New York.*

It is a pretty story, charmingly written, with cleverly sketched pictures of various types of character . . . The book abounds in keen, incisive philosophy, wrapped up in characteristic remarks. — *Times, Chicago.*

An absorbing story. It is brilliantly and vivaciously written. — *Literary World, Boston.*

The author has until now been known, so far as we are aware, only by her former story, "Alexia." Unless signs fail which seldom *do* fail, these two with which her name is now associated are simply the forerunners of works in a like vein of which American literature will have reason to be proud. — *Standard, Chicago.*

Sold by all booksellers, or mailed, on receipt of price, by

A. C. McCLURG & CO., Publishers,
Cor. Wabash Ave. and Madison St., Chicago.

MARTHA COREY.

A TALE OF THE SALEM WITCHCRAFT.

By Constance Goddard du Bois.

12mo, 314 pages. Price, $1.25.

The same material drawn upon by Longfellow for his "New England Tragedies" is here used with greater fulness and with no less historical exactitude. The story has for its background the dark and gloomy pictures of the witchcraft persecution, of which it furnishes a thrilling view. It is remarkable for bold imagination, wonderfully rapid action, and continued and absorbing interest. In short, it is too good a piece of fiction to be accepted as truth, which is to the credit of the author's imaginative powers; for "Martha Corey" is an absorbing tale. — *Public Ledger, Philadelphia.*

The story is curious and quaint, differing totally from the novels of this day; and the pictures of life among the early inhabitants of Massachusetts show that the author has been an untiring and faithful student for her work. — *Weekly Item, Philadelphia.*

The characters are well delineated; the language is smooth and refined; and from frequent change of scene and character the book is rendered very entertaining. The passions, love and hate, are carefully analyzed and faithfully described. It is a valuable little book. — *Globe, Chicago.*

An interesting tale of love and intrigue. . . . Miss Du Bois has given us a very readable book, and has succeeded where others have failed. — *Advertiser, Boston.*

The story of this book is pleasantly told; and as a picture of those sad times, when some of the worst and the best, of the darkest and the brightest, of the most hateful and the most lovable traits of human nature were openly manifested, is well worth reading. — *Illustrated Christian Weekly, New York.*

A story of marked strength, both of imagination and narration. — *Home Journal, New York.*

Sold by all booksellers, or mailed, on receipt of price, by

A. C. McCLURG & CO., Publishers,

Cor. Wabash Ave. and Madison St., Chicago.

MONK AND KNIGHT.

An Historical Study in Fiction.

By the Rev. Dr. F. W. Gunsaulus.

Two Vols. 12mo, 707 pages. Price, $2.50.

This work is one that challenges attention for its ambitious character and its high aim. It is an historical novel, — or, rather, as the author prefers to call it, "An Historical Study in Fiction." It is the result of long and careful study of the period of which it treats, and hence is the product of genuine sympathies and a freshly-fired imagination. The field is Europe, and the period is the beginning of the sixteenth century, — a time when the fading glow of the later Renaissance is giving place to the brighter glories of the dawning Reformation.

The book deals, in a broad sense, with the grand theme of the progress of intellectual liberty. Many of its characters are well-known historical personages, — such as Erasmus, Sir Thomas More, Cardinal Wolsey, Henry VIII. of England, Francis I. of France, the disturbing monk Martin Luther, and the magnificent Pope Leo X.; other characters are of course fictitious, introduced to give proper play to the author's fancy and to form a suitable framework for the story.

Interwoven with the more solid fabric are gleaming threads of romance; and bright bits of description and glows of sentiment relieve the more sombre coloring. The memorable meeting of the French and English monarchs on the Field of the Cloth of Gold, with its gorgeous pageantry of knights and steeds and silken banners, and all the glitter and charm of chivalry, furnish material for several chapters, in which the author's descriptive powers are put to the severest test; while the Waldensian heroes in their mountain homes, resisting the persecutions of their religious foes, afford some thrilling and dramatic situations.

Sold by all booksellers, or mailed, on receipt of price, by

A. C. McCLURG & CO., Publishers,
Cor. Wabash Ave. and Madison St., Chicago.

THE STORY OF TONTY.

AN HISTORICAL ROMANCE.

By Mrs. MARY HARTWELL CATHERWOOD.

12mo, 224 pages. Price, $1.25.

"The Story of Tonty" is eminently a Western story, beginning at Montreal, tarrying at Fort Frontenac, and ending at the old fort at Starved Rock, on the Illinois River. It weaves the adventures of the two great explorers, the intrepid La Salle and his faithful lieutenant, Tonty, into a tale as thrilling and romantic as the descriptive portions are brilliant and vivid. It is superbly illustrated with twenty-three masterly drawings by Mr. Enoch Ward.

Such tales as this render service past expression to the cause of history. They weave a spell in which old chronicles are vivified and breathe out human life. Mrs. Catherwood, in thus bringing out from the treasure-houses of half-forgotten historical record things new and old, has set herself one of the worthiest literary tasks of her generation, and is showing herself finely adequate to its fulfilment. — *Transcript*, Boston.

A powerful story by a writer newly sprung to fame. . . . All the century we have been waiting for the deft hand that could put flesh upon the dry bones of our early heroes. Here is a recreation indeed. . . . One comes from the reading of the romance with a quickened interest in our early national history, and a profound admiration for the art that can so transport us to the dreamful realms where fancy is monarch of fact. — *Press*, Philadelphia.

"The Story of Tonty" is full of the atmosphere of its time. It betrays an intimate and sympathetic knowledge of the great age of explorers, and it is altogether a charming piece of work. — *Christian Union*, New York.

Original in treatment, in subject, and in all the details of *mise en scene*, it must stand unique among recent romances. — *News*, Chicago.

Sold by all booksellers, or mailed, on receipt of price, by

A. C. McCLURG & CO., PUBLISHERS,
COR. WABASH AVE. AND MADISON ST., CHICAGO.

THE LAUREL-CROWNED LETTERS.

The Best Letters of Lord Chesterfield. Edited, with an Introduction, by EDWARD GILPIN JOHNSON.

The Best Letters of Lady Mary Wortley Montagu. Edited, with an Introduction, by OCTAVE THANET.

The Best Letters of Horace Walpole. Edited, with an Introduction, by ANNA B. MCMAHAN.

The Best Letters of Madame de Sévigné. Edited, with an Introduction, by EDWARD PLAYFAIR ANDERSON.

Each volume is finely printed and bound; 16mo, cloth, gilt tops, price, $1.00.

In half calf or half morocco, per vol., $2.75.

Of LORD CHESTERFIELD'S LETTERS, the *Atlantic Monthly* says: —

The editor seems to make good his claims to have treated these letters with such discrimination as to render the book really serviceable, not only as a piece of literature, but as a text-book in politeness.

Of LADY MARY WORTLEY MONTAGU'S LETTERS, the *New York Star* says: —

The selection is indeed an excellent one, and the notes by the present editor considerably enhance their value.

Of HORACE WALPOLE'S LETTERS, the *Philadelphia Public Ledger* says: —

These witty and entertaining letters show Walpole to bear out the promise of his fame, — the prince of letter-writers in an age which elevated the occupation into a fine art.

Of MADAME DE SÉVIGNÉ'S LETTERS, the *Boston Saturday Gazette* says: —

Accomplished, witty, pure, Madame de Sévigné's noble character is reflected in her writings, which will always hold a foremost place in the estimation of those who can appreciate high moral and intellectual qualities.

Sold by all booksellers, or mailed, on receipt of price, by

A. C. McCLURG & CO., PUBLISHERS,

COR. WABASH AVE. AND MADISON ST., CHICAGO

www.ingramcontent.com/pod-product-compliance
Lightning Source LLC
Chambersburg PA
CBHW031331230426
43670CB00006B/314